A GEOGRAPHY OF
TRADE AND DEVELOPMENT
IN MALAYA

BELL'S ADVANCED ECONOMIC GEOGRAPHIES

General Editor
PROFESSOR R. O. BUCHANAN
M.A.(N.Z.), B.Sc.(Econ.), Ph.D.(London)
Professor Emeritus, University of London

A. Systematic Studies

AN ECONOMIC GEOGRAPHY OF OIL
Peter R. Odell, B.A., Ph.D.

PLANTATION AGRICULTURE
P. P. Courtenay, B.A., Ph.D.

A GEOGRAPHY OF TRADE AND DEVELOPMENT IN MALAYA
P. P. Courtenay, B.A., Ph.D.

NEW ENGLAND: A STUDY IN INDUSTRIAL ADJUSTMENT
R. C. Estall, B.Sc.(Econ.), Ph.D.

GREATER LONDON: AN INDUSTRIAL GEOGRAPHY
J. E. Martin, B.Sc.(Econ.), Ph.D.

GEOGRAPHY AND ECONOMICS
Michael Chisholm, M.A.

AGRICULTURAL GEOGRAPHY
Leslie Symons, B.Sc.(Econ.), Ph.D.

REGIONAL ANALYSIS AND ECONOMIC GEOGRAPHY
John N. H. Britton, M.A., Ph.D.

THE FISHERIES OF EUROPE; AN ECONOMIC GEOGRAPHY
James R. Coull, M.A., Ph.D.

B. Regional Studies

AN ECONOMIC GEOGRAPHY OF EAST AFRICA
A. M. O'Connor, B.A., Ph.D.

AN ECONOMIC GEOGRAPHY OF WEST AFRICA
H. P. White, M.A., and M. B. Gleave, M.A.

YUGOSLAVIA: PATTERNS OF ECONOMIC ACTIVITY
F. E. Ian Hamilton, B.Sc.(Econ.), Ph.D.

AN AGRICULTURAL GEOGRAPHY OF GREAT BRITAIN
J. T. Coppock, M.A., Ph.D.

AN HISTORICAL INTRODUCTION TO THE ECONOMIC GEOGRAPHY
OF GREAT BRITAIN
Wilfred Smith, M.A.

THE BRITISH IRON & STEEL SHEET INDUSTRY SINCE 1840
Kenneth Warren, M.A., Ph.D.

A GEOGRAPHY OF
TRADE AND DEVELOPMENT
IN MALAYA

P. P. COURTENAY
B.A., Ph.D.

Associate Professor of Geography,
James Cook University of North Queensland

LONDON

G. BELL & SONS, LTD

1972

ISBN 0 7135 1624 0

Printed in Great Britain by
NEILL AND CO. Ltd., EDINBURGH

To Pamela,
who shares my nostalgia
for Penang

Contents

List of Tables

LIST OF TABLES

List of Figures

Journals Cited

The following abbreviations are used for the titles of journals cited:

Advmt. Sci.	*The Advancement of Science*
Am. Econ. Rev.	*The American Economic Review*
Am. J. Sociol.	*The American Journal of Sociology*
Br. Mal.	*British Malaya*
E. Afr. Econ. Rev.	*The East African Economic Review*
Econ. Dev. Cult. Change	*Economic Development and Cultural Change*
Econ. Geogr.	*Economic Geography*
Econ. J.	*The Economic Journal*
Econ. Rec.	*The Economic Record*
Geogr. J.	*The Geographical Journal*
Geogr. Polonica	*Geographica Polonica*
Geogr. Rev.	*The Geographical Review*
Geogr.	*Geography*
J. Indian Arch. E. Asia	*The Journal of the Indian Archipelago and Eastern Asia*
J. Mal. Brch. R. Asiat. Soc.	*The Journal of the Malayan Branch Royal Asiatic Society*
J. S. Seas Soc.	*The Journal of the South Seas Society*
J. Straits Brch. R. Asiat. Soc.	*The Journal of the Straits Branch Royal Asiatic Society*
J. Trop. Geogr.	*The Journal of Tropical Geography*
Mal. Econ. Rev.	*The Malayan Economic Review*
Mal. in Hist.	*Malaya in History*
Mal. J. Trop. Geogr.	*The Malayan Journal of Tropical Geography*
Pacif. Viewpoint	*Pacific Viewpoint*
Population Stud.	*Population Studies*
Q. J. Econ.	*The Quarterly Journal of Economics*
Scott. Geogr. Mag.	*The Scottish Geographical Magazine*
Tijdschr. Econ. Soc. Geogr.	*Tijdschrift voor Economische en Sociale Geografie*
Tin Int.	*Tin International*
Tn. Plann. Rev.	*The Town Planning Review*
Trans. Min. Ass. Inst. Corn.	*The Transactions of the Mining Association and Institute of Cornwall*

Introduction

The study of the economic geography of very many parts of the tropical world frequently is concerned with three distinct economic sectors, namely a subsistence or near-subsistence agricultural sector with its roots in a traditional past, an export sector concerned with the production for overseas markets of a limited range of raw materials, and a small modern industrial sector struggling, with greater or less success, to diversify the national economy and to provide additional employment for a burgeoning population. If the subsistence sector of such an economy is considered to be 'indigenous' (at least in the sense of being pre-colonial), the export sector is invariably, directly or indirectly, the result of a colonial experience, whilst industrial diversification is the consequence of deliberate measures taken politically.

This three-fold pattern is sufficiently common in the former colonial countries of the world for a generalized interpretation to be possible and this is attempted in the first chapter of this book. After the initial construction of a framework, the book is concerned with the analysis of the evolution of the economic geography of Malaya as a specific case—concentrating particularly on the growth of a regionally specialized export economy within a mainly laissez-faire economic environment, and on the modification of this specialization by the planned development of manufacturing industry in the period since the Second World War.

Emphasis on Malaya creates certain problems of terminology and it has proved necessary to adopt a series of geographical definitions in order to achieve clarity and consistency throughout a study that spans a number of political eras, with their own distinctive use of regional names. These definitions are listed in Appendix 1 but it should perhaps be emphasized at this point that the unqualified term 'Malaya' is used throughout as a geographical term conveniently to describe the entire peninsula, *including the off shore islands*, south of the Thai border.

I

In 1970 political terms, it therefore corresponds to West Malaysia and Singapore. It must be made clear that this use of the term is in no way intended to ignore or belittle the fact of the separate political existence of the Republic of Singapore.

Certain arbitrary decisions with regard to the spelling of Malay names have had to be taken. In general these follow the spelling adopted by D. G. E. Hall's *Atlas of South-east Asia*, except that where long established familiar forms exist they are retained. It is, in the author's opinion, excessively pedantic (as well as confusing) to prefer Melaka to Malacca, Djawa to Java or Sulawesi to Celebes.

A book of this type, which is concerned primarily with a geographical analysis of the evolution of a regional economy rather than with the publication of new material, necessarily leans heavily on the work of other writers. Of particular value have been the works of Wong Lin Ken (on the early trade of Singapore and the growth of the tin industry) J. C. Jackson (on the early commercial agriculture) and Lim Chong Yah (on the economic growth of Malaya). Malayan history, geography and economics have been well served both by expatriate and by indigenous academics, many others of whom are referred to in the references to each chapter.

The dynamic nature of economic events, especially in the developing world, condemns any piece of writing that is in any way concerned with them to be out of date before it is completed, let alone published. No one is more aware than the author that the account of industrialization in West Malaysia and in Singapore given in Chapter 5 is very incomplete, as are the accounts of the development of the three major urban complexes in Chapter 6. Nevertheless it is hoped that sufficient recent material has been incorporated to illustrate the theme and, in a small way, to be of interest in its own right.

Many people have assisted in the writing of this book. Professor R. O. Buchanan, the editor of the series, has, as always, been a sympathetic critic. In Malaya, Mr. A. L. Davis, Malaysian International Chamber of Commerce, Penang; Mr. Hoy Meng Fook, Penang Chinese Chamber of Commerce; Mr. Tan Keok Yin, State Secretariat, Penang; Che Abdul

Rahman bin Hj.Yusof, Economic Officer, Penang; Che Osman Merican bin Ahmad Merican, Penang Port Commission; Mr. Choo Kean Hin, Malayawata Steel Ltd.; Mr. V. C. de Bruyne, Ministry of Commerce and Industry, Malaysia; Che Mohamed bin Abdul Rahman, Port Swettenham Authority; Miss J. Chia and Mr. Chang Yen Yin, Investment Promotion Division of the Economic Development Board, Singapore; Mr. T. Eames Hughes, Singapore International Chamber of Commerce; Mr. J. Phillips, Jurong Town Corporation and Mr. W. Colless, Brooks, Mitchell, Peacock and Stewart, Planning Consultants, Singapore, all gave of their time. Miss Zalina Kassim of the Department of Geography, University of Singapore undertook some photo-copying on my behalf in Singapore, Professor Ooi Jin Bee and Dr. Bernard Swan provided hospitality during an all-too-short visit to Singapore. Many unnamed staff members of the Department of Statistics, Malaysia, the Department of Statistics, Singapore, the Federal Investment Development Authority, Malaysia, the Geological Survey, Malaysia, the Port of Singapore Authority and the Public Record Office, London, have all contributed by answering letters and providing data. In Townsville, Dr. B. Steveson of the James Cook University Geology Department made valuable criticisms of parts of Chapter 2, and Mrs. E. Steveson gave equally valuable assistance with calculations for Appendix 2. Mr. C. Zeeman and Mr. F. Jeffery of the James Cook cartography staff helped draft and draw maps and diagrams, whilst Mrs. G. Campbell and, especially, Mrs. P. Goodall undertook typing and re-typing. To all, I am deeply grateful. Finally, thanks are due to the University College of Townsville (as the James Cook University then was) and to the Social Science Research Council of Australia for financial assistance that made possible a short return visit to Malaya in 1968, and to the James Cook University for general financial assistance throughout the period of the writing of this book.

P. P. C.

Mundingburra, November 1970.

CHAPTER 1

International Trade & Economic Development

International trade, as a subject for economic description and analysis, has a long and respectable history. The exchange of goods and services is, of course, basic to all economic activity above the subsistence level, whilst the regional specialization of this activity that exchange makes possible is the core of economic geography. International trade, the exchange of goods and services between distinct and separate political units, has a significance more important than that arising from the fact that it often (though not invariably) takes place over longer distances than local or interregional trade. Trade which crosses national frontiers is particularly amenable to control and taxation by governments. Not only can it therefore be forced to yield revenue, but by its judicious regulation governments are able directly to influence the nature and extent of economic activity within their own frontiers and indirectly to contribute to the patterns of specialization that develop elsewhere.

The purposes for which governments may wish to control the nature or volume of foreign goods that enter their national territory are many and various. In some instances control is on what may loosely be called moral grounds, arising from the desire to restrict or eliminate the import, for example, of drugs or certain types of literature; political, cultural or hygiene reasons may also be found for regulating the movement of certain types of material across frontiers. In general, however, the motives behind the governmental control of international trade are economic, and were first developed extensively and in a systematic way in the sixteenth and seventeenth centuries. The European economic philosophy

B   5

of mercantilism, evolved during the commercial revolution of these centuries as rudimentary foreign trade grew into extensive international commerce, was designed to strengthen the power of the state, for a strong central authority was regarded as essential for the expansion of markets and the protection of commercial interests.

This philosophy was reflected in the commercial legislation of the times, so that imports of goods considered unlikely to add to national productive power were discouraged by duties or prohibited, exports were encouraged by bounties and by drawbacks of duties on imports that were re-exported, and the export of raw materials considered essential to home manufacturers was prohibited. Colonial trade was confined to the mother country, and restrictions placed on the production by colonies of manufactures which might prove competitive. The English Navigation Acts, and their continental equivalents, by restricting trade to national vessels, encouraged the growth of shipping and of earnings from the carrying trade, and also ensured a supply of ships to meet the contingencies of naval warfare.

The effects of mercantilism on the distribution of productive activity in the European nations and their colonies in the seventeenth and eighteenth centuries is of considerable interest and significance to the historical economic geography of the period, but the worldwide pattern of economic specialization that developed in the nineteenth century, and that remains of considerable importance to any understanding of present economic distributions, was related to the much more liberal trade policies that succeeded mercantilism. Mercantilism as a basis for national trade policies was strongly criticised by that group of writers and philosophers who have become known as the 'classical economists'. With certain qualifications, these economic thinkers—amongst the best known of whom were Adam Smith, David Ricardo, Thomas Malthus, Jeremy Bentham and John Stuart Mill—believed that the fewer the obstructions to trade between countries the more fully the world's economic resources would be used and the higher living standards would be. Such trade, unencumbered by tariffs, quotas or other restrictive devices, became conveniently known as 'free trade'. In the rapidly industrializing Britain of the late eighteenth and early nineteenth centuries the free trade doctrine had a powerful appeal especially to manufacturers, whose productive capacity was capable of outstripping home demand but who had little to fear from foreign competition thanks to their possession of a virtual monopoly of the new methods of manufacture.

The way in which he believed the regional specialization made possible by free trade benefited all trading partners involved was spelled out in detail by Ricardo[1] in what has become known as the theory of comparative costs. The comparative cost argument illustrates how the gain from specialization and unhindered exchange flows from *comparative* cost advantage rather than from *absolute* cost advantage. It argues that a nation or region that can produce many items more cheaply (i.e. by the use of a smaller volume of factors of production) than another, benefits both itself and its trading partners by specializing on those items in the production of which its advantages are greatest, and by importing the others from regions with the relatively smallest disadvantages in their production*. It has been pointed out by many later economists that the classical comparative costs theory in its raw form clearly begs a lot of questions, since it implies that whereas finished goods can move freely between regions and nations, factors of production such as capital and labour cannot, whilst much traditional trade theory built upon it ignores distance as a variable, and therefore also the influence of transport costs.[3] Ohlin, writing in 1933, considered that the basis of international specialization was simply the fact that productive factors enter into the production of different commodities in very different proportions and that since the relative prices of these factors are different in different countries such specialization is therefore profitable—'trade allows industrial activity to adapt itself locally to the available factors of production. Industries requiring a large proportion of certain factors gravitate towards regions where those factors are to be found in large quantities and therefore at low prices'.[4]

The importance to economic geography of these ideas is very apparent and it seems equally clear that if (in Ohlin's

* The basis of a theoretical specialization pattern based on comparative costs is reasoned out by Chisholm in *Geography and Economics*.[2]

words again[5]) trade is to 'mitigate the disadvantages of the unsuitable geographical distribution of . . . productive facilities', then that trade must be as administratively unhindered as possible, as must the movement of those productive factors such as capital, labour and entrepreneurial ability which, unlike climate or mineral resources, are intrinsically mobile. In the circumstances of free movement of mobile productive factors and of goods, as for example between a mother country and its colonies, Mill suggested that the colonies appeared to be outlying agricultural or manufacturing establishments belonging to a larger community. 'The West Indies', he suggested, for example, 'are the place where England finds it convenient to carry on the production of sugar, coffee and a few other tropical commodities' and he concluded that trade between the West Indies and England was 'therefore hardly to be considered as external trade, but more resembles the traffic between town and country'.[6] In commenting, in an article published in 1929, on this suggestion of Mill's, J. H. Williams points out how difficult it is to draw the line between trade of this sort and external trade and quotes a number of other examples of a similar kind in both colonial and non-colonial areas, indicating that, especially in the nineteenth century, England had found it convenient to produce wheat and meat (and to export capital for that purpose) in Argentina, gold and wool in Australia, and minerals and other products in Africa.[7] In just the same way it may be argued that the United States chose to produce sugar in Cuba, rubber in Liberia and copper in Chile in the twentieth century, and in order to make this possible mobile factors of production moved to immobile ones in combinations that, despite the additional costs engendered by distance, proved profitable.

The geographer may consequently claim that, in the evolution of regional specialization in this way, full benefit is being achieved from the inherent, especially physical, advantages of a region for a particular type of production. If all artificial (i.e. administratively imposed) restraints to the utilization of resources for the attainment of maximum immediate returns are eliminated, there will emerge production patterns which make best use of the physical characteristics of a region, whilst investment in social overhead capital—

transport systems, water and power supplies etc.—will be directed to serve the emerging productive region and will give it even greater and cumulative advantages. Certainly the early protagonists of free trade in the nineteenth century were not unaware of these implications of their objectives which they backed at times with moral arguments. In presenting the Petition of London, seeking free trade, to the House of Commons in 1820 Alexander Baring stated that 'it was one of the wise dispensations of Providence to give to different parts of the world different climates and different advantages, probably with the great moral purpose of bringing human beings together for the mutual relief of their wants'.[8] Sir William Molesworth, speaking against the Corn Laws in the 1840s, claimed that if Britain were to adopt free trade she would be imitated by most civilized nations and 'Then . . . each nation would take to itself that share of the general production for which it is best adapted by the nature of its soil and the genius of its inhabitants'.[9]

It may be questioned, however, whether the distribution of economic activity that evolved in the nineteenth century, and which has contributed so much to the current pattern, was, in general, one that made the best use of the characteristics of a region, despite its development in an environment of greater economic liberalism than previously known. There is an increasingly often voiced opinion—especially amongst the spokesmen for what is currently termed the developing world—that the present world pattern of economic specialization, that has concentrated high living standards in only a few favoured parts of the earth, is the outcome of a particular economic history rather than of the logical working out of a pattern that achieves maximum benefit from the inherent advantages of a region. To examine this proposition further it is necessary to look at the major factors that influenced the expansion and direction of international trade in the nineteenth and early twentieth centuries and the broad patterns of specialization that it created. Clearly, in one introductory chapter such as this, the examination can be a cursory one only, though it is hoped that it will provide a framework into which the detailed study of the evolution of the economic geography of Malaya—the main theme of this book—will fit.

The Growth of International Trade
and Specialization in the Nineteenth Century

It may generally be assumed that all trade—local, inter-regional or international—is carried on because the partners* involved all expect to gain some advantage from it. Usually the advantages gained, or expected, are economic though sometimes they may be political, and conceivably could even be moral. Trade may prove to be mutually advantageous to its participants in a number of ways. At its simplest the exchange of goods between regions or nations permits the acquisition by each of commodities that they cannot themselves produce by virtue of their particular natural resources or climate or, in the short run at least, of their lack of particular technology or skills. An example of such mutually advantageous trade was the exchange of British coal for Chilean nitrates in the days before the manufacture of chemical fertilizers. Such simple exchanges, even three or four cornered ones, are increasingly difficult to find, however, especially as substitute fuels and raw materials are found or developed and technology and skills more widely dispersed. Similar in type to this simple exchange is trade to make up for deficiencies in particular commodities, so British goods are traded for Argentine beef because Britain can consume more beef than she produces. The extent to which Britain imports Argentine beef because she cannot produce enough herself, and the extent to which she imports because she chooses not to produce it as there is greater advantage to be gained by using for other purposes the resources that could produce beef (the comparative cost argument) are difficult to determine, and the example illustrates the problems inherent in any attempt to state the precise purpose for which any particular trade is carried on.

Apart from the obvious benefits to be derived from the acquisition of goods (or services) that may be locally non-existent or scarce—for one reason or another—a region or nation will often find it to its advantage to produce a surplus of goods for trade, not so much because it needs to

---

* Such benefiting 'partners' may, of course, be only a small capitalistic, aristocratic or other controlling group—as has often been the case historically—or may be a whole nation.

pay for the import of scarce essentials but because it wishes to reap the benefits of increased productivity at home. By widening the market for its goods, a manufacturing region will increase the scope for its own division of labour, build a more skilled labour force and encourage technical innovation thus producing increasing returns and economic development for itself.

Trade may also stimulate economic development in an exporting region by providing a new effective demand for the output of resources which would remain unused in the absence of trade. This 'vent for surplus' principle of trade was described by Adam Smith and criticised by Mill as a surviving relic of mercantilism since he considered it erroneous ever to suppose that if certain goods were not produced for export the corresponding portion of capital would remain idle.[10] However, the point has been well made by Williams,[11] and repeated by Myint, that in the economic circumstances of a very considerable part of the world, either where specialization in production for world markets has dominated an economy (as with Britain) or especially where unemployment and underemployment are common, the situation may indeed exist that resources, particularly labour but also land and mineral resources, *will* lie idle unless goods are produced for export. 'The function of trade . . . (especially in the latter case) . . . is not so much to re-allocate the given resources as to provide the new effective demand for the output of the surplus resources which would have remained unused in the absence of trade'.[12] The planned and assisted development of manufacturing in, for example, Singapore at the present time is quite specifically intended to provide employment for a rapidly growing population that otherwise could not find work and, in the absence of a large home market, most manufactured goods will have to be exported.

It seems reasonable to presume that any trading economy, with the exception of the most primitive, will develop for a mixture of all these reasons, and that as such an economy matures and vested interests, including those associated with the social overhead capital, become powerful, the need for trade is explained by factors different from those that were relevant at an earlier period. Thus trade in manufactured goods, originally necessary to cope with the surplus from newly mechanised British factories, is now essential to pay for the import, amongst other goods, of a fuel that has replaced the coal initially so important in establishing the factories.

Whatever the combination of reasons for the development of trade, however, in normal* circumstances certain pre-conditions are essential for its development. In the first place, goods surplus to those that can be sold at economic prices in the region or country of manufacture must be available; secondly, knowledge of the existence of this surplus and of the price at which it is available must be widely known; and, thirdly, means of transport must exist to move such goods from the surplus area to their potential markets. In general, trade will not develop between areas unless the difference in the price of goods (reflecting the different balance of supply and demand) in each of the areas is sufficient to cover the cost of transport between them. The great expansion of inter-national trade that took place in the nineteenth century was made possible by major developments relevant to all three of these conditions, and occurred in response to a mixture of the reasons previously summarized.

By the end of the Napoleonic Wars, Britain was the world's major industrial power. Her achievement of this position between 1780 and 1815 is best interpreted as the result of forces that had been exerting a persistent influence over long periods of time, but in some cases—as shown by M. M. Edwards,[13] for example—the actual sequence of events, which might have taken a different course, was important and British industry had its setbacks as well as its triumphs in this period. Nevertheless, by the time of Waterloo, the British cotton industry especially was seeking overseas markets for its surplus production, as were the manufacturers of woollen yarns and textiles, hardware and cutlery, and iron and steel goods. Napoleon's encouragement of French industry, his series of treaties throughout Europe, whereby allied countries favoured French goods, and his enforcement of the Continental System, whereby British goods were successfully excluded from

---

* 'Normal' here excludes periods of hostility or national economic crisis when the need for a nation to survive may over-ride what otherwise would seem rational economic decisions e.g. a nation may export already scarce butter to import guns, or scarce grain to import machinery.

much of Europe, with the effect of causing considerable unemployment in her manufacturing regions, forced Britain to seek wider overseas markets.[14] That she was able to do this, and increase her trade with Portugal, Mediterranean entrepots such as Gibraltar and Malta, the Levant, the Americas (except the U.S.A.) and the West Indies, was possible thanks to her experience in world trade and to her control of the seas.

Between 1800 and 1850, the value at current prices of Britain's total overseas trade (including re-exports) had risen from £115 million to £186 million, and by 1900 had expanded to a total of £878 million,[15] these values representing a fairly constant 20–25 per cent. of a fast expanding total world trade. France, following a period of high tariffs instituted after 1815 and largely having recovered from the dislocation caused by the 1848 revolution, moved after 1850 into a period of rapid economic development and commercial expansion, and although remaining second to Britain as a trading nation throughout most of the rest of the century, was responsible on the average for about 11 per cent. of total world trade. In the last decade of the nineteenth century, the rapidly industrializing Germany and United States of America each raised its share of world trade to over 10 per cent., whilst the Low Countries had a smaller but substantial portion.[16]

Payment for the goods exported from Europe during the nineteenth century, which were primarily manufactures (especially textiles and iron and steel goods) and coal, was made possible by, and helped stimulate, the production of raw materials (including gold) in all parts of the world to which trade penetrated. The invention and development of transport and communications systems created a world market so that not only could goods, even bulky ones such as grain, be moved across continents and oceans by the railway, clipper and steamship but the electric telegraph, whose cables snaked out from Britain from 1850 and had reached as far as Australia by 1872, established world, as distinct from purely local or national, prices especially for raw materials. Commodities produced in such diverse conditions as those prevailing in Europe, America, Asia and Africa brought approximately the same prices in Europe. This was true of wheat, cotton, wool, rubber, copper, oils, tea, coffee and sugar—for all these commodities the world became one market. It was this kind of trade and the investment and transport facilities that accompanied it, that provided the most effective stimulus to the economic development of the rising parts of the world.[17] Ragnar Nurkse has described international trade as having acted in this era as

the engine of growth, by serving as the medium through which the industrial centres of the world in Western Europe transmitted their economic growth to the periphery of the underdeveloped countries, through a vigorous expansion of demand for primary products.[18]

By the end of the nineteenth century, there had evolved in the world a pattern of economic specialization bound together by an international trade focused predominantly on north-west Europe and the north-east of the U.S.A. In these latter areas, the mining of coal and the manufacture, particularly in the coalfield areas, of iron and steel goods, textiles, transport equipment and increasingly sophisticated machinery were the major specializations and were accompanied by the growing urbanization of rapidly increasing populations. The temperate grasslands and ranchlands of the New World, populated almost entirely from western Europe, were providing grain, meat and wool for the urban populations and factories of the old continent, whilst the tropical lands that were politically controlled but not settled from Europe developed dual economies with commercial sectors based on mines, plantations and seaport cities existing alongside indigenous agriculture and producing raw materials for export.

There seems little doubt that, in the context of the period and remembering that much of the world (for example China beyond its merest fringe, Japan, Asiatic Russia, much of Africa and south-west Asia) were beyond the influence of international commerce, the specialization that had emerged by 1900 appears based substantially on comparative cost advantage. The European manufacturing regions had the necessary accumulations of capital acquired from generations of trading (much of it based on mercantilist philosophy), fuel and iron ore beneath their feet, innovating entrepreneurs and an increasingly adaptable and educated labour force. The temperate plains of Canada, the United States' mid-west, Argentina, south and south-east Australia, and New Zealand possessed massive land resources in proportion to their small immigrant populations and were able by extensive and mechanized agriculture to earn high returns per man from their soil, herds and flocks, the products of which, even when moved across thousands of miles to markets in Europe, could readily compete with the latter's intensive but higher-cost-per-unit production. The tropical and sub-tropical parts of the world, with their climatic advantages for the growing of crops such as cotton, rubber, tea, sugar and coffee*, their rich deposits of rare minerals such as copper and tin, and their labour forces drawn from a subsistence economy where they were normally surplus to available land (whether locally or as immigrants from India or China) were therefore able to specialize on the production of relatively labour-intensive commodities.

That these patterns were able to develop owed a great deal to the political and economic links between large areas of the world and the European industrial powers and to the liberal commercial policies operated especially by Britain during the second half of the nineteenth century, and to some extent by France and other European nations for a somewhat shorter period. The reduction and simplification of British tariffs, begun by Pitt in the late eighteenth century but reversed by the war of 1793–1815, were renewed by Huskisson, President of the Board of Trade, in 1823. Huskisson's tariff reforms, which included a working system of preferential duties for colonial goods, laid the foundation of the British free trade policy which was finally implemented by Peel and Gladstone in the 1840s and '50s. The 1842 budget aimed to remove all absolute prohibitions on the import of foreign goods, to reduce prohibitory duties to a moderate competitive level, and to reduce other duties to maxima between 5 and 20 per cent. In 1845 520 customs duties were swept away, and by 1849 all wheat, the commodity causing greatest controversy, was admitted to Britain at a nominal registration duty of 1/- per quarter, which was itself removed in 1869.[19]

* Though in many ways the major coffee producer, Brazil, had more in common with the temperate grasslands in its economic organization, since production was organized on an extensive basis using immigrant European labour.

In France, Napoleon III, a firm believer in free trade, reversed the policy of protection that had characterized French commerce since Waterloo and in 1860 negotiated the Cobden Treaty with Britain. Under the Cobden Treaty, highly protectionist France not only abandoned its position, but agreed to a 'most-favoured-nation' clause. This forced other European nations to offer to and secure from France trade concessions to avoid Britain's enjoying overwhelming advantages in what was the major continental market. The Cobden treaty was thus followed by a whole series of treaties between France and the other major European trading nations, which also made treaties with one another and with Britain, and since each treaty contained a most-favoured-nation clause, any concessions became general for all. The European nations also followed the French example in abolishing shipping restrictions and throwing open their colonial trade. By 1870 there had been a general levelling down of restrictive trade barriers all over Europe.

After the Franco-Prussian war of 1871, and during the depression of the 1870s and 1880s agitation against the renewal of the various treaties was strong in France and in 1892 she returned to a policy of strong protection. Germany, under Bismarck, also reversed the tendency to free trade that had been marked in the 1860s and 1870s, though, as an industrial nation of growing strength desiring cheap food, she pursued more conciliatory policies in the last decade of the century with the object of extending her markets.

Despite the reaction against free trade in Europe towards the end of the nineteenth century, the fact that her markets were readily accessible to the raw materials of the other economically developing continents for some twenty to thirty years, and in Britain until 1914, at a time when they were attracting settlers and/or opening up their agricultural and mining lands for commercial purposes was a stimulus of the highest order.

The Influence of Free Trade and Protectionism
on Patterns of Economic Specialization

If it is true that the generally liberal trading policies of the major European nations eased the international flow of goods and contributed to the development of the truly global trade that took place between about 1865 and 1914, it is equally true that most of the European and European-settled nations were less firmly convinced of the appropriateness, for them, of free trade than was Britain. Both France and Germany, as has already been noted, vacillated between protectionist and low tariff policies, and the United States, following the civil war of 1861–65, in general adopted a policy of protection for both her agriculture and her industries. Canada and Australia, with dominion status, introduced measures to protect and nurture their infant industries, whilst the Japanese government was very active in stimulating and guiding industrial development after 1870. Russia, aiming to transform herself into a modern industrial state, was generally protectionist after 1878 and in 1912 had the highest duties in the world.

The desirability of protectionist policies in France, Germany, the United States, Canada, Australia, Japan, and Russia, in the period when a relatively liberal world trade, revolving especially around the British Empire, was helping create a particular pattern of economic specialization, raises more than a suspicion that the governments of those countries did not fully believe that the law of comparative costs, operating in a free trade world, would benefit them economically to the extent that the classical economists had claimed it should. By the mid-twentieth century these made up a group which, with Britain and a few smaller states, represented the world's richest and most advanced industrial nations. As a further move away from a free trade world in the economically troubled years between the two world wars, a number of the richer of these leading industrial, trading and investing nations contributed to the erection of a series of substantial barriers to the free operation of market forces with the prime intent of defending their own and their imperial economies.

Although total world trade increased between 1914 and 1929 (it rose by more than 50 per cent. of the 1913 level measured at constant prices[20]), it fell drastically during the 1930s as economic activity slowed down in the industrial states of the western world and as their reduced demand for raw materials affected the primary producing nations. Trade restrictionism, which in the 1920s was motivated largely by the desire of individual industries in numerous countries to perpetuate the natural protection they had enjoyed during the First World War, was extended in the depression years of the 1930s from simple tariff protection to the quantitative regulation of imports and the control of exchange dealings, in order to protect national balances of payments. Protective walls of one sort or another were raised around existing industries and home agriculture in the older industrial nations, and around infant industries, considered essential for diversification, in the newer ones. Following attempts at the establishment of private and national cartels in the 1920s, a range of international schemes was adopted to restrict the export of raw materials, such as tin (1931), sugar (1931), tea (1933), wheat (1933), rubber (1934) and copper (1936) in order to prevent their prices from dropping to or remaining at completely ruinous levels.[21] At the same time, the desire for self-sufficiency, as exemplified most strongly by Germany, and advances in science and technology, making possible the substitution of, for example, chemical fertilizers and artificial silk for the 'natural' commodities, limited further the demand for various raw materials in the older industrial states, whilst the development of alternative sources of power to coal and the diffusion of industrial capital and of the knowledge of industrial techniques were contributing to a much wider spread of manufacturing industry. In 1937, Sir Dennis Robertson raised the query whether international trade would ever play again the same dominant part in the economic life of the world that it had played in the nineteenth century, and seemed convinced that the world would have to learn to accommodate itself permanently to a smaller relative volume of such trade.[22]

In so far as any generalizations that deal with the economic policies of a large number of politically independent nations in a trading community as large as the world can be valid, it seems that the last forty years of the nineteenth century constituted a period of relatively liberal world trade whilst the first forty of the twentieth was one of general protectionism, with some countries, for example Britain, being more liberal than most in the protective era and others, for example the United States, more protective than most in the liberal.

If it is accepted that the 'power house' of the world economy in both these eras consisted of the industrial nations of the North Atlantic basin, the economic policies of these nations could be expected significantly to have influenced developments in most corners of the commercially organized world, and therefore the character and advantages of international economic specialization.

The free trade era, if it may conveniently be so called, was the one in which, as has been seen, economic specialization developed throughout much of the world, and this specialization was determined to a considerable extent by the cost advantages, either absolute or comparative, possessed by the various parts of the world *at that time* and thus within the framework of the technological knowledge and achievements of the period. Its contributions both to economic specialization and to economic growth cannot be denied, though these specializations and growth were sometimes founded on a reckless mining of the soil or ignorance of climatic hazards. Even in the 'free trade era', however, a marked difference is recognizable between certain rather limited areas of the world, and these were invariably politically and economically independent, and others that were tied, either as political colonies or by the existence of a large measure of foreign economic control, to overseas—predominantly North Atlantic—nations. In the former—and Canada, Japan and Russia can be cited as examples—economic policies were adopted that were believed to be in the national interest and frequently were protectionist to a less or greater extent. The theories of Friedrich List,[23] who wrote in 1841 in Germany after some years of working in mining and railway organization in the expanding American economy, favoured the protection of infant industries which were seen to be necessary for economic growth but which, in their early stages, were characterized by high production costs owing to the lack of industrial, business and organizational experience, of a skilled labour force and established market. Such youthful industries, whatever their future prospects, could not be expected to compete with those of a country, such as Britain, whose own manufacturing had passed through these stages and which was benefiting from the advantages of large scale production. List's theories carried great weight with manufacturing interests in continental Europe and Russia and had considerable influence on national policies.

In a number of the independent nation states industrial growth thus took place which, in many instances, enabled them in due course to compete very effectively with Britain against whose manufactures protection was earlier necessary. The advantages that Britain had acquired from her earlier industrialization were thus counterbalanced, and the comparative advantages of, for example, the Ruhr or Cleveland, Ohio, were equal to or greater than those of Tees-side. It cannot be claimed, of course, that protection of infant industries is the sole or even the major requirement for the successful establishment of a manufacturing economy. The conditions necessary for economic, especially industrial, 'take-off'—the analysis of which is particularly associated with the economic historian W. W. Rostow[24]—are many and varied, touching on not only the availability of raw materials,* but also of industrial capital and entrepreneurial ability, of the existence of a social system that permits mobility of all kinds, and of a legal one that clearly defines rights of property, person and contract. The existence of many of these conditions in the European states and their daughter nations of the New World, and their deliberate creation in Japan, helped make possible industrial growth but it seems generally true that, even where these economic and social pre-requisites existed, competition from older established manufacturing areas had to be contained by restrictions on trade if such industrial growth was effectively to take place. Rostow admits, amongst others, the undoubted service to take-off in leading sectors performed by the American textile tariffs of 1828† and rail-iron tariffs of 1841–42 and the Russian tariffs of the 1890s, but claims they usually reflected an energy and purpose among key entrepreneurial groups which would, in any case, 'probably have done the trick'.[25]

The contrast between the nature of the economic activities

* Indeed in many cases, these have proved of rather minor significance e.g. in Japan, Hong Kong.
† Rostow's point of view is not universally accepted, nevertheless. D. C. North makes the point that America was exporting cheap cotton textiles by 1830 and that Manchester merchants were complaining of American competition in the cotton trade of Mexico and South America as early as 1883. See North, D. C., 'A Note on Professor Rostow's "Take-off" into Self-Sustained Economic Growth', *Manchester School of Economic and Social Studies*, 26, 1958.

that developed in the 'free trade era' in the independent nation states quoted and that characteristic of many of the political and economic colonies is, however, most marked. This latter group of territories included the Asian, African and West Indian colonies of the European powers, and the majority of the Latin American republics, which were ruled by what nowadays would be called 'settler' governments and the developed sectors of whose economies were frequently under the financial and usually managerial control of overseas companies. Such territories frequently possessed what have been described as 'export economies'.[26] The demand for a variety of raw materials from the industrial nations first of Europe, then of North America and elsewhere, was responsible, as has been seen, for providing a considerable stimulus to the economic development of many parts of the world whose indigenous economies were largely rural and stagnant. Investment in mining and plantation enterprises was accompanied by the development of transport and communications facilities (including railways, roads, ports and telephone and postal systems), and power generation, and in due course, as a result of the increased income accruing to government from economic expansion, the development of at least some basic social services such as education and medicine. Increased income was undoubtedly also earned not only by the labour force directly involved in the export enterprises, which, although often an immigrant one, demanded goods and services of which some at least were locally provided, but also by the employees of public utilities, builders and contractors, wholesalers and retailers, craftsmen, market-gardeners and small-holders, clerks and messengers etc. Even, as in much of South-east Asia, where the majority of these personnel were also immigrant, real development cannot be denied to have taken place, and its effects cannot have failed to have widened the opportunities for economic betterment available to the indigenous peasantry. However, the production of plantation crops and minerals and, in some cases, of foodgrains was almost entirely destined for overseas markets, and a great deal of the demand engendered by export earnings was satisfied by imports, of food as well as of manufactures.

Criticism of such export-oriented economies arises not from

C

any misunderstanding of the benefits that economic specialization produced in the free trade era (except deliberately in
certain politically motivated cases), but from the fact that
development in these instances appears to have stagnated at a
particular point. F. F. Clairmonte, in criticizing the effects of
economic liberalism on the under-developed world, claimed that

> international specialization has brought in its train a
> 'freezing' of the economic endowments of a given country
> at a certain historically conditioned stage of development.
> Far from constituting a dynamic force in economic develop-
> ment in the less developed areas it has operated in the
> interests of the larger nationally integrated and better
> established industrial communities.[27]

Whereas it may be claimed that the nationally integrated
industrial communities were able to, and did, modify to their
own advantage* by many of the devices already described the
extent to which free trade operated, modification of this kind
was mainly denied to the countries with export economies,
since—as a consequence of the nature of the origin of these
economies—they had little real local control over them.

The disadvantages for growth of the export economies beyond
a certain point have been analyzed by a number of writers.
J. V. Levin,[28] for example, claims that for the majority of the
export economies, their entry into international trade was
sudden and that—in the absence of local social and economic
systems to supply needed factors of production—capital,
entrepreneurship and managerial help were necessarily provided
from the advanced countries of Europe and America, and
labour frequently from over-crowded less developed countries
such as India and China. The overseas origins of many or most
of the factors of production, as well as the overseas destinations
of practically all the products, had important influences not
only on the locations of the export industries but also on their
patterns of development. As a consequence of the remittance
overseas of much of the income earned by the export industries,
a substantial portion of the effective demand generated by them
leaked abroad. Foreign shareholders received dividends
abroad, foreign managers and labour remitted much of their

---

* or at least to what they believed it to be.

savings abroad, and whenever accumulated funds were used for the replacement of, or for new investment in, capital equipment, they were spent abroad.

Shu Chin Yang, in describing the 'backward' and 'forward' linkages that represent inter-industry demand and supply, indicates that although primary production has very low backward linkages, its forward linkage (i.e. its potential for generating further economic growth such as in processing and manufacturing industry), is very high but that in the cases of the export economies this potential was exported rather than retained in the home sectors of the economies.[29] According to Levin, the lack of domestic investment opportunities in the home sectors discouraged savings and led to a high level of what he calls 'luxury imports' by the wealthy groups associated with the export industries, and a further boost was thereby given to the vicious spiral of 'circular and cumulative causation'.[30] In general, where the structure of an export industry was characterized by foreign factors of production and luxury importers, and the political situation which permitted it persisted i.e. where free trade, free immigration and free exchange existed, high export earnings contributed little to the diversification of domestic economic growth.

The arguments presented by Levin and Shu, which contend that the multiplier effect engendered by primary production occurs in the 'metropolitan country' from which the foreign factors of production came and to which the factor income returned, may be considered typical of those seeking an explanation of the relatively slow economic growth of the export economies by pointing to the existence of the foreign 'economic enclave'. Other economists have laid heavier emphasis on the argument that the long term commodity terms of trade turn against economies based on the export of primary products, and that therefore such countries have been deprived of most of the gains from trade. This approach is particularly associated with R. Prebisch[31] and points to the familiar inelasticity of demand for primary agricultural commodities and metals, the secular tendency to overproduction of such goods and the development of alternatives and substitutes, compared to the high income earning capacity and infinite variety and rapid adaptability of manufactured goods.

Related to this terms-of-trade argument is the observation by R. Nurkse that whereas during the nineteenth century exports of primary products were expanding more rapidly than those of manufactured goods, in the mid-twentieth century there is a tendency for food and raw material exports to lag behind exports of manufactured goods. In consequence, the forces that made for the diffusion of economic growth from advanced to less developed countries are not as powerful in the twentieth century as they were in the nineteenth century.[32]

Unfortunately, the theoretical discussion concerning the role of overseas trade in the economic development of the export economies has been supported by only a very limited amount of empirical evidence. One interesting and revealing study, of Ceylon, casts some doubt, however, on the validity of many of the theoretical assumptions. Youngil Lim,[33] using statistics that are more reliable than those of many under-developed countries, shows that in Ceylon the export sector grew to augment market demand for domestic output rather than to form an economic enclave and that for the period 1948–54 about 2·5 rupees of domestic income was created for every rupee's worth of exports. He further shows that no downward long-term trend in the commodity terms of trade since 1900 is apparent and that the annual growth rate of Ceylon's exports since 1900 (mainly of tea, rubber and coconuts i.e. highly typical export commodities) has averaged 6 per cent. compound, a rate higher than the growth rate of income in industrial countries, of exports of industrial countries or of population in Ceylon for the same period.

There seems little doubt that the explanation of the limited diversification of the export economies cannot be given in a few simple economic terms, however attractive these may be for certain purposes and without denying their very great importance in contributing to the maintenance of particular patterns of specialization (their 'freezing' in Clairmonte's terminology) whose evolution occurred primarily in the nineteenth and early twentieth centuries. Social, institutional, and psychological factors at least, although often more difficult to measure, contribute to the existence or lack of the opportunities and incentives that seem essential for economic growth. Thus H. G. Johnson, whilst emphasizing the crucial role that the international economic relations of a country can play in the process of transformation, states clearly that economic development and industrialisation require the transformation of the society and the economy, and the transformation must be largely an internal one.[34] In retrospect, it may well be that the major criticism that can be levelled at colonial (in the broadest sense) economic policies in this context was their failure to stimulate such internal transformation more than they did, whilst, in fairness, remembering that much colonial theory aimed at disrupting indigenous society as little as possible.

Available data indicate conclusively that the total value and the physical output of exports from the 'export economies' expanded rapidly once they were brought into the ambit of international trade, and that in many cases the rate of increase in export production was well above any possible rate of increase in population, thus resulting in a considerable rise in output per head.* Equally, an analysis of the economic structure of the export economies in the mid-twentieth century, either before or after the achievement of political independence, indicates the extent to which they remain specialized.† It is perhaps possible to create a crude model that incorporates various of the notions discussed above and that helps explain both the rapid growth and lack of diversification of the export economies.

The export economies evolved as commercial, and frequently political, dependencies of distant nations, acting as outlying producing regions whose distinctive climatic conditions or mineral resources gave them advantages in the production of certain commodities. Such production was comparable to that

* For example, Myint quotes the annual value of Burma's exports, taking years of high and low prices, as having increased at a constant proportional rate of 5 per cent. p.a. on the average between 1870 and 1900—during this period the area under rice cultivation in Lower Burma more than trebled whilst the population, including immigrants from Upper Burma, doubled. Cocoa output in the Gold Coast expanded over forty times during the period 1905–30.[35] Similar examples can be quoted for many other Asian and African states.

† A measure of the degree to which the exports of a country are specialized may be achieved by the use of an export specialization index, whereby a value of 100 represents complete specialization (i.e. all exports fall into one category, however that category may be defined) and a value of 0 represents complete diversification (i.e. all categories are equally represented). Using a specialization index based on a Lorenz curve (see Thoman R. S. and Conkling E. C. *Geography of International Trade* pp. 175–179 for example), the following values were obtained for 1965: West Malaysia 79·9, Ceylon 91·0, Burma (1964) 98·1, Liberia 99·7. These may be compared with (also for 1965): Canada 62·2, West Germany 71·0.

within the various regions of a single nation and was made possible by the free movement, as within a nation state, both of the mobile factors of production—labour, capital, entrepreneurial ability—and of the commodities produced.

Under the stimulus of growing demand in the metropolitan nations and of the flow of capital investment from the increasingly prosperous north-west Europe and North America, export production expanded rapidly. That the productivity of agriculture and mining in the colonial economies was readily increased was perhaps partly due to increased division of labour and specialization leading to innovations and cumulative improvements in skill and productivity per man hour (the Smithian theory). In Myint's terminology, however, more likely it was, first, the result of once-for-all increases in productivity accompanying the transfer of labour from the subsistence economy to the mines and plantations and the ready exploitation of accessible mineral resources or previously untilled soil, and, secondly, the increase in working hours and in the proportion of gainfully employed labour relative to the semi-idle labour of the subsistence economy. Where local labour was scarce or unsuitable, it was imported from subsistence economies elsewhere, often from increasingly far afield as production expanded.

Indigenous production of the export commodities, especially agricultural ones, was often stimulated, even in remote areas, by the growing demand for such goods and by the supply of manufactures, especially cotton piece goods and ironware, that could be obtained in exchange for them. The technical knowledge obtained from the 'foreign' sector and the growth of commercial marts capable of handling the output of small-scale indigenous producers were essential additional stimuli.

The increase in population and in purchasing power of the exporting region led to a growth in the demand for foodstuffs—some locally produced and some imported—and for manufatures which were readily imported rather than locally made. Contributing factors to the limited development of local manufactures to supply the growing local demand certainly included the ready availability of imports, both varied and cheap as a result of their mass production for the large markets accessible to the industrial nations, the inability or unwillingness of local capital, where available, to combine for the establishment of local manufacturing, and the lack of skill of the local labour force, especially in machine operation, engineering and management. The shortage of supporting industries and perhaps of cheap, local raw materials were often significant also. Unlike the situation existing in the commodity export sector, there was clearly no incentive for the overseas investor or entrepreneur to devote his funds or skills to manufacturing industry in the colonial economy since, in general, returns were higher in either the export sector itself or in metropolitan manufacturing.

Emphasis on the export commodities, by both the foreign sector and the often increasingly important indigenous producer contributed to the growing volume of exports of raw materials, despite periods of economic recession that, temporarily at least, struck them particularly hard. This expanding export trade provided local governments, in various ways, with revenue for the creation and improvement of the economic and social infrastructure which, understandably, was designed to reinforce the export sector from which the bulk of such revenue was derived.

The geographical consequences of this model can readily be recognized. At points from which trade could effectively be controlled and at which exportable products could conveniently be assembled for shipment, colonial settlements were established as overseas appendages of the metropolitan economy. Although several of such settlements began as indigenous foundations, they developed as foreign enclaves with a dominantly trading function and an access and site adopted largely or entirely for that purpose.[36] European urban styles, of warehouse, bank, hotel and office, were constructed as the physical expression of the metropolitan economy along waterfront or tidal estuary whilst buildings of indigenous or non-European immigrant style housed the majority of the burgeoning populations whose activities were equally detached from those of the subsistence cultivator.

From these footholds or gateways were opened up mineral or plantation areas, their locations determined partly by the physical circumstances of the particular environment, such as the occurrence of minerals or of particularly suitable soils, but also by accessibility to the seaports. Prior to the invention and development of the railway, such locations were closely associated with seaboards and navigable waterways, but with the improvement of land transport links, mining and commercial agricultural developments took place in more remote, often continental areas. As in the temperate lands, railway development made possible the commercial exploitation of interior areas, though these remained focused on the essentially alien trading city. Control of mines and plantations was predominantly non-indigenous, since the local economy had neither the skills nor the capital to initiate or sustain such developments on any scale and often even the labour force was imported for similar reasons.[37]

In areas within reach of the transport facilities, however, and as the development of commercial arrangements in the trading city or in more local country centres made possible the marketing, and where necessary processing, of relatively small quantities of a mineral or commercial crop, small scale production of export commodities was stimulated. There thus evolved a 'grey zone' of semi-subsistence, semi-commercial activity, undertaken by indigenous or self-employed immigrant people, which was perhaps less intensive and less efficient (in terms of effort involved) than the foreign undertaking, but which often was able to work smaller patches of less accessible ores or to cultivate less tractable or fertile terrain.

In the region tributary to the seaport city, that was linked to it by railway and, later, road and within which was concentrated the production of commodities for export, came also to be concentrated the various services necessary for its efficient functioning. Postal and telecommunications services, water supply, medical and educational facilities—the latter restricted and usually in the 'metropolitan' language but laying the basis for at least a reasonably educated middle class and indigenous aristocracy—and relatively incorrupt administration and justice spread from the seaport and gradually penetrated the region of export production. As they did so they contributed to the creation of a limited number of small urban settlements, as centres of administration, railway junctions and local trading posts. The possibilities for employment in these services as well as in the export industries, the improved facilities for handling local export commodities and for local petty trading, perhaps even better chances of survival, thanks to at least minimal health facilities and famine avoidance measures, were all significant in accounting for a more rapid population growth by both immigration and natural increase in the region of export production than in neighbouring subsistence areas.

The essentially intermediate economic role of the seaport city was responsible for the fact that its occupational structure was characterized by the dominance of the tertiary sector.[38] Primary and secondary industrial development was limited to the essential processing of raw materials, especially in cases where a considerable loss in weight or bulk was involved and such processing was often on a large scale employing some hundreds of people, and to the small scale manufacture of consumer goods such as foodstuffs and furniture that, for various and differing reasons, were more efficiently provided locally than by imports. Other primary and secondary manufacturing was absent, items such as textiles, hardware, machinery, electrical goods and vehicles all being readily obtainable from overseas. The industrial landscape of the seaport city was thus one of a very few large, and frequently or usually alien-controlled, processing works, such as tin smelters or oil mills, and a large number of small scale workshops, operating in often inadequate or unsuitable premises, making cheap cigarettes, soap and sauces, pastas and confectionery, furniture and shoddy footwear for the local market.

The introduction of diverse peoples of markedly different cultural habits into the seaport cities, the mines and plantations and the smaller local towns of the export region contributed not only to its obvious social and ethnic variety but also to its landscape by the creation of houses, shops, places of worship and recreation in imported architectural styles or in new styles that attempted to provide for the distinctive cultural needs of immigrants in an environment of unfamiliar climatic elements and building materials. Well into the 'grey zone' of small scale commercial activity, and even beyond into the fully subsistence areas, petty traders carried the products of the seaport city or its imports so that rural landscapes were modified by at least the existence of a small shop and by the use of alien tools, flashlights, canned foods, soft drinks, cotton piece goods and sandals, and, in due course, bicycles, sewing machines and radio sets.

Policies for Economic Diversification
in the Export Economies since the Second World War

In very many ways, politically, economically and socially, the Second World War completed the destruction of the 'nineteenth century' pattern of life that the First had begun. As a consequence of a very complex series of factors, the full details of which have yet to be unravelled, the vast majority of the political and economic colonies of the Atlantic powers achieved far greater control* over their destinies in the twenty years following the war than they had had in the decades that preceded it. Local reactions to political independence, which clearly was far more readily achieved than economic, varied widely but in the export economies almost universal dissatisfaction was expressed with the existing economic structure.

The lack of relevance of the pre-war economic patterns and policies to the post-war problems of the former colonial countries and the economic objections to their continuation were widely agreed. The assumptions that underlay the classical doctrine of international trade seemed hardly applicable to the newly independent nations of the developing world[39]—as indeed thay had not been considered wholly applicable to most of the nations of Europe and the temperate world in general since at least the beginning of the twentieth century. It seemed highly unlikely that a mere continuation of the production of raw materials for overseas metropolitan markets in exchange for manufactured goods could possibly bring about the substantial rise in employment opportunities and living standards of fast expanding populations that were the prime expectations of all newly 'liberated' or enfranchized peoples. As a result of the use of substitutes, the constant development of synthetics made possible by the highly sophisticated technologies of the industrial countries themselves, and more efficient (thus less extravagant) use of many raw materials, the world demand for the products of the traditional mining and plantation industries was, in general, likely to grow less fast than that for manufac-

---

* At least nominally and apparently—it is a question, far beyond the purpose or competence of this book to discuss, whether this meant anything beyond the right to hold the wheel of the ship of state that was really being carried along in the powerful current of wider events.

tured goods. This expectation was, of course, no reason for ignoring the contribution that the traditional export sector could still make—in view of the urgent need in most developing countries for enlarged foreign exchange earnings, substantial expansion of agricultural and mineral export production would frequently be a rational policy even though the world market might be unfavourable,[40] whilst technological advances and industrial growth in many parts of the world were certain to demand increasing quantities of new and different raw materials that the developing countries could often provide (e.g. petroleum, iron-ore, bauxite)—but clearly commodity exports could only in rare cases provide the sole basis of economic advance as they had done in earlier eras.

The failure since the 1920s and 1930s of international trade to continue as the 'engine of growth' was perhaps related to the displacement, as the world's leading dynamic centre, of Britain, with her considerable need of imports, by the United States, whose enormous natural resources and resolutely protectionist policies made her less needy of raw material imports.[41] An alternative stimulus to that provided by the raw material demands of the industrial nations was required by most developing economies and the consensus of opinion amongst many economists and politicians was that this would best be provided by local manufacturing industry. The expansion of food production, although a very high priority in most developing countries, depended on improved cultivation methods, better water control and new crop strains, and, in some overcrowded areas of subsistence agriculture, increased productivity often required a reduction of the farming labour force. Rural development, particularly where it involved the construction of large engineering projects (irrigation systems, roads and bridges etc.), could certainly provide an economic stimulus but one that tended to be local and short-term.

The arguments favouring industrial development as a sound and desirable basis for economic advancement and stability have been thoroughly examined elsewhere,[42] and these arguments have had the added force that the advanced nations of the world were all observed to have diversified their economies and raised their standards of living by the development of manufacturing industry. Increasingly it is coming to be realized that the change from a traditional economy, based on near-subsistence agriculture and the bulk export of a few primary commodities, to a growth-oriented modern economy involves a large number of readjustments in the society concerned, and that 'industrialization' is an economy-wide phenomenon, the essence of which is the conscious pursuit of economic growth. Industrialization in this broad sense requires far more than the investment of capital in the establishment of industrial facilities and their supporting infrastructure. It requires a skilled, disciplined and acquisitive labour force, a professional managerial class, efficient resource allocation and many institutional and social changes affecting land tenure, the distribution of income and the abandonment of close social control over economic life. The understanding and acceptance, greater in some countries than in others, of the importance of these factors is one major reason for the necessary involvement of the state in economic development planning.

The first and most popular type of manufacturing industry encouraged in developing countries has been concerned with import substitution. A number of countries, especially the temperate zone nations of the southern hemisphere (Argentina, Union of South Africa, Australia and New Zealand), attempted to counteract the imbalance of their overseas trade created by the contraction of their exports during the Great Depression by means of import substitution and continued this policy during the Second World War. Import substitution serves to retain a large proportion of demand at home amd also prevents further increases in domestic demand (resulting from rises in population and per capita income) from leaking too greatly abroad—it thus both counteracts tendencies towards unfavourable balances of payments and provides domestic industrial employment. It necessarily demands, however, the abandonment of the free trade policy and the free monetary exchange system. Restrictionist trade policies of various kinds were therefore adopted by countries pursuing industrial activity of this type during the Great Depression and have been followed by many developing countries since the Second World War.

Import substitution, or inward-looking industrialization in the terminology of Prebisch, comes sooner or later to face growing difficulties. These arise, in the first place, from the smallness of many national markets whose capacity to absorb import-substitutes (typically items such as tooth-paste, cotton goods, torch-batteries, stationery etc.) is limited both by population and spending power, and secondly, because the further substitution proceeds in respect of some imports, the more other imports grow because of the heavier demand for capital goods and, subsequently, because of the effects of higher income. The simple and relatively easy phase of import substitution reaches its limits fairly quickly in countries which make satisfactory economic progress and the need then arises for more complex and difficult substitution activities that need much capital and large markets.

The problem of breaking into export markets is probably the most difficult that a newly industrializing country has to face. The relative smallness of national markets and other adverse factors, such as the absence of skilled labour or suitable ancillary services, usually results in high cost production by local industry. Such industry needs considerable protection, for example by high tariffs, which encourages the establishment of small, often uneconomic, plants and weakens incentives to introduce modern techniques. Any attempt to export the products of such industry encounters great difficulty because of the size of internal costs which, however, could be reduced, by means of greater production, if export markets were available. If industrialization is to be more than a temporary palliative to the economic problems of the developing countries, they need to move beyond the stage of import substitution and into export markets—international trade becomes, therefore, once again a prime concern.

The problem of export markets for manufactured goods is greater than that of the often high price of the goods offered for sale overseas by developing countries. Possible markets clearly include both other developing countries and the developed countries. In the former, markets are still small owing to limited purchasing power and, unless regional preferences were granted, competition with the products of the developed world would be difficult. In the long run, regional economic groupings to guarantee wider markets for strategically located industries could overcome the problem of the smallness of national markets in regions such as South-east Asia, Central

America and the West Indies, East Africa etc., but at present
economic nationalism seems to preclude any major advance in
this direction.* From the point of view of the size of the
potential market, the developed countries appear as a much
more favourable destination for manufactured goods and, in
these markets, the developing nations will often have a cost
advantage once they can operate on an optimum scale. Lower
wage rates, often cheaper raw materials (minerals may be less
worked out, many raw materials may be local rather than
imported) and modern production methods should then make
it possible for production costs to be considerably lower than
those ruling in the developed industrial nations. The cost, for
example, of Indian textiles and of a whole range of Japanese
goods suggests this is already the case in these instances.
However, the fear of this very situation and the desire to
protect often long established and increasingly uneconomic
home industries has led to the erection of many protective
devices by the developed nations. Such protectionism can be
justified by the same economic nationalism as that invoked by
the developing countries when protecting their own infant
industries but, in H. G. Johnson's words,

> The difference is that whereas nationalism in less developed
> countries justifies protection as a means of establishing new
> industries at the apparent expense of the foreigner and actual
> expense of the consumer, nationalism in developed countries
> justifies protection as a means of preserving old industries at
> the expense of both the consumer and the foreigner, particu-
> larly the poor foreigner, who could supply the products
> cheaper.[44]

The marketing problems faced by any developing countries
once their industrialization reaches the point where they need
to move beyond import substitution was one of the major
themes developed by Raul Prebisch, the first Secretary-
General of the United Nations Conference on Trade and
Development (UNCTAD).[45] Since the Second World War,
international trade has operated under the general control of
the General Agreement on Tariffs and Trade (GATT),

---

* In the oil refining industry, for example, Odell comments on the fact that of
the 118 existing or planned refineries in Latin America, South-east Asia and Africa,
only 26 exceed the capacity recognized as the minimum at which a reasonably
economic refinery can still be built.[43]

membership of which pledges a country to the general expansion of trade on a multilateral and non-discriminatory basis. The basic general rules of GATT are that there should be no trade discrimination among fellow members (except by members of free trade areas and customs unions) and that protection should be by means of tariffs only i.e. not by means of quantitative restrictions and similar devices. The rules of GATT apply equally to trade in agricultural and industrial products, but in the early 1950s the United States, increasingly worried by foreign agricultural competition that was attracted by the high support prices for farm products in the U.S.A., insisted on a waiver allowing her to apply quantitative restrictions on a larger range of agricultural products. This waiver was later to provide an unarguable precedent for the agricultural policy of the European Economic Community.

Dissatisfaction with the differential treatment of agricultural and industrial protectionism under GATT* became the major focus of the criticism by the developing nations of the policies of the developed countries, and in 1964 the first United Nations conference on trade and development was held in Geneva and attended by 120 governments. At this conference 77 developing nations achieved an unprecedented show of diplomatic unity and turned the conference into a confrontation that approved resolutions regarding generalized preferences that none of the developed countries could accept. The second UNCTAD conference, held in New Delhi in 1968, more specifically sought acceptance of a policy of tariff preferences by the developed countries for the manufacture exports of the developing countries, by setting lower tariffs against imports of manufactures and semi-finished goods from the less developed countries than against similar imports from one another. This policy, which may be seen as a step towards freer entry of manufactured goods from the developing countries whilst recognizing the hard fact that the developed countries will continue to protect their uneconomic home industries, received limited enthusiasm from the 1968 conference, most of whose members from developing countries were more concerned about trade in commodities. This attitude no doubt reflected the fact that only

* *The Economist* of March 16th, 1968, commented that it would be easier for a poor country to sell a computer to the United States than a can of orange juice.

a dozen or so developing countries, at the time, had strong prospects of exporting manufactured goods but the policy will become increasingly attractive as more countries become less inward-looking in their manufacturing.

The general acceptance that the free-trade model, which explains the initial growth but limited diversification achieved by export-oriented colonial economies before the Second World War, is in no way applicable to the new conditions and problems of the post-war world requires its replacement by one more relevant. Although every opportunity offered the commodity export industries should be taken—and this will often involve the exploitation of new resources—further economic growth appears to require the development of a manufacturing sector hand-in-hand with agricultural improvements that will raise rural living standards and provide a marketable surplus for the growing industrial population. Except in rare cases the manufacturing sector will require protection from overseas competition and initially will concentrate on import substitution. When the limits of import substitution have been reached, expansion into more sophisticated manufactures will often depend on the development of overseas markets which could feasibly be based on regional trading agreements or on preferences granted by the developed countries of the world in instances where operations below the optimum scale result in high cost products. Where the manufacturing costs of the developing countries are low, the development of overseas markets will be very dependent on the attitudes of potential trading partners who frequently will be strongly tempted to defend those home industries with which the developing countries may compete.

Any attempt at assessment of the geographical consequences of development along these lines is necessarily very tentative at such an early stage but certain tendencies are becoming apparent that permit an initial appraisal. In the export economies, the functions performed by the big seaport cities are of greater importance to the newly independent nations than they were to the colonial regimes that created them. The universal desire of these nations to improve living standards and opportunities by diversifying and expanding their economies adds new importance to the foreign income that can be derived from the export of their traditional colonial products and therefore to the services provided by the seaport cities. In addition to the necessary maintenance of the trading cities as commercial centres and links with the world market, many have acquired increased significance as administrative capitals. National planning with its unavoidable degree of centralized direction and administration, makes the need for location of planning and administrative bodies in the major centres of communications, commercial activity and overseas contacts very apparent.

Import substitution industries are most likely to be located in or near the great seaports where are to be found both the labour force and the major home market. Location in the ports also eases the import of necessary raw materials, part-manufactured goods or components and machinery, and the distribution of finished goods elsewhere in the home region by means of the transport links focused on the port which serve the areas of dense population created by the export sector. The factors influencing the location of the more sophisticated industries that are likely to develop after the import substitution phase will also favour the seaport cities. The necessary more highly skilled labour force will have been trained in the earlier industries or in technical colleges and trade schools established in the cities, the need for export markets in which the products must be as competitive as possible makes such locations preferable, whilst proximity to ancillary industries, financial and commercial services and government departments increases their desirability. Of necessity, therefore, the seaport cities have retained and indeed increased their importance to the nations on whose edges they stand but, although they retain many characteristics from their colonial days, certain changes, apart from increased size, are apparent. Diversification of functions, especially by industrialization and an increasing association of interest with national hinterlands are perhaps the most significant. If the ports were originally grafted onto areas to whose indigenous populations they were entirely foreign, it could perhaps be said that in recent years the graft has begun to 'take'. The growing concern of governments with the development of rural areas, the gradual commercialization of subsistence agriculture, often by smallholder production of

D

export crops, and the encouragement where possible of rural industries are forging new links between the seaport cities and the countryside. The danger remains, however, that, unless strong efforts are made to the contrary, the rural areas that were barely touched by the colonial economy will remain economically neglected by its successor. Perhaps one of the biggest national problems of the developing countries attempting to industrialize will be the achievement of balance between making their new industries as efficient as possible, and thereby favouring the already most developed parts of their nations, and carrying at least a minimum of social and economic justice to their outlying rural areas. The world-wide problem that lies behind the whole concept of the developing world repeats itself on the national scale.

It might finally be considered whether the concept of comparative costs has any validity at the present time, and whether economic specialization of the kind familiar in the nineteenth century retains any advantages to offer the world economy. If the economic disadvantages suffered by many parts of the world as a consequence of the fact that Britain and north-west Europe were the first parts of the world to develop industrial economies can be overcome, by the protection of infant industries, preferential trade policies as favoured by Prebisch, international aid etc., then a situation might be foreseen in which certain industrial advantages will lie with the present developed countries—in highly sophisticated industries that demand a high degree of research talent and very skilled labour forces for example—and others with the present developing countries, where less skilled labour and greater amounts of raw materials are needed. For such readjustment to take place, the developed countries will need to assist the modification of their economies more readily than many are at present willing to do—for example by accepting further declines in fields such as textile manufacturing—and the developing countries to plan their growth with more attention to regional specialization than many at present are willing to give.

REFERENCES

1   Ricardo, D., *The Principles of Political Economy and Taxation*, (first published 1817), Everyman's Library, London, J. M. Dent & Sons Ltd., 1911, reprinted 1962, Ch. VII

2   Chisholm, M., *Geography and Economics*, London, G. Bell & Sons Ltd., 1966, pp. 40–44
3   A fusion of trade theory and the distance variable is undertaken by Isard, W. and Peck, M. J., 'Location Theory and International and Interregional Trade Theory', *Q. J. Econ.*, 68, 1954
4   Ohlin, B., *Interregional and International Trade*, revised edition, Cambridge (Mass.), Harvard University Press, 1967, p. 26
5   *Ibid.*, p. 29
6   Mill, J. S., *Principles of Political Economy*, London, Longmans, Peoples' Edition, 1867, p. 415
7   Williams, J. H., 'The Theory of International Trade Reconsidered', *Econ. J.*, June 1929
8, 9 Quoted by Bosanquet, H., 'Free Trade and Peace in the Nineteenth Century', Kristiania, Publications de l'Institut Nobel Norvegien, 1924, pp. 41–42
10 Mill, J. S., *op. cit.*, pp. 579–80
11 Williams, J. H., *op. cit.*
12 Myint, Hla., 'The "Classical Theory" of International Trade and the Underdeveloped Countries', *Econ. J.*, June, 1958
13 Edwards, M. M., *The Growth of the British Cotton Trade 1780–1815*, Manchester University Press, 1967
14 Knowles, L. C. A., *Economic Development in the Nineteenth Century*, London, Routledge and Kegan Paul Ltd., 1932, pp. 130–132
15 Mitchell, B. R., *Abstract of British Historical Statistics*, Cambridge University Press, 1962, tables 2 and 3, Overseas Trade, pp. 282–3
16 Woodruff, W., *Impact of Western Man*, London, Macmillan and Co. Ltd., 1966, table VII/12, p. 313
17 *Ibid.*, p. 268
18 Nurkse, R., 'Patterns of Trade and Development' Wicksell Lectures 1959, Stockholm, 1959
19 Redford, A., *The Economic History of England, 1760–1860*, 2nd edition, London, Longmans, 1960, pp. 192–197
20 Thoman, R. S. and Conkling, E. C., *Geography of International Trade*, New Jersey, Prentice-Hall, Inc., 1967, p. 3
21 Rowe, J. W. F., *Primary Commodities in International Trade*, Cambridge University Press, 1965, pp. 136–155
22 Robertson, Sir D. H., 'The Future of International Trade', *Econ. J.*, 48, March 1938
23 List, F., *Das Nationale System der Politischen Oekonomie*, Stuttgart and Tubingen, Cotta, 1841
24 Rostow, W. W., *The Stages of Economic Growth*, Cambridge University Press, 1960
25 Rostow, W. W., 'The Take-Off into Self Sustained Growth,' *Econ. J.*, 66, March, 1956
26 Levin, J. W., *The Export Economies: their Pattern of Development in Historical Perspective*, Harvard University Press, 1960
27 Clairmonte, F. F., *Economic Liberalism and Underdevelopment*, Bombay, Asia Publishing House, 1960, p. 41
28 Levin, J. V., *op. cit.*, pp. 4–10
29 Shu Chin Yang, 'Foreign Trade Problems in Economic Development,' *Advmt. Sci.*, 21, 89, May, 1964
30 Myrdal, G., *Economic Theory and Underdeveloped Regions*, London, Duckworth, 1957

31 Prebisch, R., *Towards a New Trade Policy for Development*, New York, United Nations, 1964

32 Nurkse, R., *Patterns of Trade and Development*, Oxford, Blackwell, 1961, p. 53

33 Lim Youngil, 'Trade and Growth: The Case of Ceylon', *Econ. Dev. Cult. Change*, 16, January, 1968

34 Johnson, H. G., *Economic Policies Towards Less Developed Countries*, London, Allen & Unwin Ltd., 1967, p. 47

35 Myint, Hla., *op. cit.*

36 Murphey, R., 'New Capitals of Asia', *Econ. Dev. Cult. Change*, 5, 1957

37 Courtenay, P. P., 'An Approach to the Definition of the Plantation', *Geogr. Polonica* 19, 1970

38 McGee, T. G., *The Southeast Asian City*, London, G. Bell & Sons Ltd., 1967, p. 58

39 Faber, M., 'Is the Classical Theory of International Trade Applicable to Under-developed Economies?', *E. Afr. Econ. Rev.*, June, 1960

40 Johnston, B. F. and Mellor, J. W., 'The Role of Agriculture in Economic Development', *Am. Econ. Rev.*, 51, 4, 1961

41 Prebisch, R., *op. cit.*, p. 7

42 *for example*, Mountjoy, A. B., *Industrialization and Underdeveloped Countries*, London, Hutchison & Co. Ltd., 1963
Myint, H., *The Economics of the Developing Countries*, London, Hutchinson & Co. Ltd., 1964
Mandelbaum, K., *The Industrialization of Backward Areas*, Oxford, Blackwell, 1955

43 Odell, P. R., *An Economic Geography of Oil*, London, G. Bell & Sons Ltd., 1963, p. 122

44 Johnson, H. G., *op. cit.*, p. 79

45 Prebisch, R., *op. cit.*

CHAPTER 2

The Background to Trade in the Malayan Region

The previous chapter has attempted, in general terms, to provide a model or framework as a basis for the analysis of the evolving economic geography of what have been termed the 'export economies'—i.e. those areas of the world, frequently tropical or sub-tropical, whose resources were developed and usually controlled by overseas interests to serve overseas markets, and in which there often, though not invariably, developed dual economies with subsistence and commercial sectors co-existing. The rest of this book is a study of certain important aspects of the evolution of the economic geography of Malaya—a term* used to describe the peninsular region known politically since 1963 as West Malaysia together with the island of Singapore—which illustrates well the general theme, and which highlights both the opportunities and the problems facing young nations who are seeking to build viable modern economies on colonial economic bases. The book necessarily is concerned throughout with the commercial sector though it is fully appreciated that many of the developments described and of the factors analysed have interacted with the subsistence sector (for example in the production of the 'grey zones' mentioned in Chapter 1) and that many of the economic problems and changes in the economic geography associated with present day development are intimately concerned with subsistence and semi-subsistence areas.

There is no doubt that the commercial economy of Malaya is overwhelmingly the product of its recent colonial past. Never-

* In view of the varied use of names by different political entities at different times it has been necessary, for the purpose of this book, carefully to define the geographical areas to which names refer. These definitions appear in Appendix 1, p. 266.

theless commercial activity, both the exploitation of mineral resources and the conduct of entrepot trade, was not unknown before the penetration of the Malayan region by the European powers and, indeed, the early decades of the colonial era, particularly in the Portuguese phase, had more in common commercially with the pre-colonial period than with later developments.

Trade has been a major activity in the Malayan region for over a thousand years, and its early development was associated both with the region's geographical position vis-a-vis India and China and with its natural resources, especially minerals. The purpose of this short chapter, therefore, is to provide a general background, both physical and historical, to the Malayan region as an essential preliminary to the much more detailed analysis of the pattern of economic activity that was to emerge in Malaya in the nineteenth and twentieth centuries. Most of the material summarized here will be familiar to the reader who possesses an acquaintance with the geography and history of South-east Asia and there are many readily accessible sources that cover both in detail.[1] For the tin belt, however, rather more detail is provided, since the nature and location of tin deposits have been of particularly great significance to the economic geography of Malaya.

Physical Characteristics of the Region

The core of the Malayan region consists of the Sunda Platform, an ancient continental massif, much of which is now submerged but which, in post-Miocene times, existed as an extensive tract of land joining present day Malaya to Sumatra, Borneo and Java. The platform consists largely of sedimentary rocks of Carboniferous and Triassic Age into which were intruded great masses of igneous rocks, especially granites, in post-Rhaetic times. Much of the land area of the western Sunda Platform is underlain by a large batholith of granite, ridges of which form the backbones of mountain ranges thrusting up through the older sedimentaries that were folded and altered by the igneous material and by the earth movements that accompanied its intrusion.[2]

As a result of compressional movements between the Sunda Platform on the one hand, and the somewhat similar Sahul/

Australian massif and the stable floor of the Indian Ocean on the other, a major phase of folding took place in the South-east Asian region in Cretaceo-Tertiary and more recent times. Great thicknesses of soft sedimentary rocks that had accumulated

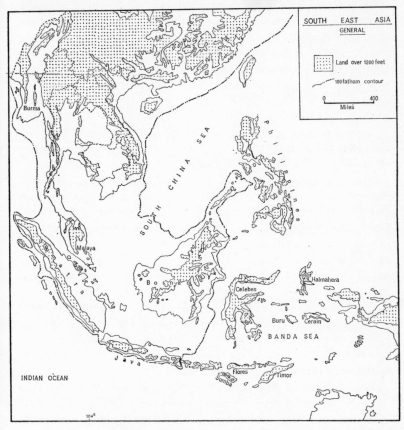

Figure 1. South-east Asia—General

around the margins of the Sunda Platform were crumbled and elevated to become dry land, and were then uplifted into two major series of folds which largely determined the pattern and relief of the East Indian islands. The first series of folds, dating generally from the mid-Miocene, is responsible for the outer line of ranges and islands, extending from the western mountains of Burma, through the Andamans, the islands off the west coast of Sumatra, Sumba and Timor, to Seram and Buru in the Moluccas and probably continuing into eastern Celebes, Halmahera and the eastern Philippine ranges. The second arc of rather later folds runs roughly parallel to its predecessor and may be traced through the medial hills of Burma, the main central axes of Sumatra, Java and the lesser Sunda islands and then through the curve of islets surrounding the Banda Sea and, conjecturally, into western and northern Celebes and the Philippines. At various points along this inner line, but especially in the eastern islands, occur the region's two hundred or more volcanoes, including ten active in the island of Flores alone.

Tectonic movements, changes in sea level, particularly those related to the melting of the Pleistocene ice sheets, sedimentation of river mouths flowing into the shallow seas of the partly submerged Sunda Platform and the modification of land surfaces by erosion and volcanic eruption have together produced in the region an extremely intricate pattern of large and small islands. These are separated from one another by shallow seas or narrow straits and divided within themselves by rugged mountain ranges or volcanic cones rising in places to above 10,000 feet. Extensive coral reefs occur off the west coast of Sumatra and also along the edge of the Sunda Platform in the Macassar Straits and Flores Sea and, in conjunction with minor reefs and swift currents between the islands of the eastern archipelago, produce navigational hazards that deflected sailing routes to the generally coral free seas between Sumatra, Malaya, Java and Borneo.

The climate of this vast archipelago is dominated by the monsoon wind system, or more accurately by the interplay of air-streams from three main directions—south, west and north-east.* During the northern winter, approximately from October to April, surface air-streams from the north-east ('the north-east monsoon'), originating as trades flowing under the influence of the sub-tropical Pacific anticyclone and reinforced by outflows of cold air from the vast Siberian anticyclone centred near Lake Baikal, advance southwards

---

* Dobby prefers to avoid the use of the term monsoon 'because the connotations given it in various parts of Asia differ so much that the term has become the "woolliest" in Asiatic geography.'[3]

over the South China Sea pushing the boundaries with the other air-streams ahead of them, and by January dominate

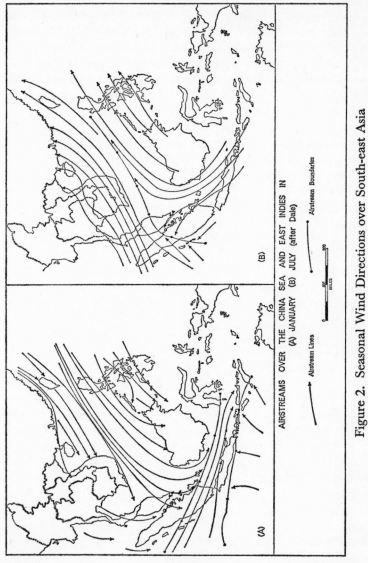

AIRSTREAMS OVER THE CHINA SEA AND EAST INDIES IN
(A) JANUARY (B) JULY (after Dale)

Airstream Lines ——▶

Airstream Boundaries ●—●

Figure 2. Seasonal Wind Directions over South-east Asia

the entire region as far south as the Java Sea. In the northern summer, from June to September, air-streams from the south and west reverse the process and by July and August converge over the South China Sea. At this season the whole of South-east Asia is influenced by south-westerly winds ('the south-west monsoon') except Java, southern Sumatra and the south coast of Borneo where the prevailing wind is south-easterly. The times of beginning and ending of the seasons vary with distance from the equator, so that in October, for example, the north-easterly air-stream has reached Indo-China although Malaya is still dominated by the south-westerly, and between the two seasons of predominantly north-easterly and predominantly south-westerly winds occur transitional periods lasting for about one month when wind directions are indeterminate. These transitional periods are frequently the times of heaviest convectional precipitation.

Associated with the surface winds that sweep across the South China Sea are complicated water movements. In the South China Sea the system of surface currents is completely reversed twice a year. Although the Luzon Strait faces the open ocean of the North Pacific with a width of more than 250 miles, and a sill depth of 7,500 feet in places, it is several degrees too far north for the North Equatorial Current to penetrate the South China Sea and establish a permanent circulation, while the disposition of the Philippines isolates, to a great extent, the South China Sea from the strong circulations of the western North Pacific.[4]

Surface drift currents on the western side of the South China Sea (i.e. paralleling the coasts of south China, Annam and south-east Malaya) show a marked seasonal rhythm, with a north-setting drift current flowing from April or May until September, and with a south-setting drift from September or October until March or April. In July and August a broad steady drift between 200 and 500 miles wide flows north-eastward across the South China Sea from the equator to Formosa; in November a south-setting western drift flows strongly and with marked constancy of direction between Hong Kong and the Anambas islands. On the eastern side of the South China Sea, along the coasts of Luzon, Palawan and northern Borneo, the seasonal rhythm is not so regular since gaps in the continuity of the land permit flows to and from the Sulu Sea but there is a clear northerly drift in October and November contributing to an anti-clockwise gyration in the South China Sea basin as a whole at that time.

The South-east Asian Tin Belt

Although metallic minerals occur in a number of places in the fold mountain zone of South-east Asia (for example gold in the Philippines and Sumatra, and copper in the Philippines) and there are considerable petroleum reserves associated especially with the area of gentler folds between the main regions of uplift and the stable edge of the Sunda Platform, by far the most important mineral resources exploited to date are those of the Platform itself. Within the core region of the Sunda Platform from southern Yunnan to the Sumatran off-shore islands of Singkep, Bangka and Billiton, by way of northern and peninsular Burma, Thailand and Malaya, stretches an 1,800 miles long metallogenetic province that contains valuable deposits of gold, copper, zinc, silver/lead, iron, manganese, chromium, cobalt, vanadium, molybdenum, and tungsten. The minerals ilmenite, zircon, and monazite are also present. The main economic value of the province, however, lies in the rich tin deposits, on which most mining activity has been concentrated. This mineral-rich province is the result of a complex series of geological events that occurred within a north-south trending belt. During the Proterozoic a complex series of mainly calcareous sediments, with intercalated volcanics, accumulated. Emplaced in this sequence are granites of various ages associated with migmatisation.[5] The granites now form the elongated, composite batholith that extends the length of the metallogenetic province and with which mineralization is associated.

Tin mineralization of this geological zone seems to date at least from the late Carboniferous and anomalously high concentrations of tin* may well have been present in the region much earlier than this.[6] Not all the granites are tin-bearing. Their history has never been worked out in detail, but it is known that intrusion took place in several stages, and that the

---

* Throughout this section reference to tin should be understood as being to cassiterite, the dioxide of tin (SnO_2), which is the principal ore of tin found in South-east Asia. Stannite, a primary sulphide of copper, iron and tin, a secondary tin mineral identified as calcium-tin-silicate, and the hydrated oxide varlamoffite, all occur but none is of any economic significance.

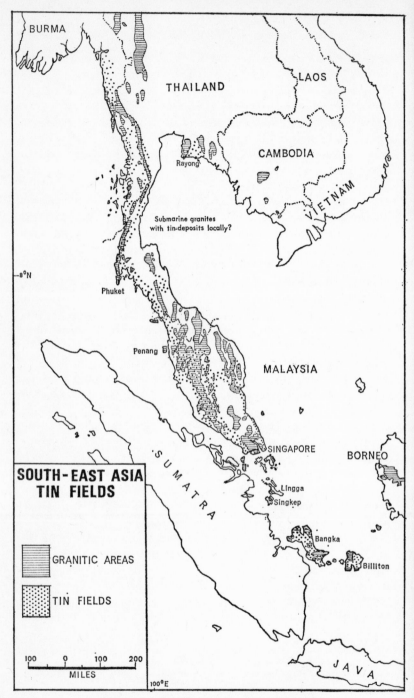

Figure 3. The South-east Asia Tinfields

granites of the latter stages are those which brought in the tin. As the granite magmas cooled and crystallized, the tin became progressively concentrated in highly mobile fluids which made their way along the joints and fractures, both in the consolidated granites and in the adjacent sedimentary rocks. Wherever temperature and pressure conditions were favourable, tin minerals separated out from the fluids and primary tin deposits were formed. The most favourable places for deposition were close to the 'contacts' between granite and the sedimentary rock.

Some of the primary tin deposits were disseminations of cassiterite through aplite, granite or pegmatite. Some took the form of stockworks, veins, or well-defined lodes in granite or schist. Some were highly irregular ore bodies filling 'pipes' in limestone. In many of the primary deposits, the cassiterite was associated with tourmaline or topaz, in others with quartz, and in some with arsenopyrite and other sulphide ore minerals. Most of the cassiterite crystallized in fairly small grains, but in some deposits crystals over two inches in length developed, while massive granular aggregates formed in many places. [7]

In Malaya, tin deposits are disposed in two well-defined parallel belts on the western and eastern sides of the country, separated by a zone that is virtually devoid of tin (Figure 3). The western tin belt, which is the larger and richer, extends beyond Malaya throughout the length of the former Yunnan-Malaya geosyncline and into south-east China. To the south this western tin belt extends into the Sumatran tin islands. The eastern tin belt of Malaya is best developed in Trengganu and the adjacent parts of Kelantan and Pahang and is continued further south in south-west Pahang and east Johore. Northwards this belt disappears into the Gulf of Thailand, but tin reported at Chantaburi and Rayong may represent the same belt exposed over a limited area before passing beneath the horizontal strata of the Korat plateau.

The Thai-Malay peninsula appears to have experienced a sequence of seven plutonic episodes since the Pre-Cambrian, and tin mineralization was probably associated with three of them viz. in late Carboniferous, early Triassic and late Jurassic/early Cretaceous times. Tin was possible migrant in the Pre-Cambrian and middle Cretaceous, and the pre-existing tin deposits of the western tin belt must certainly have been affected by the extensive granite emplacement of the late Triassic. Whilst the eastern tin belt was affected by four of the plutonic episodes, all seven probably affected the western tin belt which is, largely in consequence, the most highly stanniferous zone in the world. The concentration of tin during the course of plutonic evolution has probably reached its terminal stage in the Thai-Malay peninsula, since the region has been tectonically stable for nearly 200 million years and the last granites were emplaced some 60 to 80 million years ago. The tin deposits seem destined, therefore, for a protracted period of transport, corrasion and dispersal, and the exceptional richness of the deposits of this region would seem to be due to the co-incidence in geological time of their working by man and of the final stage of exposure of primary tin, by the forces of tropical erosion, and the beginning of the stage of transport.

The means of formation of the rich deposits of secondary tin (placers) in Malaya, which have been the principal sources worked by man*, is still somewhat uncertain but, according to Hosking,[8] it is difficult to escape the conclusion that major fluctuations of sea level during the Pleistocene played a major part by inducing the rejuvenation of rivers, a process that was accompanied by rapid valley erosion and followed by marine transgressions that re-worked already developed onshore placers. During the Pleistocene, eluvial cassiterite accumulated on valley slopes and hillsides, where primary deposits were subject to weathering, and then, under the influence of gravity and run-off, either formed base-of-slope colluvial deposits or was concentrated in streams that sorted the downwash. As a function both of water velocity and of grain size, varying amounts of tin were transported downstream but as a consequence of the rapid reduction of cassiterite to exceedingly small particles in running water, and also of the progressive dilution of the sediments by tin-barren debris as the distance from primary sources increased, the richest concentrations were formed relatively near to the primary sources. This has resulted in the fact that

---

* Though Scrivenor comments that owing to tropical weathering many non-detrital ore deposits can be and have been worked as if they were alluvial.[9]

economically worthwhile alluvial deposits are rarely found at distances greater than about 5 miles from a primary source.[10]

Cassiterite from primary sources near the coast was tran-

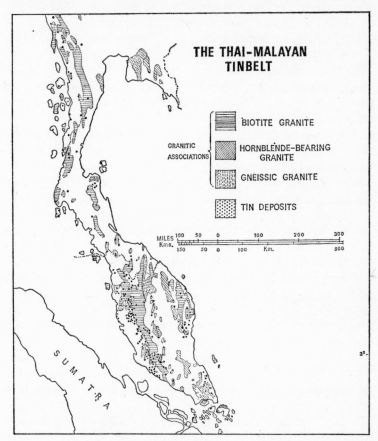

Figure 4. The Thai–Malayan Tinbelt

ported by rivers to the sea, and although larger grains tended to remain in the valleys, the finer particles were transported by longshore currents and deposited in elongate zones below low-water level parallel to the coast. Eluvial, colluvial and valley-type deposits that have been reworked by the sea, together with those deposits that were originally transported by rivers and concentrated in valleys before being reworked and drowned, constitute offshore placers of major economic importance.

The western tin belt of Malaya extends from the Thai border with Perlis to north-western Johore in the vicinity of Muar, with three major areas of concentration of alluvial cassiterite in the Kinta valley, in Selangor and in the Main Range extending from Ulu Selangor to Bentong (Figure 4). This last includes a wide area of mineralized granitic rocks, rising at one point to over four thousand feet and embracing the whole range, while mineralization decreases both to the north and to the south.

The Kinta tinfield, which has yielded nearly half of Malaya's total recorded tin production and which is by far the world's most productive single field, lies between the Kledang and Main Ranges in Perak and, in a former period of higher sea level, was most probably a sea strait. On both sides of the tinfield the normal granite is porphyritic, and on the margins aplite, frequently stanniferous and rich in kaolin, is found in several places. The bedrock of the valley floor is a crystalline limestone, believed to be of Carboniferous age,[11] which outcrops especially along the eastern margins in rugged hills with well developed karst features and often vertical or over-hanging cliffs, in some cases rising sheer for a thousand feet. The valley floor typically is composed of alluvium which conceals the limestone bedrock and fills crevices and solution hollows in the limestone to variable depths, in some places exceeding one hundred feet. Between Batu Gajah and Lahat the limestone is overlain by phyllites, quartzites and schists of comparable age. Tin ore has chiefly been won from the alluvium which is almost universally stanniferous, but granitic rocks with tin-bearing veins or lodes have also been worked and the chances of finding rich deposits of ore are much enhanced in areas of granite/sedimentary contacts. From Batu Gajah to the mouth of the Perak River stretches an extensive area of swamp land, resulting from the sinking of alluvial deposits over the limestone and the very gentle gradient of less than 1 in 7,000 characteristic of the lower course of the Kinta River, which has been extensively dredged for tin.

In Selangor, tin-bearing alluvial deposits are associated

with the valley of the Selangor River and its tributaries, particularly the Garing, Serendah and Kuang, and especially with the upper Klang Valley. A long tongue of granite extends southwards from the Main Range to beyond Puchong and results in the almost complete enclosure by granite of the upper Klang. Only in the south, between Puchong and Sungei Basi, does the continuity of the outcrop break and the high mineralization of the area is certainly in part due to the shallow depth of the granite under the environs of Kuala Lumpur.[12] As in the Kinta Valley, the margins of the upper Klang basin are flanked by limestone especially in the east.

The eastern tin belt is less productive than the western and known occurrences of tin-ore are further apart with a large gap in the belt south of the Pahang River. As in the west, tin deposits are all associated with granite but the more widespread occurrence of hornblende-granite in the east may account for the relative paucity of cassiterite. By contrast with the west, the most productive mines of the eastern tin belt are those working the tin lodes at Sungei Lembing, where veins cut granite and metamorphosed allied igneous and older sedimentary rocks. The tin occurs in the wall-rock alteration zone between the quartz veins and the country rock.

Early Trading Patterns: Pre-European Trade

Unlike the great sub-continental areas of India and China, between whose bordering oceans the isthmus of Kra and the Malay peninsula stretched as a mountainous, jungle-covered barrier, the Malayan region had no major alluvial lowlands or river valleys capable of supporting large populations and advanced cultures. Except for the northern plain of Java, where the Indianized civilization of Majapahit thrived for a short period in the fourteenth century, the lowlands of the peninsula and of the archipelago were small and isolated from one another by intractable rainforest, mountain ranges, or by the sea.

To the traders from the south China ports, who were venturing across the South China Sea as early as the first century B.C., the Malayan region was a source of supply of certain luxuries acceptable in China, such as pearls and scented woods, 'holy things' (e.g. fragrant woods for incense),

E

drugs and spices,[13] and the Thai-Malay peninsula itself was both a land barrier to direct trade with the Indian Ocean* and a useful entrepot for the exchange of China goods for commodities from further west. Although Chinese vessels are known at certain periods to have continued into the Indian Ocean†, most trade to the west of the peninsula was conducted by Indian and Arab merchants who similarly both sought the products of the archipelago and used its landfalls as convenient entrepots for the collection of local and China goods.

By the fifteenth century an exceedingly sophisticated pattern of trade had evolved that linked Europe with China by way of a series of entrepots in western Asia (such as Aden and Ormuz), India (especially the ports of Gujerat i.e. Surat, Randar, Diu and Daman) and South-east Asia (especially Malacca). The movement of goods between Europe and China was closely related to the seasonal wind patterns and normally spread over a number of seasons. It was impossible to traverse the entire Indian Ocean in one monsoon and the importance of the Gujerati ports was much dependent on this fact. The western half of the Indian Ocean was dominated by Arab traffic which collected European goods—precious metals, arms, glass and glass-ware, beads, quicksilver, dyes, copper nails, coloured woollen clothes—from Aden, and opium, gold, silver, pearls, rosewater, raisins, carpets, horses, seeds and grains from Arabia, Syria and East Africa and carried them to Gujerat where they were exchanged principally for South-east Asian spices.

Traffic between Gujerat and Malacca was almost exclusively in Gujerati hands. An extensive fleet of merchant shipping designed to meet the requirements of the Indian Ocean and the monsoons had been built with large cargo holds and capable both of running well before the wind and of manoevring against it. In addition to western goods, this shipping carried the products of Gujerat itself—many varieties of textiles, indigo, opium, soap, grain, butter, dried and salted meat. Ships could leave the Indian coast for Malacca from January

* Use was made of a portage that crossed the neck of the Malay peninsula either north or south of the Kra isthmus.[14]

† In the twelfth century Chinese junks reached even as far as Quilon on the coast of Malabar.[15]

until the best time to sail in March, the later date enabling travellers from further west to embark in the Gujerati vessels. This programme allowed a short time only in Malacca since it was necessary to be back on the Indian coast by the end of May before it was sealed by the full force of the south-west monsoon which made the arrival or departure of ships impossible between May and the end of October.

The importance of Malacca as an entrepot appears to have been based primarily on its position vis-a-vis the seasonal wind patterns of both the Indian Ocean and the South China and Java Seas which made it equally accessible, though at different seasons of the year, from India, China and the eastern archipelago. The most authentic account of the foundation of Malacca is that of Tomé Pires who attributes the establishment of the port to a band of Bugis corsairs who commandeered a fishing village at the mouth of the Malacca River at the very beginning of the fifteenth century.[16] The marketing of pirated goods in due course apparently stimulated more orthodox trade and by 1409 the Malacca settlement, having offered annual tribute to the Chinese empire, was given the status of a kingdom. The harbour itself enjoyed a good reputation.* It occupied a sheltered estuary with a mangrove-free shore, was accessible in any monsoon and free of storms and dangerous shallows. It also controlled the narrowest part of the Strait over which it had ensured supremacy by about 1420 by means of a fleet of patrol boats that forced vessels passing along the Strait to call at Malacca. Its economic base was, however, a narrow one. It had few domestic products for export, these being mainly gold and tin from subordinate states on the peninsula and fish, and the small area of agricultural land in the vicinity of the town was totally inadequate for its population which was probably in the vicinity of 40,000–50,000 in 1510.[17]

The period of greatest activity at Malacca was from December to March when ships were arriving from the Far East as well as from western Asia. Between November and February Chinese vessels were arriving, having crossed the South China Sea on the north-easterlies and been aided by

* Malacca harbour had silted so much by the later nineteenth century, however, that landing was difficult except at nearly high water.[18]

the strong south-setting drift current. If early, they could proceed on to Java from Malacca taking advantage of the strong westerly airflow that persisted in the Java Sea until March. It was necessary to leave Malacca by the end of June for the return voyage to the China coast on the south-westerlies.

Between May and September native craft from the eastern archipelago arrived in Malacca propelled by the south-easterlies that pre-dominate over the Banda, Flores and Java Seas at that season. These came from the Banda islands, which acted as a minor entrepot for the cloves of the Moluccas as well as for the nutmegs of the Banda group itself, and from Macassar, Timor, Java and southern Sumatra with a variety of spices, precious woods, and other local products of forest and seashore. These commodities were bartered and stored for later resale in Malacca during the waiting period until January when the native craft could return east on the now favourable north-westerlies, and the vessels began to arrive again from India and China. An early arrival of the north-easterlies in the Java Sea, however, or delays en route, could easily upset the timing of trading vessels from the eastern archipelago and prevent their arrival at Malacca, a problem met more frequently by the English East India Company when it set out to attract the native trade to its new entrepot of Penang at the northern end of the Straits of Malacca after 1786.

From the beginning of the second millenium, therefore, and possibly from even earlier, the Malay peninsula, as a consequence of its position and resources, has performed the joint functions of entrepot and exporter of raw materials. Of her mineral wealth it was the gold, produced especially from the mines and placers of Pahang, that attracted the principal attention of merchants and travellers, particularly from the west, and accounted for the term 'Golden Khersonese' used of the peninsula on early European maps. The exploitation of readily accessible tin deposits along stream courses, however, probably has as long a history. Tin mines, probably on the Tenasserim coast, were described by Arab voyagers towards the end of the first millenium whilst a fourteenth-century Chinese account of the countries of the South Seas*

* The Tao-i Chih-lioh of Wang Ta-yüan compiled after travels in the 1330s and 40s.

makes frequent reference to tin as an indigenous product and item of trade.

Early European Trade

The European penetration of the South-east Asian region was the direct result of the Portuguese desire to re-route the eastern trade around the Cape of Good Hope to Lisbon, and their first abortive contact with Malacca in 1509, when Diego Lopez de Sequeira's squadron of five ships withdrew after a disturbance, was followed by the capture of the town by Alfonso d'Albuquerque's expedition from Goa in 1511. The objectives of the Portuguese in Asia, being commercial and missionary rather than imperial, hinged on the concentration of trading and naval power in a limited number of strategic bases or 'factories', often fortified for the greater security of their persons and their merchandize in an actually or potentially hostile environment, and only to a limited extent did their rule spread beyond the main fortress centres. Malacca, thanks to its situation and its existing control of trade, became Portugal's principal fortified factory in South-east Asia and a model for later European headquarters in the region. Other similar but generally smaller fortresses were constructed elsewhere on the Malayan coast, in the islands of the eastern archipelago and ultimately as far as at Nagasaki (1570).

Portuguese trading policy in the Straits followed the traditional lines of monopolistic control laid down by their indigenous predecessors which they maintained with a narrow margin of superiority thanks to better techniques and equipment. Besides direct trade between Portugal and Asia, the Malaccan administration sought to control the valuable Asian inter-port trade by maintaining surveillance over the narrow sea lane of the Straits and compelling all traffic to turn in to the port of Malacca.

The ousting of the Portuguese from their monopoly trading position in Asia by the Dutch was a direct outcome of political re-alignments in Europe, but was also an understandable consequence of the great strain of Portugal's far-flung interests (in Brazil and Africa as well as in Asia) on her limited manpower. The unification of the Portuguese and Spanish crowns under Spain from 1580 to 1640 rendered the Portuguese colonies open to depredations by the Low Countries, still hostile to Spain following the independence of the seven United Provinces (the modern Netherlands) in 1579, and the closing of the port of Lisbon to Dutch merchants in 1594 sent them to India on their own, piloted round the Cape by a compatriot erstwhile in the service of Portugal. Spain tacitly surrendered Portuguese interests in the east thus whetting the appetite of the Dutch for general invasion of the overseas monopoly of the Iberian states. Particularly after 1590 there was a steady increase in Dutch overseas trade and in Dutch influence in the South-east Asian region until their seizure of Ceylon and Malabar (in 1655–63) spelt the final eclipse of the Portuguese empire in Asia.

The ships of the Netherlands East India Company, which was founded in 1602 to exploit systematically the newly won commercial interests of the Low Countries in the east, at first sailed to the Indies along the route pioneered by the Portuguese, which hugged the east African coast as far north as about Mombasa and then followed the traditional Arab and Gujerati sea lanes to the Straits of Malacca by way of Malabar. In 1611, however, the 'roaring forties' route across the Indian Ocean was first sailed and was made the officially authorized route for eastward bound Indiamen in 1617. After leaving the Cape of Good Hope, the Dutch Indiamen steered due east between 36°S and 42°S, thus leaving the African coast and sailing into open ocean, until, picking up the south-east trade winds, they set a northerly course for the Straits of Sunda. In sailing for Java many vessels actually made North-West Cape, New Holland, before heading northwards.[19]

The new Sunda Straits route into the South-east Asian archipelago and the fact that the Portuguese clung tenaciously to Malacca until 1641 made necessary the establishment of a Dutch factory in the vicinity of the Straits, where trade routes converged and where homeward and outward-bound vessels could load and unload their cargoes, and goods from the islands be collected, stored or transhipped. The ideal location for this station was somewhere on the north-west coast of Java, and, in May 1619, Jan Pieterszoon Coen seized the small Javanese port of Jakarta and constructed the castle and fortified town of Batavia that was to remain the focus of the Dutch empire in the Indies for over three centuries.

Initially the Netherlands East India Company was able to satisfy its European markets, and its directors in the Low Countries, by monopolizing the archipelago's trade in tropical crops, forest products and valuable metals, and by exploiting intensively the native producers who were accustomed to handing over part of their output as tribute to local chiefs. The Company had no intention at first of acquiring territorial sovereignty beyond its factories but in due course the insatiable European market made it necessary to compel the native farmer to grow those crops desired by the Company— such as coffee, sugar and indigo—and Dutch administration inevitably followed. Java, by far the richest agriculturally of the East Indian islands, thanks to basically fertile and often renewed alluvial and volcanic soils, a rather lower rainfall than the equatorial islands and a long history of settled agriculture, became the main area of Dutch influence and ultimately the most valued of Holland's possessions.

For the greater part of the seventeenth and eighteenth centuries, Holland dominated the trade of the Indies (though effectively 'monopolized' only the trade in spices thanks to the resourcefulness[20] of the Asian trader and of the European country trader) and became increasingly involved in organizing the production of tropical crops, especially in Java. Although in control of Malacca after 1641, the Dutch retained it as a fortress dominating the Straits rather than as a trading post. As an entrepot it was firmly overshadowed by Batavia, though it continued to import Indian textiles and to export the tin produced in its immediate hinterland—the only tin exports from the peninsula over which the Dutch were able, in practice, to maintain their monopoly. By the second quarter of the eighteenth century an important exchange centre, which the Dutch Company was only partially and occasionally able to control, had been established at Riau, largely under Bugis authority, and was conducting a thriving trade in Bangka tin, opium, pepper, piece-goods and China goods.[21] The Dutch finally drove the Bugis out and garrisoned Riau in 1784, but within less than two years the English establishment of a settlement on Penang island introduced another element in the undermining of the Dutch controlled trade. The successful penetration of the English into the Malayan region was to create a new trading pattern in the Straits of Malacca. It was gradually to draw the Malayan peninsula, and in due course much of the archipelago, into the ambit of the English industrial economy, which was in the early stages of its phenomenal growth and whose demands for raw materials and markets were to be responsible for a quickening of economic activity throughout the region and for the emergence of a pattern of economic specialization with far-reaching consequences.

REFERENCES

1 Standard basic texts include:
  Dobby, E. H. G., *South-east Asia*, 10th ed., University of London Press, 1967
  Fisher, C. A., *South-east Asia*, 2nd ed., London, Methuen, 1966
  Robequain, C., *Malaya, Indonesia, Borneo and the Philippines*, 2nd ed., London, Longmans, 1958
  Hall, D. G. E., *A History of South-east Asia*, 3rd ed., London, Macmillan, 1968
  Harrison, B., *South-east Asia—a Short History*, 3rd ed., London, Macmillan, 1966
2 Scrivenor, J. B., *The Geology of Malayan Ore Deposits*, London, Macmillan, 1928, p. 1
3 Dobby, E. H. G., 'Winds and Fronts over South-east Asia', *Geogr. Rev.*, 35, 1945
4 Dale, W. L., 'Wind and Drift Currents in the South China Sea', *Mal. J. Trop. Geogr.*, 8, 1956
5 Hosking, K. F. G., *Aspects of the Geology of the Tin-Fields of South-east Asia*, London, International Tin Council, 1969, p. 2
6 Burton, C. K., *The Geological Environment of Tin Mineralization in the Malay-Thai Peninsula*, London, International Tin Council, 1969, p. 14
7 United Nations, *Tin Ore Resources of Asia and Australia*, Mineral Resources Development Series, No. 23, New York, 1964, p. 38
8 Hosking, *op. cit.*, p. 28
9 Scrivenor, *op. cit.*, p. 152
10 Emery, K. O. and Noakes, L. C., 'Economic Placer Deposits of the Continental Shelf, pp. 95–111 of Technical Bulletin 1 of E.C.A.F.E. Committee for co-ordination of joint prospecting for mineral resources in Asian off-shore areas, Geological Survey, Japan, 1968.
11 Ingham, F. T. and Bradford, E. F., 'Geology and Mineral Resources of the Kinta Valley, Perak', Federation of Malaya Geological Survey District Memoir No. 9, Kuala Lumpur, Government Printer, 1960, p. 20
12 Scrivenor, op. cit., p. 106
13 Wang Gungwu, 'The Nanhai Trade. A Study of the Early History of Chinese Trade in the South China Sea', *J. Mal. Brch. R. Asiat. Soc.* 31, 1958

14 Wheatley, P., *The Golden Khersonese. Studies in the Historical Geography of the Malay Peninsula before 1500*, Kuala Lumpur, University of Malaya Press, 1961, p. 10
15 *Ibid., op. cit.*, p. 61
16 *Suma Oriental of Tomé Pires*, London, Hakluyt Society, 1944 (Hakluyt Society, second series, nos. 49–50), 2v. v. ii, p. 238.
17 Meilinck-Roelofsz, M. A. P., *Asian Trade and European Influence in the Indonesian Archipelago between 1500 and about 1630*, Martinus Nijhoff, The Hague, 1962, p. 339
18 'Malacca Harbour', *J. Straits Brch. R. Asiat. Soc.*, 52, 1909
19 Parkinson, C. N., *Trade in the Eastern Seas, 1793–1813*, Cambridge University Press, 1937, p. 102
20 Bassett, D. K., 'Dutch Trade in Asia', *J. S. Seas Soc.*, 14, 1958
21 de Bruijn, P. G. (trans. B. Harrison), 'Trade in the Straits of Malacca in 1785', *J. Mal. Brch. R. Asiat. Soc.*, 26, 1953

CHAPTER 3

Free Trade & the Pattern of Economic Specialization in Malaya

As is well known, the economic geography of modern Malaya—outside the subsistence sector, which largely is not the concern of this book—has for long been dominated by the tin mining and rubber planting industries of the mainland and by the commercial activities of the two island entrepots of Penang and Singapore, much of whose trade has been concerned with the products of the peninsula's mines and plantations and with the demand for imports that they have engendered. The nature and pattern of this economic specialization evolved during the nineteenth and early twentieth centuries, particularly between 1869 and 1914, and in many ways appears as the development of activities and functions for which the region had outstanding advantages.

From the foundation of the free port of Penang in 1786 until the outbreak of the First World War, the Malayan economy grew within the increasingly free trading British Empire, in which few administrative limitations were placed on trade or on economic activity in general. Within this economic environment, the very real physical advantages possessed by the peninsula for the production of commodities that were subject to a rapidly growing demand were able strongly to mould its economic geography and were assisted by a combination of additional favourable factors. The indigenous population, consisting essentially of wet-rice farmers, was sufficiently small in numbers* for land to be available for other than subsistence activities without the necessity for any form of forced cultivation and with the

* Estimated at only 400,000 as late as 1830.[1]

minimum disruption of the subsistence sector. Immigrant labour which consequently was needed to man the mines and work the plantations had unrestricted entry. The guarantee of law and order that accompanied the British forward political movement into Malaya encouraged confidence and trade and, in due course, overseas investment, whilst the small size of the peninsula and the relatively easy terrain assisted the development of an efficient infrastructure of railways, roads, power generation and distribution to serve the emerging economy. Its ports were on international trade routes and the commercial, marketing and financial functions that grew up initially in connection with the entrepot trade were ready and able to handle all the requirements of their peninsular hinterland as its economy grew.

The Foundation & Early Growth of the Free Ports

As has been recounted in Chapter 2, the Malayan region had been actively concerned with commerce from an early period, but during the greater part of the seventeenth and eighteenth centuries much of the trade both within the archipelago and with Europe was dominated by the Dutch. By the 1780s, however, the English East India Company, which for the best part of a century had taken little direct interest in the Malayan region apart from maintaining an undistinguished station at Bencoolen on the west coast of Sumatra and some shortlived settlements in Borneo, was seeing the archipelago in a new light. One reason for this renewed interest was the rapidly developing trade with China which was especially stimulated by the passing of the Commutation Act by the House of Commons in 1784. This act, designed to kill the smuggling trade on which the Danish, Swedish and Imperial East India Companies all thrived, reduced the duties payable on tea from over 100 per cent. to only 12½ per cent. and thus enabled what had previously been an expensive luxury to come more within the reach of the less affluent. The increase in the demand for China goods, particularly tea, resulted in the trade between Britain and China being more than doubled in the next few years.[2] Whilst the demand for China goods remained small, payment in gold and silver bullion and coin had been the rule, but towards the end of the eighteenth century the East India Company was finding increasing difficulty in procuring enough specie to finance the growing trade. The acceptability of Straits tin and Indian cotton and especially opium to the Chinese made these commodities suitable alternatives and they were carried between Bengal and Canton, and tea and silk brought back, both by the Company's ships and by 'country traders'—private merchants licensed by the East India Company to trade east of Calcutta.

The establishment of the Company's settlement on Penang island in 1786 has often been explained as a strategic decision, created by the necessity for a naval base on the eastern shore of the Bay of Bengal during the north-east monsoon when ships were unable to re-fit on the exposed Coromandel coast of India. It seems as likely, however, that Penang was intended as a port of call for the country ships on the China run, who found the Dutch ports of Malacca and the archipelago expensive and frequently hostile and the native ports usually of limited assistance. The desire to develop commercial contacts with the native states of the region was almost certainly also a consideration, since, amongst other commodities, they produced tin.[3]

The selection of the island of Penang as the site of the East India Company's settlement was based on the initiative of Francis Light, the captain of a country ship trading out of Madras, who for some years had been exploring the commercial prospects in both Kedah and Achin on behalf of his employers. His suggestions for a British trading station on either Penang or Junk Ceylon (Ujong Salang)—a small island, now known by its Thai name of Phuket, off the western coast of Siam— were received with indifference by the Company, apparently wary of the political involvement with Siam that either settlement would create, until the re-emergence of Dutch influence in southern Malaya including their occupation of Riau, which followed the Anglo-Dutch peace terms of 1784, seemed to force their hand. In 1786, following negotiations with the Sultan of Kedah, Penang's overlord and nominal vassal of the Siamese, the island was ceded to the East India Company and Light took possession.

Sir John MacPherson, acting Governor-General of India

at the time of the cession, wrote to Light on the 22nd January 1787 setting out the Company's purposes in founding the station:

> At present our great object in settling Prince of Wales Island* is to secure a port of refreshment and repair for the King's, and Company's and the country ships, and we must leave it to time and to your good management to establish it as a port of commerce.[4]

Light himself considered that Penang was eminently suitable as a harbour for refitting ships, as a centre for the commerce of the archipelago and as a mart where the ships engaged in the China trade could buy those products of the archipelago that were suitable for the Canton market.

The advantages of Penang for these purposes were certainly considerable. It was situated—unlike Bencoolen—on the direct route from India to China, and was thus a suitable port of call for the country traders, and it was an admirable place for developing trade with northern Malaya (particularly the tin producing areas of Perak and Kedah), south Siam and Achin. The physical nature of Penang helped it provide, almost uniquely among the many islands off the west coast of the Malayan peninsula, a good anchorage. Most of the islands bordering the Straits of Malacca are low lying stretches of alluvium and mangrove swamp largely built up from the silt carried by the sluggish rivers of the peninsula and of Sumatra, and the inlets and rivers that separate them from one another and from the mainland are shallow and treacherous. Penang, however, is basically a granite island, geologically a part of the Malayan Ranges but separated from them as a consequence of sea level changes. The channel (averaging 2–3 miles in width) between the island and the mainland is deep, in some places exceeding ten fathoms, and, apart from the relatively minor Prai river on the mainland side, receives no sediment loaded streams. The channel shallows towards the shores of the island, with the result that large ships had to be unloaded by lighter, but the roads are admirably protected

---

* The island was so christened by Light, on its acquisition by the East India Company, in honour of the birthday of Prince George, but the name was largely ignored, except by the pedantic and official, in favour of the more melodic, convenient and appropriate Malay 'Pinang'.

from both monsoons thanks to the alignment of high ground to both east and west, whilst a mudbank or flat not more than four and a half fathoms at low water breaks the force of waves from the north-west—the direction of maximum fetch. A senior naval officer of the period considered that 'an advantage which Prince of Wales Island possesses beyond any other part of the Eastern Coast is the excellence of its harbour'.[5]

Whatever strategic considerations may have been in mind when it agreed to the foundation of a settlement on Penang, there seems little doubt that the Company hoped it would thrive as a trading centre, and MacPherson was quite explicit in instructing Light to 'refrain from levying any kind of duties or tax on goods landed or vessels importing at Prince of Wales Island',[6] since it was the Company's wish to make the port free to all nations. This first reference to a British free trading policy in the Malayan region suggests the adoption of an expedient for the specific purpose of attracting trade to Penang rather than any major liberalization of the Company's general commercial policy, but it was to have far reaching effects. Light, still trading on his own account while super-intendent of the settlement, was only too well aware of the advantages of keeping the port free since he was conscious of the practical difficulties that faced trade in the Straits of Malacca and the archipelago at the end of the eighteenth century and realized that every encouragement was needed if native merchants were to be attracted to Penang. The greater profits to be made, thanks to the freedom from duties, were the magnet to overcome the difficulties created for commerce by wars in the native states of Malaya and Sumatra, and by Dutch attempts to maintain Malacca's monopoly of Straits trade. James Scott, friend and trading partner of Light, thought it 'wiser to trust to a sure revenue from an increase of capital and population consequent to a free trade, than trust to one on a passing commodity which impediments may move elsewhere'.[7]

Increasingly, however, manufacturing and commercial interests in Britain were seeking freer trading with India and the East for the purpose of the ready disposal of the surpluses of their factories, and free trade in the Malayan region not only made this easier but, by encouraging native commerce, was likely to raise the local propensity to consume. Furnivall, in reference to Java, made a striking contrast between Dutch and British interests in this matter when he wrote:

> The Dutch had nothing to sell to the people ... But by 1800 England was producing vast quantities of cheap cotton goods which could undersell local produce even in British India and, whereas Dutch interest in the East centred in the supply of Eastern produce, British interest looked also to the demand for Western produce. An increase in the welfare and consuming power of the natives was prejudicial to the Dutch but profitable to the English. ... [8]

British cotton interests, with confidence in their competitive power, began agitation about 1808 for free trading with India and the East, and, according to H. R. C. Wright, this agitation was made exceedingly potent by a fear that unemployment in the British cotton manufacturing districts might have violent social and political consequences.* A free intercourse with India and with the 'rich, populous and extensive countries further east' would ensure 'peace of the community' and 'give full employment to the operative classes'.[9] When Singapore was founded in 1819 it followed the free trade example set by Penang and in keeping with Britain's overseas commercial interests.

The foundation of Singapore was the outcome of the recognition by Stamford Raffles that Penang's situation was too peripheral to South-east Asia as a whole to serve its avowed purpose as a British entrepot for trade in the archipelago and as a counter to Dutch monopolistic trading practices. Despite the fact that Britain had occupied Malacca in 1795 and controlled Java between 1811 and 1816, so that Dutch influence was all but annihilated in the region for a while, the annual volume of Penang's trade between 1810 and 1819 was stationary.[10] Penang's lack of success in attracting trade especially after 1810 has been attributed to a variety of causes.

---

* M. M. Edwards describes the problems facing the English cotton manufacturers especially after 1803 when the home market 'was exceeded far too often' and 'those in the trade had to be constantly searching for new outlets for their wares'.—*The Growth of the British Cotton Trade* 1780–1815, Manchester University Press, 1967, p. 29.

The increase in piracy in the Straits of Malacca which compelled many native traders to avoid those waters, the refusal of the East India Company, still wary of political involvement, to permit any attempt by the settlement to extend its political influence among the Malay states of the peninsula, the depressed nature of the China market for Straits produce,* maladministration, and the imposition of various though generally small revenue-raising duties to support the administration, have all been claimed as circumstances contributing to, or accounting for, the economic difficulties that were undoubtedly faced by Penang in the second decade of the nineteenth century. The basic geographical disadvantage of Penang, however—so clearly recognized by Raffles—was also apparent to the historical writer J. Crawfurd who, in 1820, declared:

> (Penang) is a small spot of barren soil, having a good harbour, but too far to the west, or, in other words, too remote from the most populous and productive parts of the Archipelago, and entirely out of the way of the easiest and safest avenue, the Straits of Sunda.[11]

The return of Java and Malacca to the Dutch by the Anglo-Dutch Convention of 1814 confirmed Raffles in his conviction that, unless Britain's commercial interests were to be lost to a re-asserted Dutch monopoly, a British station more central to the archipelago than Penang wss essential. Writing in 1818 he stated:

> The Dutch possess the only passes through which ships must sail into the Archipelago, the Straits of Sunda and Malacca; and the British have now not an inch of ground to stand upon between the Cape of Good Hope and China, nor a single friendly port at which they can water and obtain refreshments. It is indispensable that some regular and accredited authority on the part of the British Government should exist in the Archipelago, to declare and maintain the British rights. . . . At present the authority of the Government of Prince of Wales Island extends no further than Malacca, and the Dutch would willingly confine that

---

* Straits produce included areca-nuts, birds' nests, coconuts, gambier, mother-of-pearl, pepper, rattans, snake and lizard skins, tapioca, tin and tortoise shell.

of Bencoolen to the almost inaccessible shores of the West coast of Sumatra.

To effect the objects contemplated some convenient station within the Archipelago is necessary; both Bencoolen and Prince of Wales Island are too far removed, and unless we succeed in obtaining a position in the Straits of Sunda, we have no alternative but to fix it in the most advantageous position we can find in the Archipelago; this would be somewhere in the neighbourhood of Bintang.[12]

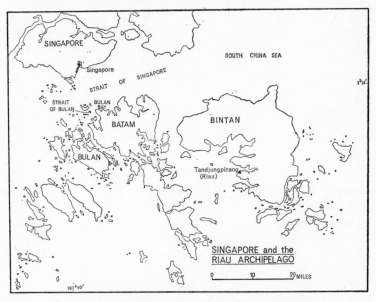

Figure 5. Singapore and the Riau Archipelago

Bintang (Bintan, Figure 5) is the largest island in the Riau group, and lies some thirty miles south-east of Singapore.

Despite strong opposition from Calcutta, where the East India Company was still unhappy about acquiring new responsibilities in South-east Asia, and from Penang, whose early support for a second settlement in the Straits turned to hostility when it was realized that the new station would not be under its control, Raffles obtained agreement in 1819 from members of the ruling house of Johore to found a settlement on the practically uninhabited island of Singapore.

The site, used by native traders in the past, and earlier even considered but never adopted by the Dutch, had sound advantages for Raffles's purpose. For similar physical reasons to those applying to Penang, it had a harbour of deep water protected by small islands, it was focally placed for trade from the Malayan peninsula, Sumatra, Java, Borneo and the eastern islands, and was also on the China route. Raffles considered that 'its position in the Straits of Singapore is far more convenient and commanding than even Rhio, for our China trade passing down the Straits of Malacca and every native vessel that sails through the Straits of Rhio must pass in sight of it.'[13] The new settlement was viewed with enthusiasm by the China merchants. James Matheson of Canton, for example, considered its situation 'truly delightful, being within four miles of the direct tract for China,'[14] whilst the *Calcutta Journal* of 19th March 1819 stated that 'the commercial world will rejoice in our having occupied the position which was required as a fulcrum for the support of our Eastern and China trade.'[15]

From the first, Singapore was a free port. Raffles's instructions to Farquhar, who was installed as the first Resident, were that it was not necessary to subject the trade of the port to any duties since it was still very small and that it would be impolitic to incur the risk of obstructing its development by such measures. If the port was to become a success and serve Raffles's main purpose it had to attract the local trade as swiftly as possible. In order to do this, it was not enough that Singapore was in a convenient position, it had to offer better trading prospects than any Dutch port, and the simplest way to guarantee such prospects, as Penang had earlier shown, was to keep it free from duties. As early as nine months after Singapore's foundation, Farquhar was able to report encouraging progress and to comment on the gratification of native traders 'at the opening prospect of a free and advantageous commerce.'[16]

There seems little doubt that the duty free status of the two British trading ports, located at each end of the Straits of Malacca, was established for the simple purpose of drawing as much trade as possible away from the Dutch ports and, equally, that the policy succeeded. Trading vessels from all parts of South-east Asia converged especially on Singapore—

within less than a year of its foundation ships from Siam, Cambodia, Kelantan, Trengganu, Pahang, Brunei, western Borneo, Celebes and eastern Sumatra were recorded at Singapore[17]—and its volume of trade and its population increased rapidly.

The initial attractions of both British ports, but especially of Singapore, were reinforced by the provision of properly conducted auctions and markets, of banking and insurance facilities and of shipping. The ports, again particularly Singapore, became collecting and redistributing centres for the produce of the Straits and of much of the archipelago—the products of local jungle, sea-coast, mines and fields were exchanged for British piece goods of wool, cotton and silk, for steel goods, gunpowder, iron and china ware. European merchant houses became important for providing finance, often for Chinese merchants who traded on credit, and in intercontinental shipping, whilst the Chinese merchants became prominent in directing the flow of goods within the archipelago.

1824 is the earliest year for which reasonable commercial statistics exist for Singapore, and was also the year of the Anglo-Dutch Treaty that finally achieved Dutch recognition of Britain's paramountcy in the Malay peninsula as well as stipulating the terms under which the merchants of Singapore were to conduct their trade in the archipelago. With the removal of any lingering doubts as to the political future of the settlement and the regularization, at least on paper, of its trading rights, the trade of Singapore entered a phase of immense progress, punctuated by only occasional setbacks, from each of which it rose to even greater prosperity.[18] For the first thirty or so years of its existence, Singapore was one of the freest of the contemporary world's free ports. Not only was trade exempt from import and export duties, tonnage and port dues, wharfage and anchorage duties, but also from the payment of port clearance fees and stamp duties. Even the Navigation Acts and the East India Company's monopoly of the trade with China, both increasingly anachronistic, were flouted, the former with official connivance and the latter by commercial sleight-of-hand. One of the few occasions when the Navigation Laws were enforced, against an American vessel by an over-zealous naval officer, led to the subsequent use of Booland Bay* on Batam in the Riau archipelago and Riau itself as anchorages for United States shipping and the lightering of goods fourteen miles or so across the straits to Singapore. Direct trade between China and Britain in other than Company ships was manipulated by the issue in Singapore of fresh bills of lading to London consignees for commodities from China which then proceeded on their journey usually in the same ship.

The far greater accessibility of Singapore than either Malacca or Penang for trade in the archipelago and the energy and initiative of its merchants, both European and Chinese, soon reduced the older ports to commercial dependencies of the newer settlement. The trade of Malacca had long ceased to be of any but local significance, whilst that of Penang was limited to business with the west coast of Malaya, Sumatra, southern Siam and southern Burma—regions for which Penang was more conveniently situated than Singapore. Commodities from Europe for distribution within the hinter-lands of Malacca and Penang were transhipped from Singapore to the smaller ports, but the growing prosperity of Singapore was a strong stimulus to the development of their local trade as it was to trade throughout the archipelago.

Singapore soon became the most advantageous port to which the native traders of the archipelago could take their goods. The Dutch ports of the East Indian islands began to lose that portion of their local trade that could readily be handled through Singapore. The east Borneo ports, for example, Sambas, Mampawa and Pontianak, lost their eastward trade to Singapore whilst the Dutch protective tariff wall throughout the archipelago was undermined by the introduction of British cotton piece goods. Established in order to provide a protected market for the products of the Belgian cotton industry that had developed during the Napole-onic period, the Dutch tariff was almost powerless to keep out contraband British cottons carried by native traders up the numerous creeks and rivers of the islands. Surveillance

* It has not proved possible to locate Booland (or Bulan) Bay with certainty. All evidence suggests, however, that the bay used was that on the north side of Batam island at the entrance to the Bulan strait, part of which is now known as Djodoh Bay (Figure 5).

of the long coastlines of innumerable islands was virtually impossible.

With Singapore as the major international link, the Celebes port of Macassar became the entrepot for the distribution of British goods further east, and the Bugis* the major traders throughout the archipelago. Through the medium of the Bugis, British manufactures penetrated the remote regions in the archipelago inaccessible to European merchants or hardly visited by them. The inhabitants of Timor, for example, consumed almost no British manufactures until they were distributed from Singapore by the Bugis. In transacting business between the European commercial houses and the Bugis taders, the Chinese middlemen of Singapore proved their worth, especially those Malacca-born Chinese who could speak tolerable English and Malay.

The full economic and geographical significance of Singapore in the first half of the nineteenth century is not to be measured solely or perhaps even mainly in terms of the profits it brought to the mercantile population of the city and the creation of a major seaport on what previously had been an almost uninhabited island. Singapore's significance is to be found rather in the extension of trade to practically every corner of the archipelago from which a native *prahu* could set out for the port. In 1830, an article in the *Singapore Chronicle* spoke of Borneo and Celebes in the following terms:

The establishment of Singapore, free of duties, and the known facility with which the native population can transact business at that port have created an unusual sensation amongst all ranks of people; even the Diaks in the centre of Borneo and those of Celebes are aware of its establishment and advantages. On the eastern coast of Borneo, from point Salatan to the Sooloo Islands, an extent of little less than one thousand miles, new prows are building in almost every week; the same on the western coast of Celebes, where the inhabitants, generally speaking, are much more enlightened, enterprising, and industrious. In all parts of both these coasts, the natives are moving from the interior districts, towards the sea; in hopes of

* The true Bugis are the inhabitants of the south-western peninsula of Celebes, on which Macassar stands, but the term came to be used in Singapore to describe all Malaysian traders from the east.

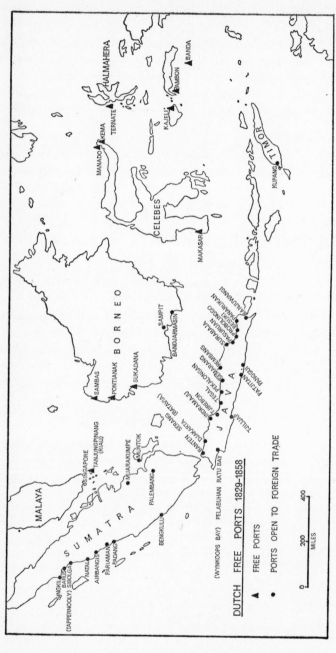

Figure 6. Dutch Free Ports, 1829–1858

participating in the benefits so plainly derived by those who send prows to Singapore. . . .[19]

The very obvious commercial success achieved by Singapore's

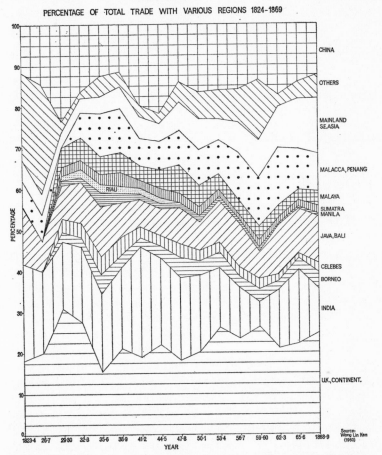

Figure 7. Singapore—Percentage of Trade with various Regions, 1824–1869

liberal trading policy and the inroads that it was clearly making into their earlier monopoly of trade in the archipelago, led the Dutch to attempt to counteract this success by establishing free ports of their own and by opening a large number of other ports to foreign trade. Between 1829 and 1858, ten free ports were established by the Dutch and over thirty others opened to foreign trade (Figure 6). The first of the Dutch free ports was at Riau (1829) on the doorstep of Singapore, and the others on the east Borneo coast, whence trade had early been lost to Singapore, and in the Moluccas. It would seem that Riau was intended as a direct challenge to Singapore but statistics indicate that its trade *with* Singapore expanded rapidly, and the principal long-run effect of the more liberal Dutch trading was to make Singapore's trade with the archipelago easier and to help draw the region into closer contact with the contemporary economic growth of western Europe.

Singapore was, of course, more than an entrepot for the south-east Asian region since, as Figure 7 illustrates, it carried on a very considerable trade with China, North America, India, Britain and Europe, much of which was unrelated to its immediate region. In 1868-69, however, 46 per cent. of a total trade valued at 59 million Spanish dollars (about £12¼ million sterling) was with the region bounded by Burma in the west and the Philippines and Celebes in the east.[20] Penang's trade at about the same time was worth some 20 million dollars (about £4 million sterling)*, 65 per cent. of which was with Burma, Siam, Sumatra and the Malayan peninsula but, of this, half was with Singapore.

During the 1860s, the trade of the Straits ports (which is a convenient term to describe Malacca, Penang and Singapore— especially the latter two) was generally sluggish. Although the total value of Singapore's trade rose by 13 million dollars between 1860 and 1869, few new British firms were established and there were several important failures in the middle of the decade. In 1870, however, in one year, imports increased by more than 7 million dollars and exports by nearly 5 million dollars, a burst of activity that initiated a decade-long trading boom made possible by the opening of the Suez Canal in 1869 and the establishment of telegraphic communication with Britain by the successful laying, in 1870, of a submarine cable from Madras.

Commercially, the opening of the Suez Canal, the increasing

---

* Cameron gives £4,076,707 for 1862–63,[21] Mills gives 19,983,000 dollars for 1864.[22] The intrinsic value of 100 Spanish dollars was about £20.16.8.[23]

use of the steamship that the shorter route made economic and the rapid transmission of market intelligence and trade decisions by telegraph, greatly increased the volume of business that could be undertaken with a given amount of capital. Transit time between Singapore and London, by steam via Suez in place of sail round the Cape, was cut by an average of ten weeks. This represented a saving in interest on the capital involved of 2½ per cent. but, more important, released the money tied up in goods in transit much more quickly for use in further business. It has been calculated that the change-over from sail via the Cape to steam via Suez more than doubled the earning capacity of a Singapore merchant's capital.[24] Thanks to telegraphy, goods could be bought and sold whilst in transit and this, too, made possible the handling of a larger volume of business with the same capital.

Geographically, the opening of the Suez Canal reaffirmed the strategic positions of the Straits ports but also had the effect of modifying and re-aligning their trading links. The use of the Suez route helped both France and the Netherlands to strengthen their holds on their colonial territories and Singapore's trade with Indo-China and Borneo fell off considerably during the 1870s. Until the 1860s nearly all the trade between Indo-China and Europe was conducted via Singapore, but with increasing French control over Indo-China, the traffic passed into their hands and the trade with Singapore fell away sharply. Equally the Netherlands government began to tighten its control over the archipelago by a series of treaties and military conquests. Low freight rates in the mid-70s consequent on over-expansion of the world's mercantile fleet also helped reduce Singapore's entrepot trade somewhat by encouraging speculative voyages by some shipping owners to the smaller ports of the region.[25] As many of the local markets began to fall away in the 1870s, they were replaced, however, by a steady increase in the trade with the Malayan peninsula itself. In 1879, 2,569 coasting vessels from the Malay states reached Singapore, compared with 417 in 1871.[26] A great deal of the increased traffic was related to the development of the peninsula's tinfields, the exploitation of which, on a rapidly expanding scale, was a major outcome of the existence of the Straits ports.

The Expansion of Tin Mining on the Malayan Mainland

The physical occurrence of the Malayan tin deposits has been examined in Chapter 2, where it was seen that rich accumulations of cassiterite are found along stream beds and their associated flood plains, in swamp areas, especially where underlying limestone has partially dissolved causing subsidence, and in cups or trough-like cavities where limestone has dissolved along joints. Tin ore was most readily recovered by primitive means from stream beds and flood plains, and was already being traded, according to Arab sources, as early as the 10th century A.D.[27] Until tin became an important industrial raw material in Europe, production and trade in the Malayan region was on a limited scale, though of sufficient value to cause both Portuguese and Dutch, in their turn, to attempt to monopolize it. After the discovery of tin on the Sumatran island of Banka in 1711 and its development by Chinese miners and smelters, this Dutch controlled island, thanks to the higher quality of its product,* was the main source of tin traded from south-east Asia. Its major market in the eighteenth century was China, since the relatively small needs of Europe were met by the protected industry of Cornwall.

When Britain began to develop a renewed interest in trade in the archipelago in the mid-eighteenth century, that in tin was of especial interest, partly because of its intrinsic value but also because it was one of the few commodities in demand in the China market. As a consequence of Dutch control over the tin production and trade of Banka at this period, Britain's interest was focused on handling the output from Malaya and south Siam, especially Junk Ceylon (Ujong Salang), where the mines appear to have been especially productive.[28] By 1790, four years after its establishment, Penang had attracted from the Malay states so much of the trade in tin, previously monopolized by the Dutch, that the latter admitted the East India Company's mastery of the Straits tin trade.[29] In 1806, 16 per cent. of Penang's trade by value was accounted for by tin[30] and this proportion had risen to 20 per cent. by 1816.[31]

The importance that tin had clearly acquired in the trade of Penang was illustrated by the efforts undertaken by the

---

* Banka tin was especially suitable for beating into fine leaves that were burnt by the Chinese as sacrificial offerings.

settlement government in 1818–19 to stimulate the supply from the Malay states. At this time the trade had received a setback as a result of Dutch attempts to re-establish their monopoly following the post-Napoleonic settlements that had returned

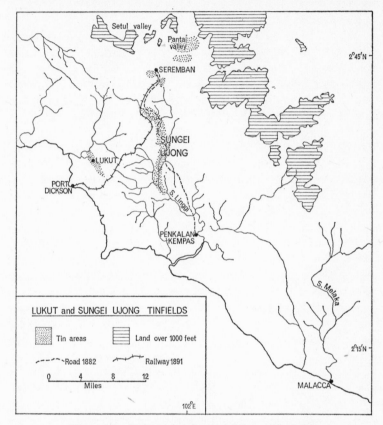

Figure 8. Lukut and Sungei Ujong Tinfields

Malacca and Java to their rule, and also as a consequence of unsettled conditions in the Malay states themselves. This direct intervention by the East India Company was evidence of a particular official concern since, with the major exception of the tea trade, it had been Company policy to leave commercial activities east of Calcutta strictly to private merchants. In order to ease the flow of tin to the British settlement, Governor

Bannerman of Penang, on his own initiative, sent representatives to negotiate treaties with Perak and Selangor, and in 1818 treaties were made with these two states, and also with Johore, which aimed at obtaining most-favoured-nation status for British merchants and forbade the exclusion or interruption of the trade of British subjects.[32]

Despite early accounts that suggest the contrary, it seems probable that large scale tin production for export depended on the presence of Chinese miners in the Malayan peninsula even in the eighteenth century.[33] After the establishment of Penang and the final cession of Malacca to Britain in 1824, both the financial backing for the tin mines and the physical working of the tin deposits were effectively in the hands of the Chinese, though nominal control over the mines at first remained with Malay chiefs. Chinese merchants in Malacca and Penang advanced capital to Malay chiefs who worked the mines with Chinese labour, also often supplied by the merchants to whom the chiefs undertook to consign all tin produced.

In 1815, Chinese miners were already working in Lukut,[34] then a province of Selangor and now part of Negri Sembilan (Figure 8), a district some five miles inland from the coast and forty miles from Malacca town, and by 1824, when sustained Chinese mining in Malaya may be said to have begun, there were about 200 Chinese miners in the district.[35] Of the various regions within easy reach of Malacca that possessed accessible tin deposits, Lukut was the closest to the sea, and in an era when transport both of tin and supplies was either by river or porter it was logical that such a location ideally should be preferred by the capitalists involved. Over the next thirty-five years, Chinese mining enterprise in central Malaya fanned out from Malacca and Lukut. Chinese mining interests benefited from the strong desire of local Malay chieftains to obtain the exploitation of their territories' resources in order to pay for the upkeep of the armed men that were necessary in the troubled local conditions of the time. Such exploitation was far more effectively undertaken by Chinese, willing to risk their lives and capital, than by the local Malays who were only part-time and uneconomical miners and who had no incentive to be otherwise.

By 1828–30, Chinese mining activity was well established in Sungei Ujong along the Linggi River. Though details of the actual numbers of miners involved vary, it appears that there were between 600 and 1,000 working in the Sungei Ujong district in 1828, but following a temporary depopulation of the mines caused by Malay attacks, the total had recovered to only 400 by the early 1830s.[36] Tin mined in Sungei Ujong was transported down the Linggi River then carried by Malay traders to the Chinese merchants of Malacca. Between 1830 and 1850, Chinese mining was recorded as active in a number of places in Malacca territory and in the state of Selangor.[37, 38]

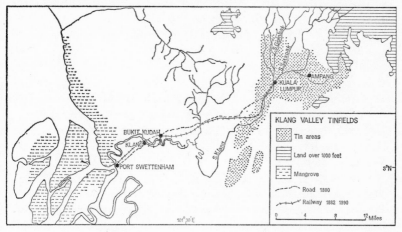

Figure 9. The Klang Valley Tinfields

Penetration was invariably by river and groups of miners followed streams to their sources in search of tin bearing ground. Mining enterprise in Malacca passed its peak in the 1850s, however, since the ore deposits were neither extensive nor rich and by 1860 fresh mines in the neighbouring states were being sought.

In the later 1850s, a large group of 87 Chinese, financed from Malacca under persuasion from the Malay rulers of Lukut and Klang, prospected up the Klang River and cleared jungle for mining in the Ampang area. Despite large numbers of deaths from malaria, countered by the import of more labour from Lukut, developments were continued and in 1859 the first tin was exported from the upper Klang. A trading settlement to serve the area was established at the highest point on the Klang

River to which supplies could conveniently be taken by boat—the site of Kuala Lumpur.[39]

Tin mining developments in north Malaya followed a rather similar pattern. Financed by Chinese merchants in Penang, Chinese miners were working the Larut area of coastal northern Perak by 1850, and in 1879 there were reported to be 80 mines each averaging 86 men active in the district.[40] The development of the Kinta Valley fields was a little later as a consequence of their somewhat greater remoteness from Penang and the coast. In the 1870s, the valleys and foothills drained by the Kinta, Bidor and Batang Padang rivers (Figure 12) were known to be rich in tin, and by 1875 this region of interior Perak was being worked by over 3,000 Chinese miners. Transport within and from the Kinta Valley was, however, much more expensive than in Larut. Whereas a road connected the Larut mining area to the port of Telok Kertang and facilitated the use of bullock drawn carts, either elephants or human porters were the only means of transporting tin from the interior mines to the Kinta River, down which it was carried to the port of Durian Sabatang for shipping to Penang. In 1882 it cost about five times more to transport a pikul of tin from Gopeng (Kinta Valley) to Penang, than from Taiping (Larut) to Penang.[41] Between 1880 and 1885, considerable sums were allocated by the British administration (which had assumed the protection of Perak in 1874) for clearing the Kinta River and its tributaries and for connecting mines with their nearest river ports by road and bridle path. New fiscal arrangements gave preferential treatment to tin produced in Perak Proper (i.e. interior Perak) and succeeded in narrowing the differences between production costs in Kinta and Larut to only about 9 per cent. per bahara of 3 pikuls. By 1882, the Chinese had penetrated as far as Ulu Kinta and were working the deposits on the Sungei Pari and Sungei Chemor, which focused on the site of Ipoh. In 1885 there were some five hundred registered mines in the Kinta Valley,[42] concentrated especially along the Sungei Terap, Sungei Kampar and Sungei Chenderiang, and although most of these were Chinese the Malays retained control over a number of so-called 'ancestral mines' and there had appeared a few European workings.

Chinese superiority in the Malayan tin mining industry for

much of the nineteenth century owed a great deal to the greater efficiency of their mining methods over those of the Malays and to their greater willingness than European investors to risk capital in the unruly conditions that existed in the Malay states before British intervention. Chinese mining efficiency was based partly on certain technological achievements, such as the chain pump (chin chia), a pump driven by an overshot water wheel, with which opencast workings could be mechanically drained and thus worked to greater depths,

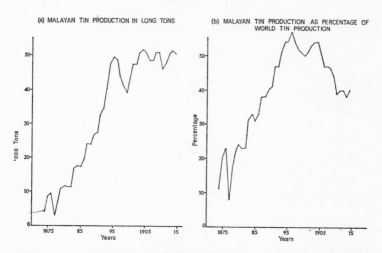

THE RISE OF THE MALAYAN TIN INDUSTRY
1874-1914

(a) MALAYAN TIN PRODUCTION IN LONG TONS

(b) MALAYAN TIN PRODUCTION AS PERCENTAGE OF WORLD TIN PRODUCTION

Figure 10. The Rise of the Malayan Tin Industry, 1874–1914
Source: Wong Lin Ken, 1965

and partly on the effective organization and protection of mines through the medium of their secret societies. These organizations were also effective as instruments for coercing newly arrived Chinese immigrants into working in the mines. This tight organization and supply of cheap labour no doubt made investment in Malayan mining for Chinese a less risky and more profitable business then it would have been for Europeans, and the declining yield from entrepot trade in the archipelago, especially in the 1870s (see p. 77), encouraged many Chinese merchants to seek alternative outlets for their capital in the peninsula's tinfields.

Until the period of British intervention in the political affairs of the tin producing Malay states—a circumstance that arose from the suppression of armed clashes over mining rights in Larut—the pattern of mining developments in Malaya appears to have been closely controlled by the physical accessibility of the tin deposits from the two Straits ports of Malacca and Penang. The high cost of transport favoured the early development of those deposits which were nearest the ports and to which access by river was possible, and only when these were worked out, at least in terms of the techniques of the times, or when tin prices were particularly favourable, were more remote fields penetrated and opened up.

In the 1850s, '60s and '70s, the output of the Malayan tin fields was comparable with that of Cornwall,[43] but following the establishment of British political control over the tin producing states after 1874, Malaya's total production of tin and her share of world output both increased phenomenally (Figure 10). The demand for tin from the industrializing countries of Europe and North America was expanding at a rapid rate throughout the nineteenth century, especially for the manufacture of tinplate for food canning (after about 1820) and for barrels for storing and transporting petroleum. The annual consumption of tin in Britain multiplied fivefold in the course of the first half of the century.[44] Until the 1840s this demand was met almost entirely by the Cornish mining industry, which was protected against foreign tin by prohibitive import duties. In 1853, however, following reductions over a period of eleven years, the duty on metallic tin imported for British consumption was removed, and by 1871 more imported than Cornish tin was being used in the fast growing tinplate industry.

The statement concerning Larut, written by Patrick Doyle in 1879,[45] could well have referred to western Malaya as a whole:

> The tin industry is fast developing, under British protection in Larut, and bids fair to eclipse, in a period far from remote, the productions of the other parts of the Peninsula and islands of the Archipelago. There is no exaggeration in the statement that its deposits (which exceed in richness

those of any other tin-producing country in the East), if worked with British capital and enterprise, with appliances of modern machinery, would surpass the production of any other part of the known world.*

Despite the greater stability guaranteed by British control, there were only abortive attempts at establishing mining

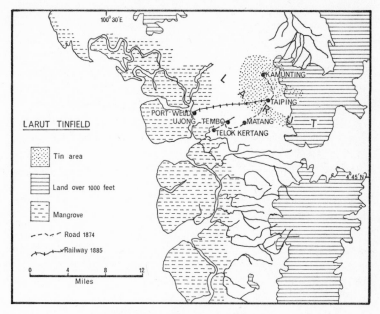

Figure 11. The Larut Tinfield

companies by Europeans until the mid-1880s. The failure of most early European mining enterprises in Malaya has been attributed to bad management, such as inadequate prospecting

* If the remarks made by a member of the Mining Association and Institute of Cornwall were any indication, even as late as the early 1890s the Cornish tin industry was ignorant of the scale of the competition it was already facing. Following a paper on Mining in Perak, the chairman of a meeting of the Association said that, although tin was coming from Perak and the Straits, they as Cornishmen need not fear that they would be driven out of the field. They had produced, and would still continue to produce large quantities of tin and he did not know that the speaker had said anything to dishearten Cornishmen generally.[47] However, by 1895 after one Cornish mine after another had been driven beyond the margin of profitable mining by competition from Malaya, the Cornish tin industry was seeking government action to save i from extinction, without success.

G

and the installation of unsuitable machinery, and to the difficulties of obtaining and controlling Chinese labour.[46] The
importance of British political control to the economic growth
and areal spread of the Malayan tin mining industry in the '70s
and '80s lay mainly in the policy of encouraging the industry by
providing the inducements and the free entry of capital and
labour necessary for its development.

The improvement of communications was high among the
inducements. In 1874, there were 13 miles of poorly surfaced
roads in Larut which were under constant repair because of
their inability to withstand the tropical climate and the heavy
cart traffic. In 1875 Kamunting, where the tin deposits were
amongst the richest in Larut, was connected by road to Ujong
Tembo, whence ore was shipped to Penang, and by 1870,
Taiping had a road link with Telok Kertang. The high cost of
road maintenance in Larut, however, forced the government to
decide on the construction of a railway, and in 1885 after over
four years of difficult work, eight and a quarter miles of metre
gauge line were opened between Taiping and the anchorage of
Sapetang (re-named Port Weld)[48]—the first railway in Malaya.
Government subsidy of steam communications ensured a daily
steamer service to Penang.

A severe drop in tin prices in 1884 forced many mines in
Larut out of business and Chinese capital and labour began to
move to the richer tin fields of the Kinta Valley. A marked
recovery in the tin price over the next few years and an intensive
road building programme contributed to the 'Kinta tin rush' of
1889–95. By 1891 every important mining area in the Kinta
Valley was linked by road to the Kinta River where existing
villages or new settlements (such as Batu Gajah) acted as
transhipment points.[49] By 1889, a trunk road linking the Kinta
tinfields to the railhead at Taiping had been constructed but
its use was expensive and the Kinta River continued to be
used as the main transport artery serving the district until its
serious disadvantages—which included a tortuous narrow
channel made increasingly shallow by mining effluent—led the
government to agree to construct a railway. Begun in 1891, a
line connected Tapah with Telok Anson* by 1893, and in 1896

* First known as Telok Mah Intan, Telok Anson replaced the shallower
Durian Sabatang previously used.

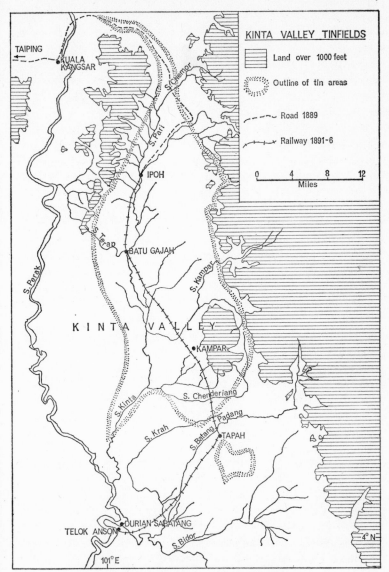

Figure 12. The Kinta Valley Tinfields

direct rail communication between Ipoh and the deep anchorage at Telok Anson was established. The richness of its deposits and its improved transport network permitted the

Kinta mining industry in general to weather the depression of the 1890s, though many mines were abandoned and recorded output fell for the first time in 1896.

In central Malaya expansion was also dependent on the improvement of communications, but the inland location of the mines and their greater distance than those of Perak from a major Straits port burdened them with heavier transport costs and greater difficulty in raising capital. Mining enterprise in Selangor was also hampered by a more short-sighted fiscal policy than that followed in Perak, including taxes which raised the cost of feeding and clothing labourers. Smaller mining profits meant lower revenue and consequent lower government expenditure on infrastructure. The mines of Selangor were served by the Klang River and the port of Klang near its mouth, but river transport was expensive partly owing to navigation difficulties and partly to a shortage of boats. By 1880 Kuala Lumpur was connected by road to Damansara, the head of launch navigation on the Klang, and in 1883 a coherent road construction programme was implemented to link together with a trunk road the mining districts from the northern to the southern end of the state. As in Perak, however, climatic and physiographic factors in an era of poor surfaces and bullock cart traffic, contributed to the failure of roads substantially to reduce transport costs, and a railway from Kuala Lumpur to Bukit Kudah was built between 1882 and 1886 and then carried over the Klang River by the Connaught Bridge to Klang in 1890. The importance to the Chinese miners of the rail link was well evidenced by the fact that to accelerate its completion, which had been delayed by labour shortages, the principal Chinese miner supplied the government with 300 labourers from his mines.*

Developments in Sungei Ujong and Jelebu after the establishment of British control expanded only slowly as a result of the early working out of the small patches of richer tin deposits and the unprofitability of exploiting poorer resources until prices

---

* This action was hailed by the Resident of Selangor when opening the Selangor Railway as 'public spirited . . . although the removal of so large a body of men from their mines must have caused them serious inconvenience, more especially having regard to the present high price of tin'.[50] It may be suspected that the desire to benefit from high tin prices was even more inconvenienced by the non-completion of the railway!

were high (as after 1885). Attempts at improving communications produced a cart road from Seremban to Pengkalan Kampas on the Linggi River in 1882. Road communications into the interior Pantai and Setul valleys of Sungei Ujong helped the revival of mining from 1886 onwards, and in 1891 a privately built railway linked Seremban to Port Dickson.*

The principal effect of British administration on the pattern of tin mining in western Malaya after 1874 was brought about by its encouragement of private enterprise.[52] This was undertaken primarily by its conventional role of maintaining law and order and by the provision of social overhead capital. Fiscal policy varied, for example between Perak and Selangor, and in the former certainly contributed to the initial development of Kinta, but the richness of interior Perak's tin deposits would certainly have led to expansion of their exploitation once transport had been eased. By 1895, almost all the tin areas known today in Perak, Selangor and Negri Sembilan had been discovered and worked. Apart from its construction of transport facilities, the main contribution that government made to the expansion of mining lay in its labour policy. Until the 1890s fundamentally this protected the employer by controlling within Malaya the movements of labour in the interests of the capitalists who had imported or collected their labour force at great expense and who exploited them to the full. Certain marginal mining areas might well not have been profitable had it not been for the very intensive use made of labour which, for example in Larut in 1880, represented about 75 per cent. of production costs.[53] In general, it may be concluded that the pattern of tin mining operations that developed in western Malaya during the nineteenth century was very largely determined by a combination of economic circumstances in Europe which influenced the price for which tin could be sold and the

* The creation in 1896 of the Federated Malay States, which linked politically those states with British Residents (i.e. Perak, Selangor, Pahang and Negri Sembilan), led in due course to a policy of amalgamation of the state railways of Perak and Selangor and the privately owned Ujong railway into the F.M.S. Railways, and to the construction of a north-south trunk line that linked the various state railways so that, by 1903, through running was possible from Port Dickson, via Seremban, to Prai opposite Penang.[51] The political distinctiveness of the Federated Malay States from the Straits Settlements, appears to have been a significant factor in the creation of an ocean port at Port Swettenham (previously Kuala Klang) to which the F.M.S. railway was extended from Klang in 1901 and which was administered as a railway port.

varying richness and accessibility of the tin deposits themselves. The freedom with which labour and capital could move into the industry and profits and earnings be transferred abroad, the construction of transport facilities and the marketing contacts and experience of the Straits ports made possible the profitable exploitation of the tinfields and provided the essential links between the fields and their overseas customers.

The participation of western enterprise in the Malayan tin mining industry was very limited until almost the end of the century. The investing public in Europe was generally ignorant of the nature and potentialities of the peninsula and funds could profitably be employed in mining, or alternative ventures, elsewhere. The 'Pahang boom' of the late 1880s had attracted European capital in a minor tin-rush to what was believed to be a land of great mineral potential and for a few years there was a scramble for concessions, which, however, were often vaguely worded and the areas to which they referred poorly defined.[54] The boom had collapsed by 1896 as a consequence of difficulties encountered in raising funds after initial paid-up capital was exhausted by the costs of prospecting in what often turned out to be concessions with limited mineral resources of economic value.

In the west coast states there was no active interest in tin mining by western concerns between the collapse of the short-lived Malayan Peninsula (East India) Tin Mining Co. Ltd. in 1875 and the formation of the French Société des Mines d'Etain de Perak in 1881. Whilst labour-intensive methods were the rule, European companies found it very difficult to compete with the Chinese and therefore sought techniques that would make possible a reduction of their dependence on Chinese labour by an increasing reliance on western technology. European companies had some success with hydraulic mining, as developed on the goldfields of California, but the technological break-through that assured the success of capital-intensive European mining in Malaya was the introduction of the tin dredge in 1912. Until that year, 80 per cent. of Malaya's tin had been produced by the Chinese.

The first tin dredge in south-east Asia, based on the principle employed in recovering gold from river beds in New Zealand and Australia, was set up by an Australian to recover tin from

Tongkah harbour, Phuket, in 1907. Fabricated in Renfrew, Scotland, the dredge was shipped in sections to Prai, on the mainland opposite Penang, re-assembled and then towed to Phuket. By the end of January 1908, 20 tons of tin ore had been recovered from thirty feet or more below the sea bed, and the potential of dredging established with sufficient confidence for five dredges to be operating in southern Thailand in 1910.[55] The first dredge erected for mining in Malaya was in the Kinta Valley at Batu Gajah, where extensive swamp areas were now open to exploitation. The use of dredges not only permitted operations in wet or swampy land but also made possible the recovery of tin from ground of a lower ore content than could profitably be worked by any other method, including areas already worked over to only shallow depths by Chinese. Dredging made heavy demands on capital resources, however, and needed technical knowledge and sound management. The dredges were expensive and could not be employed efficiently in the absence of leases of large areas of payable ground. The limited experience in large scale enterprises of the Chinese miners and their inability to raise adequate capital to finance dredging left the development of tin dredging to European companies and although the First World War somewhat delayed expansion, the share of total tin output derived from European mines increased markedly after 1912, as did the area of western Malaya devoted to mining.

European capital moved into processing at much the same period as into mining. During the era of small scale Chinese domination of tin mining in Malaya, smelting of the ore, i.e. its chemical reduction to metallic tin by the use of charcoal, was usually carried on at the mine in order to minimize transport costs to the Straits ports where the slab tin was refined. In 1886, a European partnership established a small furnace at Telok Anson. Converted into a limited liability company, the Straits Trading Co. Ltd., in 1887, the partners moved their operations to Pulau Brani, an island off Singapore where coal imports were cheaper and where adequate storage space was available for fuel. Operating under monopoly conditions for eight years, the company had the incentive to establish a modern smelting works and by 1896 had the capacity to smelt nearly one fifth of the world's tin output. At the end of 1901, the Straits Trading Co. installed a second smelting works at Butterworth, across the Prai River from the new railhead to be reached by the F.M.S. Railways in 1903.

The dominant position in the smelting industry of the Straits Trading Company, based on an exclusive right to export tin ores produced by non-European companies in Selangor and Sungei Ujong for eight years from 1886, was challenged in 1897 by the establishment in Georgetown, Penang, of a Chinese-owned smelting works. Rising labour costs and a growing shortage of fuel were reducing the competitive position of small scale Chinese smelters in the Malay States and the percentage basis for computing the duty on tin ores discriminated in favour of exports of ore rather than of slab tin from the Malay States to the Straits ports.* There were therefore decisive advantages in smelting tin ores in the Straits ports rather than in the Malay States. The Penang works proved very successful. In 1907 it was turned into a local limited liability company with modern smelting processes, eventually to be bought out by British interests and floated in 1911 as the Eastern Smelting Co. Ltd. By 1914, the two British smelting companies, located in the Straits ports and protected against competition from outside the Straits Settlements and Britain by discriminatory export duties on tin ore and by legislative action, handled 85 per cent. of the tin produced in Malaya.

The Development of Commercial Agriculture in Malaya

Unlike the Netherlands East India Company, which actively encouraged and coerced the indigenous peoples of the Indies to grow commercial crops, or the Dutch colonial government which, in the era of the 'culture and consignment system' between 1830 and 1860 was directly involved in aspects of agriculture, the British Company and the Settlements government that succeeded it left such development strictly to the individuals, and for much of the nineteenth century strongly resisted any territorial responsibility that would have been involved by officially-encouraged agricultural development

* Whereas the percentage of tin in the tin ores was approximately 72 per cent., the basis for computing the percentage of duty on metallic tin that should be payable on ores was still only 68 per cent. when raised in 1898. This clearly favoured the export of ores rather than of slab tin, especially since ores were usually dressed up to a percentage well exceeding this figure.

beyond the immediate environs of the Straits ports. Commercial agricultural development in Malaya in the early nineteenth century was therefore spasmodic and, except on Penang and Singapore islands where European spice plantations were established with only limited success, early commercial agriculture, like early tin mining, was undertaken by Chinese.

The Chinese went to Malaya, as to other parts of South-east Asia and elsewhere, strictly for economic reasons. Although relatively few succeeded in making fortunes and returning to China, this was the normal ambition and the activities to which they devoted their attention in Malaya were those that offered prospects of achieving this ambition. Subsistence agriculture and associated permanent settlement, along the lines followed by the Malay wet rice farmers, offered no inducements since it was no more likely to give a quick return on small capital than was the intensive cultivation typical of the homeland they had left. The Chinese immigrants who turned their attention to agriculture consequently devoted their energy to the cultivation of export crops on an extensive rather than on an intensive basis.[56] As in the contemporaneous mining developments on the Malayan mainland, the Chinese merchants of the Straits ports were involved in the financing of Chinese commercial agriculture and in organizing the labour supply, while the overseas trading links of the ports provided the essential market contacts.

The Malayan mainland offered extensive tracts of land for commercial development by anyone prepared to accept the risks inherent in agriculture undertaken in unknown terrain only nominally under the control of the Malay rulers. The small population of subsistence farmers in the peninsula was concentrated almost entirely on the alluvial lowlands suitable for wet rice farming and, apart from small local pockets along river flood plains and at valley mouths, these were located in the north-western and north-eastern coastal plains and deltas of Malaya. In Johore, the immediate mainland hinterland of Singapore, Malay settlement was very sparse. In order to obtain a quick return in this environment from a limited supply of mainly unskilled labour, the early Chinese agricultural investor in Malaya developed a system of commercial shifting cultivation. This exploited previously virgin land for the production of crops such as gambier, pepper and tapioca until such times as yields ceased to be sufficiently economic, when the plantings were abandoned in favour of new clearings. Tapioca

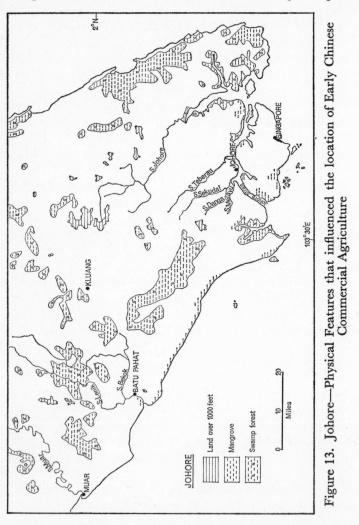

Figure 13. Johore—Physical Features that influenced the location of Early Chinese Commercial Agriculture

and gambier, especially, gave quick returns under this system. Initially, plantings of pepper and gambier were made on Singapore island. Some gambier production, by both Malays and Chinese, was apparently in existence at the time of the foundation of the British settlement in 1819, but the expansion of commercial agriculture on the island was most rapid after this date. Gambier and pepper proved particularly profitable during the 1830s and the area devoted to them on Singapore island had reached to between five and six thousand acres by 1841.[57] Although not interplanted, the production of gambier and pepper on the same planting was common, since the almost continuous collection of gambier foliage integrated well with the seasonal cycle of pepper production, the refuse from gambier boiling provided manure for the pepper vines and the relatively rapid returns from gambier provided income in the two to three year period before the pepper reached maturity. Gambier was an exhausting crop, however, and under the cultivation methods of the day, land yielded an adequate return for only about fifteen years. Pepper vines were past their peak of production in fifteen to twenty years, whilst the supply of timber, required as fuel for boiling up gambier leaves to produce tannin, was used up within an economic distance of the planting after twenty-five years at the most.[58] In the mid-1830s many of the early Singapore plantings were close to abandonment. The declining area of land available for new plantings in Singapore and the rising tide of Chinese immigration led, in the 1830s, '40s and '50s, to a considerable expansion of Chinese agricultural interest into Johore.

As in the early tin industry, penetration was necessarily by river, and the valleys of the Sungei Skudai, Sungei Melayu, Sungei Danga and Sungei Tebrau—all of which streams drained into the Johore Strait—located the new areas of agricultural development. Small settlements and river depots were established as bases from which cultivation extended, in a sequence of exploitation and abandonment, to the nearest watershed. The movement of crops and supplies to and from Singapore was by river.

Outward pioneering from the initial areas of concentration in south Johore occurred along the west coast of the state in the 1870s, especially along the Muar and Batu Pahat river systems, south of which a swampy coast inhibited penetration, and into areas drained by rivers flowing into the South China Sea in the 1880s. The major topographic limitation to the distribution of plantings at this period was their complete

dependence on the rivers as a means of communication with
Singapore.[59]

Commercial agricultural development in the vicinity of
Malacca occurred from the 1850s. By the middle of the nineteenth century the trade of Malacca, which had dominated
earlier Chinese interest, was eclipsed by that of Penang and
Singapore, and the meagre local tin deposits were hardly more
profitable (see p. 81). Some local entrepreneurs therefore
turned to the cultivation of export crops and especially to
tapioca, which combined the advantages of being easily grown
with limited supervision and of requiring only simple processing.
It could also profitably be combined with the rearing of pigs
which fed on the factory waste. Newly cleared land was planted
with tapioca for three to five years and then abandoned. A
rapid expansion of the industry in the 1870s and early 1880s
was marked by the spread of planting outwards from the original
centres of concentration, aided by the road building of the
period. By about 1875, the crop had penetrated into Negri
Sembilan and in the late 1880s into areas of Johore adjacent to
Malacca, but its areal expansion was limited by transport costs,
and a crescent shaped area, with a radius of thirty to thirty-five
miles centred on Malacca, located most of the nineteenth-
century tapioca plantings in Malaya.

Unlike the situation in south Johore, where Malay settlement
was very sparse, the hinterland of Malacca into which tapioca
planting spread contained a sizeable Malay population concentrated in the numerous small valleys that characterize the
area. Interfluves remained jungle-clad and unoccupied, however, and utilized only as a source of jungle produce by the
Malays. It was these unoccupied hillslopes that were temporarily
exploited for tapioca planting and then abandoned.

Official concern at the undesirable effects of shifting tapioca
cultivation developed in Malacca and Negri Sembilan in the
1880s and 1890s. Prejudice against the granting of fresh land
for tapioca grew, and after 1900 Negri Sembilan included a
special cultivation clause in the titles of all new land granted
for tapioca which required the planting of a 'permanent' crop
simultaneously with tapioca. Official discouragement was
accompanied in the early 1900s by falling prices for tapioca
and a growing interest in rubber, and acreages under the

crop fell drastically throughout the first decade of the new century.

Planting also of gambier and pepper by Chinese was of some importance in the west coast states, probably from the 1850s, and expanded rapidly after British intervention. Special regulations encouraged its development, and although the cultivation of these crops in Malacca, Negri Sembilan and Selangor was by a shifting system similar to that employed by the Chinese in Johore, there were several very large concessions. In these states, however, it was only one form of agricultural pioneering and, although important for about thirty years, it operated within a framework established by British officials and declined after the turn of the century for similar reasons to those responsible for the decline of tapioca planting.

European interest in agricultural development, understandably, was first focused on spices. Pepper, nutmegs and cloves were all introduced into Penang and Singapore islands soon after their acquisition by the East India Company. Pepper, introduced into Penang from Sumatra about 1790, was planted until about 1835, with varying profitability. Nutmegs and cloves had little success on Penang, owing to the planters' ignorance of cultivation methods and to trouble from blight. On Singapore, a period of hectic nutmeg planting in the 1840s was followed by setbacks for the same reasons.

Considerably more success was achieved by European sugar planters in Province Wellesley.[60] Although pioneered by the Chinese between 1810 and 1820, the development of sugar growing on the mainland of Malaya opposite Penang island* dates principally from the third decade of the century. The high price of sugar at about the time of the emancipation of the West Indian slave labour force encouraged European participation in sugar production in each of the Straits Settlements, but the extension in 1846 only to Penang and Malacca of the preferential import duty into the United Kingdom for empire-grown sugar effectively accounts for the industry's lack of success on Singapore (Singapore's exclusion was, of course, a consequence of its large trade in Javanese sugar). Attempts

---

* Province Wellesley, a 280 square mile strip of territory on the mainland opposite the island, was ceded to Penang by the Sultan of Kedah in 1800.

at European sugar planting in Malacca proved abortive and interest came to be centred on Province Wellesley.

Province Wellesley, south of the Prai River, had a number of physical characteristics that were favourable for cane sugar production. Climatic conditions, at about 5° north, produce greater seasonal variation in rainfall than is the rule in central and southern Malaya, and a distinct dry season during the period of the north-east monsoon from December to March was beneficial for the concentration of sucrose in the ripening cane as well as for harvesting activities. The heavy alluvial soils were sufficiently fertile, and the level terrain, although requiring artificial drainage in places, made the movement of harvested cane possible along natural waterways and drainage canals. Coastal mangrove forest provided accessible fuel for local mills. Similar physical advantages for sugar production existed north of the Prai River but the occupation of the land by padi planters from Kedah in the 1820s effectively prevented its commercial utilization.

Between 1870 and 1900, sugar growing in southern Province Wellesley developed into a highly capitalized, European-controlled enterprise. Towards the end of the century, however, the industry, which at its peak had spread into the Krian district of neighbouring Perak, was encountering local problems of disease, labour shortage and diminishing fuel supplies at a time when world sugar prices were slumping, and the now unprotected British market was the recipient of large dumpings of export bounty beet sugar by European continental producers. Between 1900 and 1914, the sugar industry of north-west Malaya declined to extinction, and much of the former sugar estate land was converted to coconut or rubber production.

Of all the crops introduced into Malaya in the nineteenth century, the one that had greatest significance for the future development of commercial agriculture in the peninsula was coffee. European coffee planters from Ceylon were attracted to Malaya after the destruction of their estates in the early 1870s by the virulent fungus *Hemileia vastatrix*. By 1896, there were over 35,000 acres of European coffee planted in Perak, where attractive land terms were offered to planters, and a considerable acreage in Selangor and Negri Sembilan. The plantations of Selangor were concentrated to the north and north-east of Kuala Lumpur especially in the valleys of the Gombak and Setapak rivers. This concentration was related to the need for accessibility at a time when suitable roads were few in number, but also to the fact that many of the estate pioneers were involved in other interests, especially road and railway contracting, in Kuala Lumpur.[61] The great decline in world coffee prices in the later 1890s brought about by Brazilian overproduction much reduced the attractiveness of coffee growing in Malaya and stimulated planters' interests in the new crop for which demand was beginning to emerge—rubber.

Although only short-lived in itself as an export crop, coffee served as an important pioneer crop in Malaya. For the first time (with the exception of the Province Wellesley sugar area), European capital was invested in agricultural development in Malaya. Land was cleared and minor roads constructed. Government policy was formulated to attract the large European planter, who was seen as the most desirable instrument for opening up virgin land for commercial agriculture. Land terms were easy and planting loans available. Channels were developed for the introduction of Tamil labour to work the estates by the institution of subsidized steamer passages from Negapatam in south India, and the opening of an official depot in Negapatam with a medical officer as superintendent. With the advent of rubber after about 1895, full advantage was taken of these earlier developments.

The first seedlings of Para rubber (*Hevea brasiliensis*) to enter Malaya reached the Singapore Botanical Gardens in 1876. Only five were alive on arrival and these all died. The following year a second consignment was successfully raised, and a small number of plants sent to Perak and, possibly, Malacca.[62] The earliest planting of rubber was unsystematic and not undertaken as a serious venture. Commercial interest in the crop dates from the 1890s, when *Hevea* was planted on the Inch Kenneth Estate, near Kajang, Selangor, a British-owned coffee estate, and by a Chinese tapioca planter in Malacca.[63] The initial lack of interest in rubber can be attributed to a number of factors, of which the profitability of coffee in the 1880s, an understandable lack of awareness of the potential of the crop for Malaya at a time when Brazil and Africa seemed more than capable of meeting world demand, and ignorance of the productivity of the rubber tree and of suitable methods of extracting its latex, were probably the most important. H. N. Ridley's enthusiasm for rubber whilst he was Director of the Singapore Botanical Gardens and his development of an effective tapping method failed to persuade Malayan planters to take up cultivation of the crop until the declining coffee prices of the 1890s forced them to consider possible alternatives.

By the late 1890s rubber had been planted on an experimental basis in various parts of Perak, mainly interplanted with other crops, especially coffee, and the first official record of a sale of Para rubber on the London market is found in 1900 when 327 lbs. of best quality and 23 lbs. of scrap were sold by Perak planters.[64] In 1905, 104 tons were exported from the Federated Malay States. Rising world demand for rubber, created by the expansion of the new motor car and electrical industries, further stimulated interest in its production and was reinforced by new land regulations in the Federated Malay States which introduced low quit rents for land granted for rubber planting. The six or seven year maturation period of the *Hevea* tree was seen by government as an excellent guarantee of the permanence of cultivation considered so desirable for land development, but it also contributed to the boom prices obtained in the first decade of the twentieth century since the expanding market could not immediately be satisfied.[65] During the rubber boom of 1905–08 virtually every estate introduced rubber by interplanting and on newly cleared fields, and in 1908 the crop was planted in every state, though especially in those of the west coast.

There is very little doubt that rubber was almost an ideal crop for the physical, economic and political conditions of Malaya in the early twentieth century and that coffee had served it well as a precursor. Early fears that, as an exotic, it could not profitably be cultivated* were shown to be groundless since the plant flourished in the suitable ecological conditions of the peninsula, and indeed the freedom of Malaya

* Expressed, for example, by Murton, one of Ridley's predecessors at the Singapore Gardens.

from the pests, such as leaf-blight, that were native throughout *Hevea's* South American habitat, enabled it to thrive better than in its 'natural' environment. Its tolerance of soils of low fertility, such as the laterized soils of much of Malaya, meant that planting was possible almost anywhere in the peninsula. Only on poorly drained soils—which often were already occupied by padi farmers anyway—and on peats, where storm damage may often be considerable, was rubber less suited, or at altitudes in excess of about 1000 feet where temperature minima were too low for healthy growth.

From core areas associated with the location of the coffee estates, rubber spread onto unoccupied land within economic reach of the lines of communication developed to serve the tinfields. The Klang Valley with its road and rail links from Kuala Lumpur to Port Swettenham was the first major axis of development in Selangor, and away from this axis rubber planting was tied to the coastal roads out of Klang and to the north-south transport lines along the foothills from Kuala Lumpur. In Perak planting was similarly related to the transport axis through Batang Padang, Batu Gajah and Ipoh, and rubber vigorously replaced sugar on the estates of Krian and southern Province Wellesley. Comparable development occurred along the roads and railways in Negri Sembilan. In 1906, eighty per cent. of the total area planted with rubber was in these three western states and the spread of planting into the other states of the peninsula was closely related to the extension of the road and rail network in subsequent years.

In a number of ways, the role played by the Straits ports in the rubber industry was similar to that which they played in the tin industry. They provided the essential banking, commercial and shipping services and acted as the gateways through which the immigrant labour, increasingly in demand for plantation work, entered Malaya. Penang particularly was the receiving depot for the Tamil labour which came to dominate the plantation workforce. From 1890 to 1904 an average of about 20,000 Tamils arrived annually at Penang, of whom between 2,500 and 3,000 each year were indentured and the rest were South Indian deck passengers whom R. N.

H

Jackson considers proportionate to the number of 'free' immigrant labourers becoming available for work.[66]

The floating of many small rubber planting companies was to a large extent undertaken by the large merchant houses, especially of Singapore, their established positions and reputations giving confidence to potential investors in what were still speculative undertakings. The merchant or agency houses played a fundamental role in attracting large sums of European capital to the rubber plantations and, especially in the case of the smaller companies, performed many services on their behalf.

The processing of latex into the smoked sheets of rubber that was the normal form in which it was exported, which was, however, a much simpler operation than the smelting of tin ore, was readily undertaken by the plantations themselves and in primitive smokehouses by the smallholders who developed in the lee of the plantations. Only in the milling of scrap did the ports have an industrial function to perform for the rubber industry, but this could be undertaken by relatively small concerns and was certainly not confined to the Straits ports as tin smelting came to be.

The Role of the Straits Ports in the Nineteenth Century

There is little reason to doubt that the free ports of the Straits of Malacca—Penang and Singapore—were founded and developed largely in order that Britain might obtain a share in the profitable trade of the archipelago, especially in commodities, such as tin, which were acceptable in the China market. The lack of duties was intended as an inducement to attract the native traders to the British, rather than to Dutch, ports, but the concept of freedom of commerce was acceptable to the growing industrial community of Britain, which, from the period of the Napoleonic wars onwards, was seeking overseas markets for the surplus products of its factories and mills. Within a relatively short time, the Straits ports, and particularly Singapore, had developed as entrepots, receiving, grading, baling and forwarding the varied produce of the East Indian archipelago, carried to their wharves by Bugis prahus, and sending the piece-goods, ironware and china of Britain to almost every harbour and creek in the islands.

Contemporary with their growing function of handling the international trade of the archipelago, the Straits ports began to stimulate the production of primary commodities. To some extent this occurred throughout the islands, in so far as the desire to obtain textiles and iron goods encouraged the more enthusiastic collection of marine and jungle produce, but on the Malayan mainland development was of a more sophisticated type, financed by the Chinese merchants of the ports. From the 1820s onwards, both mining and agricultural operations expanded in the peninsular hinterlands of Singapore, Malacca and Penang, with accessibility by river to the ports acting as the basic factor locating these developments.

The last quarter of the nineteenth century was a period of many developments that stimulated the growth of the Straits ports but particularly of Singapore. The opening of the Suez Canal in 1869 not only reinforced the advantages of the steamship over sail, which in its turn provided more rapid and punctual links between the entrepot ports, the archipelago and the rest of the world, but the international route into the archipelago by way of the Straits of Malacca took all shipping past Penang and Singapore. The British political forward movement into the native states of the Malay peninsula, begun by the Treaty of Pangkor in 1874 which established the first British Resident in Perak, provided security which begat trade, was further to encourage tin mining and produced an economic and political environment favourable to the rapid spread of rubber plantations in the early twentieth century. The establishment of the Federated Malay States in 1895 was a basic pre-requisite for the growth of the Malayan railway system, built initially to serve the tin mines, which later was a powerful factor in locating the rubber plantations and which opened up a considerable hinterland for the ports.

In the period before the expansion of British influence beyond the Straits Settlements, the economic exploitation of the peninsula was limited to that range of mineral and agricultural commodities which gave the highest immediate return for capital invested, and the location of such economic activity

TABLE 1

RICE TRADE OF THE STRAITS SETTLEMENTS, 1878–1886

1878

	Source	Imports (in piculs*)	Destination	Exports (in piculs)
SINGAPORE	British Burma	584,225	Malacca and Penang	159,380
	Thailand	548,958	Netherlands India	448,129
	French India	123,079	Malay Peninsula	187,979
	Malay Peninsula	126,872	Others[2]	72,306
	Netherlands India	91,209		
	Others[1]	77,958		
	TOTAL	1,552,301	TOTAL	867,794
PENANG	British Burma	615,082	Singapore and Malacca	86,367
	Calcutta	23,463	Sumatra	278,887
	Malay Peninsula	19,392	Malay Peninsula	65,292
	Others[3]	11,309	Others[4]	26,728
	TOTAL	669,246	TOTAL	457,274
MALACCA	Singapore	172,544	Malay Peninsula	74,836
	Penang	32,945	Sumatra	1,523
	TOTAL	205,489	TOTAL	76,359

1881

	Source	Imports (in piculs*)	Destination	Exports (in piculs)
SINGAPORE	British Burma	703,623	Penang	13,290
	Thailand	1,687,179	Malacca	152,832
	French Cochin China	355,733	East Malay Peninsula	176,199
	East Malay Peninsula	42,295	West Malay Peninsula	49,187
	West Malay Peninsula	580	Netherlands India	1,426,880
	Others[5]	98,774	Others[6]	201,703
	TOTAL	2,888,184	TOTAL	2,020,091
PENANG	British Burma	1,301,909	Sumatra	273,338
	Calcutta	23,846	Hong Kong	127,379
	East Malay Peninsula	13,820	West Malay Peninsula	100,589
	Others[7]	38,803	Others[8]	82,350
	TOTAL	1,378,378	TOTAL	583,656
MALACCA	Singapore	152,361	West Malay Peninsula	69,596
	Penang	59,026	Netherlands India	163
	British India	800		
	TOTAL	212,187	TOTAL	69,759

1886

	Source	Imports (in piculs*)	Destination	Exports (in piculs)
SINGAPORE	British Burma	1,170,740	British Burma	220,777
	Thailand	845,558	Philippines	399,992
	Java	388,915	Johore	368,093
	French Cochin China	30,696	East Malay Peninsula	78,362
	British India	29,804	West Malay Peninsula	115,346
	Others[9]	82,657	Malacca	112,438
			Others[10]	787,044
	TOTAL	2,548,370	TOTAL	2,082,052
PENANG	British Burma	1,654,841	Sumatra	520,538
	Thailand	26,346	West Malay Peninsula	381,882
	British India	45,828	Hong Kong	476,960
	Singapore	22,493	Malacca	74,437
	Others[11]	18,179	Others[12]	97,415
	TOTAL	1,767,687	TOTAL	1,551,232
MALACCA	Penang	69,414	Johore	12,301
	Singapore	164,838	Sumatra	3,724
	Others	174	West Malay Peninsula	53,874
	TOTAL	234,426	TOTAL	69,899

was also determined by this consideration. In the circumstances of the period 1820–1874, then, it may fairly be concluded that the pattern and character of commercial economic activity in Malaya was based on cost advantage. Following the establishment of British political control, the pattern and character were modified to some extent, for example by the Perak fiscal policy which aided the expansion of tin mining in the Kinta Valley, and by the introduction of cultivation clauses in land titles that encouraged permanent rather than shifting cultivation. In general, however, there was little limitation on the continued evolution of a pattern of specialization which was based on the development of the most profitable resources in the most profitable place, and this pattern, initially sketched out by the location of tin deposits, rivers and the Straits ports, was given considerable rigidity by the construction of road and railway facilities.

The comparative advantages that mining and export-oriented agriculture had over alternatives such as food production in nineteenth-century Malaya are suggested by the very limited expansion of rice production, even in the vicinity of the concentrations of population associated with tin mining, and by the growing volume of rice imports passing through the Straits ports. Gullick,[67] writing of Negri Sembilan in the 1890s, quotes figures which suggest that, in a year of average yields, padi growing was unremunerative compared with wage labour and that even in times of scarcity a day's wages would

---

FOOTNOTES TO TABLE 1.

* picul=133·1/3 lbs.

(1) mainly Cochin China, Malacca and Penang, British India, China
(2) mainly Sarawak, Natunas Is. (S. China Sea), Australia, Labuan, Philippines
(3) mainly Singapore and Malacca, Hong Kong, Sumatra and Madras
(4) mainly Hong Kong and Siam
(5) mainly Penang, British India, Hong Kong.
(6) mainly Hong Kong, Sarawak, Natunas Is., Labuan
(7) mainly Chittagong, Singapore, Malacca
(8) mainly Singapore, East Malay Peninsula, Malacca
(9) mainly Cochin China, Bali, Hong Kong, Other Dutch Islands, Penang
(10) mainly Hong Kong, Sarawak, Java, Natunas Is., Riau, Sumatra
(11) mainly Madras, Malacca, French India
(12) mainly China, Thailand, Singapore.

Source: Straits Settlements Blue Books for 1878, 1881, 1886.

buy a gantang of rice*. Fruit, vegetables, poultry and live-stock were necessarily locally produced, however, and provided the main source of money to the Negri Sembilan Malay community. In the vicinity of Kuala Lumpur, on the other hand, extensive padi cultivation was reported in the late 1870s and mid-1880s,[68] a situation which may well have been caused by the higher price of imported rice at this greater distance from the sea especially in periods of low tin prices. Despite the possibility of selling surplus foodstuffs to the urban and mining communities, Malay peasants were also growing export crops. Both Malays and Javanese were planting coffee, and some tobacco, pepper and gambier in the 1880s and, like the European estates, turned to rubber at the end of the century.

Trade figures from the last quarter of the nineteenth century reveal considerable increases in the volume of rice imports to Singapore, Penang and Malacca—originating especially in Burma, Thailand and Cochin-China—and the forwarding of considerable quantities to the Malayan mainland for consumption by the expanding labour force employed in the export industries. The Blue Books for the late 1870s and 1880s, from which the data in Table 1 are extracted, are particularly detailed and give a very thorough picture of the origins and destinations of the commodities moving through the Straits ports. Apart from the demand for rice and other foodstuffs, imports by the west coast Malay states of cotton goods, hardware and metal goods, glassware and matches appear to reflect a growing demand by the export-producing areas for manu-factured goods from Europe and seem indicative of the emergent specialization and earning capacity of the commercial sector of the mainland Malayan economy.

Despite the much closer economic relationships with their peninsular hinterlands that were possessed by the Straits ports at the end of the nineteenth century compared with those held in the early years of their existence, Penang and Singapore (and to a less extent, Malacca) continued to develop as foreign enclaves, having less and less in common with the indigenous societies on whose geographical margins they were located. As illustrated by Table 2, only a small proportion of their population was Malay; the majority of the labouring classes

* Gantang—a volumetric measure for padi, approximately equal to 5¼ lbs.

TABLE 2

POPULATION OF THE STRAITS PORTS, 1820–1911

	EURO-PEAN	MALAY	CHINESE	INDIAN	OTHERS	TOTAL
			SINGAPORE			
1821	29	2,851	1,159	132	550	4,721
1830	466	5,173	6,555	1,913	2,527	16,634
1840	1,110	9,318	17,704	3,375	3,882	35,389
1850	1,332	12,206	27,988	6,284	4,986	52,796
1860	2,385	11,888	50,043	12,973	4,445	81,734
1871	1,946	26,141	54,572	11,411	3,041	97,111
1881	2,769	33,012	86,766	12,086	4,575	139,208
1891	5,254	35,992	121,908	16,035	5,365	184,554
1901	3,824	36,080	164,041	17,823	6,787	228,555
1911	6,358	31,840	224,230	28,454	3,963	311,303
			PENANG[1]			
1820	1,328	8,681	8,270	8,198	2,373	28,850
1830	1,877	11,943	8,963	8,858	2,318	33,959
1842	1,180	18,442	9,715	9,681	1,481	40,499
1851	347	16,670	15,457	7,840	2,829	43,143
1860	1,995	18,887	28,018	10,618	438	57,961
1871	383	24,189	24,055	11,022	2,148	61,797
1881	607	27,816	45,135	15,533	2,467	91,558
1891	1,097	35,786	64,327	19,891	2,785	123,886
1901	995	34,286	71,463	18,740	3,348	128,832
1911						101,182[4]
			MALACCA[2]			
1827	2,522[3]	23,292	5,006	2,342	—	33,162
1834	1,799	20,463	4,143	2,403	452	29,260
1842	2,544	32,622	6,882	3,258	790	46,096
1852	2,283	48,226	10,608	1,182	206	62,515
1860	2,648	53,554	10,039	1,026	—	67,267
1871	50	58,126	13,482	3,277	2,821	77,756
1881	40	69,368	19,741	1,891	2,539	93,579
1891	134	70,325	18,161	1,647	1,903	92,170
1901	74	72,978	19,468	1,276	1,691	95,487
1911	340	79,066	36,094	7,527	1,756	124,952

(1) Island only. (2) Includes considerable rural area of colony. (3) This column includes Eurasians before 1871. (4) Georgetown only.

Sources: 1820–1860 Braddell, T., *Statistics of the British Settlements in the Straits of Malacca*, Penang, 1861. 1871 Straits Settlements Blue Book. 1881–1911 Census Reports.

were immigrant Chinese or Indian, and the merchants Chinese, Indian, Arab and European. The function of the ports, though they remained concerned with the native trade of the Straits and archipelago, was more to provide the points where international trade touched the periphery of a still largely undeveloped Malaya, to put the primary products from the peninsula's mines and plantations into contact with the world market and to inject cheap European, and to some extent Indian, goods into the economy. The significance of free trade in this era lay in the fact that it permitted the entry of foreign goods readily into the Malayan market, a situation which, at the time, was highly satisfactory to the export trade of Britain and one which must have been welcomed by the local inhabitants who were able to obtain a range of manufactured goods at the lowest possible price.

By the end of the nineteenth century, the Straits ports had become the essential links between the world market and the foreign-dominated mines and plantations of Malaya which, especially after the great expansion of rubber and the introduction of tin dredges, were largely financed by European capital and managed by European personnel. The ports' ties with their Malayan hinterlands, which were increasingly dominating their trade, were primarily concerned with the export of primary commodities produced by foreign capital, management and labour and which only indirectly—for example by stimulating rubber small-holdings and by making available a range of imported goods even in remote villages— touched the indigenous peoples. British colonial administrative policy, with its attempts to conserve traditional peasant Malay society, reinforced this situation. Much of the effective demand generated by foreign trade, which might conceivably have stimulated a variety of economic activities with the ports themselves, if not elsewhere in Malaya, leaked abroad. Profits from mining, rubber planting and trading were paid to foreign shareholders.* Managers and labourers alike remitted much of their earnings abroad, to Europe, China or India,

---

* For much of the late nineteenth and early twentieth centuries, nevertheless, the United Kingdom had an annual deficit on balance of payments with the Straits Settlements. This can be attributed to the heavy investment Britain was making there as well as to the fact that a high proportion of imports into the Straits ports consisted of foodstuffs from India (i.e. Burma).[69]

a situation facilitated by free exchange, the logical financial concomitant of free trade.

It would appear that, in consequence of the ready availability of freely imported goods there was little or no incentive for the development of manufacturing in the ports themselves, or for that matter elsewhere in Malaya, beyond the processing of the primary products and the small scale provision of local consumer goods. Tin smelting, at both Penang and Singapore, was by far the most important industrial activity in Malaya. The small scale consumer industries, almost entirely Chinese operated, were family businesses usually limited to a single shop-house and operating on slim profit margins. Although the processing industries, particularly tin smelting, did employ a considerable labour force, and indirectly provided livings for more people than was apparent at first sight, the fact that the raw materials were almost entirely exported meant that their potential for creating further industrial growth was denied to Malaya. Whilst it would be wrong to pretend that the free entry of foreign goods and the export after their initial processing of the country's primary products for further manufacture elsewhere were the only obstacles to the development of a greater variety of industries in the Straits ports before the First World War*, their concentration of activity— other than raw material processing—on the provision of commercial and other services and on naturally-protected secondary industries such as food and drink, suggests that free port status was a powerful deterrent to the establishment of industrial variety.

By 1914, the economic geography of Malaya, outside the subsistence sector, had been moulded by the exploitation of minerals and soil to meet an overseas demand for products that the peninsula was in a favourable position to provide in increasing quantities at competitive prices. The ports, major inland cities, lines of communication and transport facilities were oriented to this end. Unhindered by restrictive economic policies, except in relatively minor ways which in the main were considered necessary to improve the efficiency

* The small size of the Malayan market with only some three million people, many living at subsistence level, was in itself discouraging to certain possible types of industry.

TABLE 3

Manufactories in the Straits Settlements, 1911*

Classified According to the International Standard
Industrial Classification of all Economic Activities[70]
(*Corresponds to last population census before 1914)

MAJOR DIVISION 3: MANUFACTURING	Singapore	Penang	Province Wellesley	Malacca
31 MANUFACTURE OF FOOD, BEVERAGES & TOBACCO				
311–312 *Food manufacturing*				
311 Melting tallow	38			
3113 Pineapple canning and packing	11			
3114 Fish curing		72		
3114 Blachan manufacture	10	10		
3115 Coconut oil manufacture	6	24	1	20
3115 Copra ? Drying	14		8	
3116 Sago manufacture	7		13	
3116 Rice milling and rice cleaning	5	3	36	
3116 Tapioca manufacture		31	267	9
3117 Bread and biscuit manufacture	15	51		
3118 Sugar refining	18			
3118 Sugar manufacture			2	9
3121 Ice manufacture	4	2		
3121 Tea manufacture				1
313 *Beverage Industries*				
3131 Samsu Distilleries	1	1	2	
3131 Rum manufacture			1	
3134 Aerated water manufacture	17	9		
32 TEXTILE, WEARING APPAREL & LEATHER INDUSTRIES				
321 *Manufacture of Textiles*				
3211 Dye-houses	26	16	1	
323 *Manufacture of leather and products of leather, leather substitutes and fur except footwear and wearing apparel*				
3231 Tanneries	17	15		
33 MANUFACTURE OF WOOD & WOOD PRODUCTS, INCLUDING FURNITURE				
33 Carpenters' shops	304			
3311 Sawmills	20	2	4	
35 MANUFACTURE OF CHEMICALS & OF CHEMICAL, PETROLEUM, COAL, RUBBER AND PLASTIC PRODUCTS				
351 *Manufacture of Industrial Chemicals*				
3511 Gambier manufacturing				124
3511 Indigo manufacturing		10	41	
? Charcoal kilns and depots	14	27		
352 *Manufacture of other chemical products*				
3523 Soap manufacturing	9	9		
3523 Essential oil distilleries	1		33	
3529 Candle manufacturing		27		
355 *Manufacture of Rubber Goods*				
3559 Rubber manufacturing			2	
36 MANUFACTURE OF NON-METALLIC MINERAL PRODUCTS EXCEPT PRODUCTS OF PETROLEUM AND COAL				
361 *Manufacture of Pottery, China and Earthenware*				

TABLE 3—*continued*—

MANUFACTORIES IN THE STRAITS SETTLEMENTS, 1911*

Classified According to the International Standard
Industrial Classification of all Economic Activities[70]
(*Corresponds to last population census before 1914)

MAJOR DIVISION 3: MANUFACTURING	Singapore	Penang	Province Wellesley	Malacca
3610 Potteries	10	1	13	
369 *Manufacture of other non-metallic mineral products*				
3691 Brick kilns	9	⎫		10
		⎬ 19		
3692 Lime works	13	⎭		3
37 BASIC METAL INDUSTRIES				
372 *Non-ferrous metal basic industries*				
3720 Tin smelting works	1	1	1	
38 MANUFACTURE OF FABRICATED METAL PRODUCTS, MACHINERY & EQUIPMENT				
381 *Manufacture of Fabricated Metal products, Machinery and equipment*				
3811 Smithies	194			
3819 Engineers, iron and brass founders	7	81 (incl. black-smiths and copper smiths)		
382 *Manufacture of machinery except Electrical*				
3825 Engineers and millwrights	3			
384 *Manufacture of Transport Equipment*				
3841 Shipyards, slipways and docks	3	1	5	
3841 Graving docks	5			

N.B. Data on manufacturing in the Straits Settlements were compiled for the 1911 Blue Book on the basis of number of premises or works and not on numbers employed and therefore do not give any indication of the relative importance of each works listed. Thus although it is apparent that one tin smelting works employed far more people and was of far greater economic significance than one carpenter's shop each is counted as one unit in the compilation.

Certain inconsistencies exist in the collection of data from the three settlements but where possible these have been eliminated in the table above by amalgamating categories that are clearly related. Some data do not fit precisely into the I.S.I.C. and have been allocated to the most approprate category e.g. charcoal kilns. Doubt must be cast on the completeness of the data—it seems unlikely, for example, that there were no bakers in Malacca or carpenters in Penang.

Despite the unsatisfactory nature of using probably incomplete data relating to numbers of premises, there occur certain significant omissions from the manufacturing structure of the Straits Settlements in 1911. These are especially the lack of textile, wearing apparel and footwear industries, of paper and paper products, paints and varnishes and all chemical products except soap and candles, the very limited development of metal working (except tin smelting), and the almost complete lack of machinery manufacture of all types.

Emphasis is clearly on the processing of raw materials (tin, rubber, copra, indigo, gambier, tapioca, sugar, sago and tea), food preparation, and the manufacture of low value and/or bulky goods such as pottery, bricks and soap. Calculation of a specialization index from these admittedly unsatisfactory data, employing the same method as that used to obtain the export specialization indices on p. 25, gives an industrial specialization index of 93·5 for Singapore. 94·5 for Penang (excluding Province Wellesley), and 96·7 for Malacca.

Source: Straits Settlements Blue Book 1911.

of the export sector, those elements in the physical make-up of the country that were favourable to the establishment of the export economy were developed, and a pattern was established that could not fail to influence the nature and location of all subsequent economic activity.

REFERENCES

1   Fisher, C. A., 'Some Comments on Population Growth in South-east Asia, with special reference to the period since 1830', in Cowan, C. D. (ed.), *The Economic Development of South-east Asia*, London, Allen and Unwin Ltd., 1964, p. 51

2   Harrison, B., *South-east Asia—A Short History*, London, Macmillan, 1957, p. 156

3   Tregonning, K. G., 'Penang and the China Trade', *Mal. in Hist.*, 1, February, 1959

4   Mills, L. A., 'British Malaya 1824–1867', *J. Mal. Brch. R. Asiat. Soc.*, 3, 1925

5   Popham, Sir H. R., *A Description of Prince of Wales Island in the Straits of Malacca with its real and probable advantages and sources to recommend it as a marine establishment*, London, Stockdale, 1805, p. 23

6   Mills, L. A., *op. cit.*

7   Scott, J., (ed. Fielding, K. J.), 'The Settlement of Penang', *J. Mal. Brch. R. Asiat. Soc.*, 28, 1955

8   Furnivall, J. S., *Netherlands India*, Cambridge University Press, 1939, p. 68

9   Wright, H. R. C., *East Indian Economic Problems of the Age of Cornwallis and Raffles*, London, Luzac & Co. Ltd., 1961, p. 219

10 Clodd, H. P., *Malaya's First British Pioneer*, London, Luzac & Co. Ltd., 1948, p. 150

11 Crawfurd, J., *History of the Indian Archipelago*, Edinburgh, Archibald Constable & Co. Ltd., 1820, Vol. III, p. 268

12 Wurtzburg, C. E., *Raffles of the Eastern Isles*, Hodder and Stoughton, London, 1954, p. 433

13 *Ibid.*, p. 478

14 Greenberg, M., *British Trade and the opening of China 1800–42*, Cambridge University Press, 1951.

15 Wurtzburg, *op. cit.* p. 514

16 The Resident, Singapore, to Lieutenant-Governor, Fort Marlborough, 3rd November, 1819, viz. Cowan, C. D. (ed.) 'Early Penang and the Rise of Singapore 1805–1832', *J. Mal. Brch. R. Asiat. Soc.*, 23, 1950

17 Cowan, C. D., *op. cit.*

18 Wong Lin Ken, 'The Trade of Singapore 1819–1869', *J. Mal. Brch. R. Asiat. Soc.*, 33, 1960

19 Dalton, J., Singapore Chronicle, 1830, quoted in Moor, J. H., 'Notices of the Indian Archipelago and Adjacent Countries', Singapore, 1837, p. 15, and in Wong Lin Ken, op. cit.

20 Wong Lin Ken, *op. cit.*, appendix A.

21 Cameron, J., *Our Tropical Possessions in Malayan India*, London, Smith, Elder & Co., 1865, p. 195, 197

22 Mills, L. A., *op. cit.*

23 Wong Lin Ken, *op. cit.*
24 Bogaars, G., 'The Effect of the Suez Canal on the Trade and Development of Singapore', *J. Mal. Brch. R. Asiat. Soc.*, 28, 1955
25 *Ibid., op. cit.*
26 *Ibid., op. cit.*
27 Wheatley, P., *The Golden Khersonese*, Kuala Lumpur, University of Malaya Press, 1961, p. xxiv
28 Begbie, P. J., *The Malayan Peninsula*, Madras, Vepery Mission Press, 1834, pp. 430–431
29 Cowan, C. D., 'Governor Bannerman and the Penang Tin Scheme, 1818–1819', *J. Mal. Brch. R. Asiat. Soc.*, 23, 1950
30 Braddell, T., *Statistics of the British Settlements in the Straits of Malacca*, Penang, 1861, p. 5
31 Cowan, *op. cit.*
32 Tarling, N., *Anglo-Dutch Rivalry in the Malay World 1780–1824*, Brisbane, University of Queensland Press, 1962, pp. 87–88
33 Wong Lin Ken, *The Malayan Tin Industry to 1914*, Tucson, University of Arizona Presss, 1965, pp. 17–18
34 Begbie, *op. cit.*, p. 425
35 Jackson, R. N., 'Immigrant Labour and the Development of Malaya', Kuala Lumpur, Government Printer, 1961, p. 32
36 Wong Lin Ken, *The Malayan Tin Industry to 1914*, p. 18
37 Westerhout, J. B., 'Notes on Malacca', *J. Indian Arch. E. Asia*, 2, 1848
38 Croockewit, H., 'The Tin Mines of Malacca', *J. Indian Arch. E. Asia*, 8, 1854
39 Gullick, J. M., 'Kuala Lumpur 1880–1895', *J. Mal. Brch. R. Asiat. Soc.*, 28, 1955
40 Doyle, P., *Tin Mining in Larut*, London, 1879, pp 6–7
41 Wong, *op. cit.*, p. 89
42 Hale, A., 'On Mines and Miners in Kinta, Perak', *J. Straits Brch. R. Asiat. Soc.*, 16, 1885
43 International Tin Council, 'Statistical Supplement, 1965', London, 1965, Table 1
44 Wong Lin Ken, 'The Malayan Tin Industry: A Study of the Impact of Western Industrialization on Malaya' in Tregonning, K. G. (ed.) *Papers on Malayan History*, Department of History, University of Malaya in Singapore, 1962, p. 20
45 Doyle, P., *op. cit.*
46 Wong Lin Ken, 'Western Enterprise and the Development of the Malayan Tin Industry to 1914', in Cowan, C. D. (ed.) *The Economic Development of South-east Asia*, London, Allen and Unwin Ltd., 1964, p. 138
47 Wickett, J., chairman's remarks following 'Mining in Perak', *Trans. Min. Ass. Inst. Corn*, 3, 1890–92
48 Wayte, M. E., 'Port Weld', *J. Mal. Brch. R. Asiat. Soc.*, 32, 1959
49 Ooi Jin Bee, 'Mining Landscapes of Kinta', *Mal. J. Trop. Geogr.*, 4, 1955
50 Federated Malay State Railways, *Fifty Years of Railways in Malaya, 1885–1935*, Kuala Lumpur, 1935, p. 10
51 Fisher, C. A., 'The Railway Geography of British Malaya', *Scott. Geogr. Mag.*, 64, 1948
52 Wong Lin Ken, *The Malayan Tin Industry to 1914*, p. 115

53   de la Croix, J. E., 'Some Account of the Mining Districts of Lower Perak', *J. Straits Brch, R. Asiat. Soc.*, 7, 1881

54   Cant, R. G., 'Pahang in 1888. The Eve of British Administration', *J. Trop. Geogr.*, 19, 1964

55   Miles, T. A., 'Diamond Jubilee of Tin Dredging', *Tin Int.*, 40, January February and March, 1967

56   Jackson, J. C., *Planters and Speculators*, Kuala Lumpur and Singapore, University of Malaya Press, 1968, p. 5

57   Wheatley, P., 'Land Use in the Vicinity of Singapore in the Eighteen-Thirties', *Mal. J. Trop. Geogr.*, 2, 1954

58   Jackson, J. C., *op. cit.*, pp. 9–11

59   *Ibid.*, *op. cit.*, p. 28

60   *Ibid.*, *op. cit.*, p. 128

61   *Ibid.*, *op. cit.*, p. 184

62   Jenkins, R. O., 'Rubber—Introduction and Expansion with Special Reference to Malaya', *Br. Mal.*, 26, 1951

63   Marks, O., 'The Pioneers of Para Rubber Planting in Malaya', *Br. Mal.*, 2, 1927

64   *Ibid.*, *op. cit.*

65   Courtenay, P. P., *Plantation Agriculture*, London, G. Bell & Sons Ltd., 1965, p. 151

66   Jackson, R. N., *op. cit.*, p. 105

67   Gullick, J. M., 'The Negri Sembilan Economy of the 1890's', *J. Mal. Brch. R. Asiat. Soc.*, 24, 1951

68   Gullick, J. M., 'Kuala Lumpur, 1880–1895', *J. Mal. Brch. R. Asiat. Soc.*, 28, 1955

69   Saul, S. B., *Studies in British Overseas Trade 1870–1914*, Liverpool University Press, 1960, p. 60

70   Statistical Office of the United Nations, 'International Standard Industrial Classification of all Economic Activities,' Statistical Paper Series M, No. 4, Rev. 2, New York, United Nations, 1968, pp. 27–48

CHAPTER 4

The Malayan Export Economy between the two World Wars

By 1914, Malaya's economy was clearly dependent on international trade, and the export sector was dominated by the production of two raw materials, tin and rubber, which entered world markets through the Straits ports of Penang and Singapore. In 1913, the last full year of peace, the value of the total export trade of Penang was $121 million, and that of Singapore was $251 million, almost exactly twice as much. The peninsular hinterlands served by the two ports were yearly increasing in wealth as rubber replaced jungle along the western foothills of the Main Range, and plans for the extension of the Federated Malay States railway northward into the protected state of Kedah, under British influence since the 1909 treaty with Siam, and southwards into Johore offered every expectation of the spread of plantations in the two directions. Tin output was also slowly expanding. Apart from their traditional links with Europe and the archipelago, the trade of which was also growing with the development of such areas as the Oostkust and Djambi districts of Sumatra, the Straits ports had established contacts with eastern Asia, especially with the treaty ports in China and Japan, but also with Korea and Formosa, and with the United States and Australia. The British policy of active encouragement of the exploitation of the peninsula's resources within a generally unfettered economic environment had brought about major economic development in west Malaya and contributed to the emergence of a distinctive economic landscape.

The period between the outbreak of the First World War and the occupation of Malaya by the Japanese in the early years of the Second was, on the whole, one of economic difficulty. These years saw Malaya's economy influenced, as never before, by events far beyond its control as the nature of the peninsula's trade became increasingly of world significance. This situation, although it had been developing slowly during the period when tin was dominant, was stimulated by the rapid increase in the volume of rubber that was passing through the Straits ports from Malaya after 1914. Rubber, 'which is now one of our main staples of trade and which in the future bids well to rival tin in importance' (as commented the 1913 Report of the Penang Chamber of Commerce[1]), was beginning to embroil Malaya in the price fluctuations that were coming to be endemic to its production and thus directly to influence the volume of much of the other trade of the peninsula. It was an unfortunate co-incidence for Malaya that the very period when its prosperity was becoming increasingly dependent on two commodities, the supply of and demand for both of which were basically inelastic, should turn out to be one of recurring economic crises of world magnitude.

In retrospect, the period between the wars may be seen as one in which Malaya was denied the right both of benefiting fully from the comparative advantages that increasingly she possessed in the production of tin and rubber, and of diversifying her economic structure by the stimulation, with some form of protection, of a manufacturing sector along lines followed by a number of other nations that were either fully independent or were of dominion status. In fact, the move away from a freely operating economy in the 1920s and 1930s was, from Malaya's point of view, for the wrong reasons and in the wrong direction, and to use Clairmonte's terminology (see p. 22), effectively 'froze' the economy in what essentially was its earlier colonial pattern. The geographical consequences of this freezing were the maintenance of a distribution pattern of economic activity that showed few major changes between 1920 and 1940 and only a limited intensification.

When the First World War broke out in Europe in the August of 1914, tin was still the dominant item in Malaya's export trade, representing about 30 per cent. by value of the total export trade of the peninsula. Rubber, though rapidly growing in importance as a contributor to export earnings, had represented only about 8 per cent. of the total in 1912 whilst the export of other Straits produce, particularly copra, tapioca, pepper and spices, was still of considerable importance. Although Malaya was far removed from the centres of hostilities in Europe and the Middle East, repercussions were felt as a result of the shortage of shipping from the Straits to United Kingdom ports. This affected particularly the items of less strategic importance such as copra and tapioca though tin shipments were also reduced, especially during 1915. Rubber suffered less from the shortage of tonnage and, in general, exports increased gradually throughout the war, especially to American Pacific ports. By 1919, rubber accounted for 35 per cent. of Malaya's export earnings compared with the 15 per cent. earned by tin. When the armistice was signed in November 1918, the reaction of the Penang traders at least, and this was probably typical, was one of 'apprehension and anticipation of lower values'[2]—an indication perhaps of the relatively slight effect that the war had had on Malaya and of the expectation that business would revert to its pre-war normality. Indeed, apart from the increase in importance of rubber as an export item and a partial loss of Penang's spice and pepper trade to Singapore (where tonnage had been a little easier during the war), the 1918 pattern of the Malayan trading economy looked little different from that of 1914.

The Export Industries between the Wars

It has already been noted (p. 89) that, by the end of the nineteenth century, almost all the tin areas known today in Perak, Selangor and Negri Sembilan had been discovered and worked. The construction by 1903 of the continuous rail link between Port Dickson and Prai had provided a transport facility for the tinfields, and Malaya was firmly established as the world's largest tin producer, its output exceeding that of the rest of the world combined. Lim Chong Yah credits this position to a combination of forces of which growth in both world tin demand and Malayan supply, the increase in factor supply (especially labour, enterprise and capital), law and order, technical innovations and the development of infrastructure were of major significance.[3] The emergence of the regional pattern of tin mining in response to these forces has already been examined in detail in Chapter 3.

There is no doubt that Malaya's tin deposits are the richest known in the world, a circumstance arising from the particular geological history of the region and the stage in its erosion currently reached (p. 50). The introduction of the gravel pump and the bucket dredge in the first decade of the twentieth century made possible the extraction of tin ore from greater depths, from swamps, and from ground with a relatively low concentration of tin, so that areas formerly considered unprofitable to mine were opened up and abandoned areas were re-worked. The dredging sector of the industry, dominated completely by European companies, grew particularly fast and by 1929 was responsible for over half Malaya's total tin production.

Although tin shipments did not suffer so much from the lack of tonnage during the war as did some other Malayan exports, and prices reached record levels both in 1917 (£238 per ton London standard cash average) and in 1918 (£330), a tin surplus had begun to accumulate by 1919. Owing to the unsettled affairs in Europe that year, serious cable delays and an embargo on imports into America during the first six months, production was in excess of requirements and the price began to decline. In order to assist the industry, the Federated Malay States government bought tin concentrates as a price-supporting measure early in 1919 and gradually released them at the end of the year as prices improved. A similar scheme was operated again at the end of 1920, but it soon became obvious as the post-war depression worsened that the Malayan government alone was not capable of halting the downward trend of prices, a tendency no doubt worsened by the increasing inelasticity of supply of tin brought about by the larger size of the producing units. In consequence, a conference of representatives both of the Federated Malay States and of the Netherlands East Indies (the world's third producer responsible for about 18 per cent. of world output) met at Bandoeng, Java, in 1921. Under the auspices of the two governments, a stock pool was formed for the purpose of taking excess supplies of tin off the market and selling them after prices had recovered. This occurred mainly in 1923 and 1924, and both world prices and Malayan output climbed during the next few years, the former reaching a peak average of £291 per ton in 1926, and the latter a record production of 72,000 tons in 1929.

Thereafter, prices and production declined dramatically, ultimately forcing the establishment of international control over the tin industry by an agreement involving most world producers. The problems of the tin industry between the wars have been analyzed in considerable detail by a number of economists but there remains a deep seated division of opinion about the efficacy of the various attempts to stabilize prices by export control. The American, K. E. Knorr, claimed that much of the difficulty in which the tin mining industry found itself in the 1930s was due to over-investment in earlier years, to which the operation of the Bandoeng Pool materially contributed. Knorr suggested that:

The gradual liquidation of the (Bandoeng) stocks in 1923–24 disguised the fact that growing tin consumption was running ahead of the existing capacity to produce. In the absence of sales from the pool stocks, tin prices would have risen more sharply at an earlier time and would thus have pointed to the growing disequilibrium between output capacity and capacity to consume. As it happened, it was not before 1925–26 that the tin market and tin producers generally realized the insufficiency of existing output capacity. Then tin prices soared to an exceedingly high level. The violence of this reaction, in turn, overstimulated investment and thereby made for the creation of surplus production capacity.[4]

After 1927, production capacity was excessive in relation to average requirements, visible stocks accumulated and prices declined, so that, even before the Great Depression had developed, voluntary attempts at restriction by the large scale producers were attempted. These attempts were greeted with suspicion by the small, low-cost producers in Malaya and were generally unsuccessful, but as the depression worsened there was a decidedly strong drift towards support of government intervention for the compulsory curtailment of output. The International Tin Control Scheme, which aimed at restricting exports by quota, was consequently formulated by agreement between the governments of British Malaya, Nigeria, Bolivia and the Netherlands East Indies and became operative on 1st March, 1931.* The 1931 scheme was renewed in 1934, and again in 1937.

Malayan tin output over the decade of the 1920s had grown by about 11 per cent. but showed no growth in the 1930s.[5] In the rest of the world, the output growth rate of tin was greatly slowed down by the restriction schemes but still showed a growth rate of 4 per cent. due primarily to a great increase in output in the Belgian Congo and, to a smaller degree, in Thailand and China. It was Knorr's opinion that the control schemes were responsible for a deviation of production from the most economic pattern by under-assessing Malaya, a low-cost producer,† in the distribution of production quotas.[6] Malayan producers were certainly more severely restricted than producers in the other control countries, and the complex financial inter-relationships between tin smelting and mining companies with interests both in high cost producing regions, such as Bolivia, and in low cost regions such as Malaya, suggests that a degree of favour was extended to the high cost regions. Lim argues, with considerable reason, that it is difficult to measure changes in the output capacity of an industry like tin in which great fluctuations in output have been a normal feature and which is exploiting a wasting asset, and goes so far as to suggest, using ten year averages, that Malaya's share of total world tin output declined less from the 1920s to the 1930s than it had between any previous two decades.[7] Nevertheless, on the basis of annual figures (Table 4), Malaya's share of world output during the period of international control was at its lowest during the years of lowest prices when, as a low cost producer, it might have been expected to have

* Thailand joined the scheme, though on a very favourable basis, in July, 1931.
† Malaya's low cost production was and is due not only to the fact that average costs are low, because the tin is alluvial and transport is cheap compared to Malaya's chief competitors, but because marginal cost is even lower since the European section is very capital-intensive while the Chinese section, with a high labour content, employs its labour mainly on a profit sharing basis.[8]

fared better than most.* That there was no scarcity of tin-bearing ground, the leap in production, under the stimulus of high prices in later decades, was to show.

TABLE 4

MALAYAN AND WORLD TIN PRODUCTION AND
AVERAGE LONDON STANDARD CASH PRICE FOR TIN, 1920–1941

Years Before International Control	Production ('000 tons)		Malayan Production as Percentage World Production	Average London Standard Cash Price (£stg)
	Malaya	World		
1920	37	123	30·1	296
1921	36	116	31·0	165
1922	37	123	30·1	160
1923	39	126	31·0	202
1924	47	142	33·1	249
1925	48	146	32·9	261
1926	48	143	33·6	291
1927	54	159	34·0	289
1928	65	178	36·5	227
1929	72	196	36·7	204
1930	67	179	37·4	142
1931	55	144	38·2	118
Years of International Control				
1932	29	100	29·0	136
1933	25	88	28·4	195
1934	38	121	31·4	230
1935	42	138	30·4	226
1936	67	181	37·0	205
1937	77	206	37·4	242
1938	43	165	26·1	190
1939	47	168	28·0	226
1940	83	235	35·3	286
1941	79	246	32·1	262

Source: Lim Chong Yah.

* During the years of international control between 1932 and 1941 Malaya's *average* annual share of the world market was 31·5 per cent., compared with an *average* annual share of 33·7 per cent. in the years 1920 to 1931. However during the pre-control years there was a low *negative* correlation (– 0·42) between Malaya's share of annual world production and annual average price but a low *positive* correlation (0·5) between its share and average price during the years of control. Although these correlations statistically are barely significant, the fact that they are in opposite directions at least suggests that Malaya's advantage apparent in years of low prices in the period before international control did not obtain—rather the reverse—in the years of control.

Certainly the effect of the international control of tin output was to curtail production in Malaya and to lead to the suspension of operations by a considerable number of producing units, whilst others concentrated production on their relatively lower-cost areas. Whether tin production in Malaya would have fared better or worse during the Great Depression if control had been absent is one of the unanswerable questions of economic history, but it seems at least possible that, in view of the relative ease with which its alluvial deposits could be worked by large and small operators alike, it was denied the opportunity of obtaining the full share of the much reduced market that its natural advantages in tin production might have gained.

By 1916, rubber was contributing more to Malaya's total export earnings than was tin, a position that it was not to relinquish even in the depth of the Great Depression, when rubber prices had fallen to less than 7 per cent. of their 1916 level. Between 1910 and 1920 vast areas of rubber had matured in the states of west Malaya, especially in Perak, Selangor, Negri Sembilan and Johore where land accessible to the railway in the better drained foothill zones of the peninsula had been cleared of jungle and planted under the stimulus of the high rubber prices of the first decade of the century.[9] The unfortunate coincidence of the great increase in output of these acreages of rubber—which totalled over 2·3 million by 1922—and the post-war recession in the major rubber consuming countries, especially the United States, caused drastic declines in prices, on occasion to below estates' production costs.

Voluntary restriction of output by estates was followed, in 1922, by the government-enforced Stevenson restriction scheme which aimed to reduce the stocks of rubber that had accumulated and to restore prices to a reasonably profitable level. The institution of the Stevenson scheme reflected not only the real need of the estates for higher prices if they were to survive but also the fear of the collapse of the Malayan Chinese economy as the Chettiar moneylenders began to foreclose on Chinese rubber estates.[10] The Stevenson scheme, which had a short term success in achieving a recovery of rubber prices and a reduction of stocks up to 1925, was abandoned in 1928. Except during the very transitory boom of 1929, rubber prices showed a continued decline from the 1925 peak as absorption of rubber by the United States fell drastically, especially after the Wall Street crash. In 1934, an agreement to control the supply of rubber was reached by nearly all the rubber producing countries on the basis of the assignment to each participating country of a basic export quota.

The Stevenson scheme, which operated only in the British rubber producing territories, and the International Rubber Regulation Scheme of 1934, with its renewal in 1938, have been examined in detail by a number of writers[11] and, as with analyses of the tin control schemes, considerable disagreement has been expressed over their effects. It is generally agreed, however, that the Stevenson scheme, limited as it was to the British territories, stimulated the spread of rubber planting, especially by smallholders, to other parts of Southeast Asia, particularly to the Netherlands Indies, so that by 1929 the Netherlands territories had a larger acreage under rubber than Malaya, though, as a consequence of the greater maturity of the Malayan trees, Netherlands Indies production did not equal Malayan until 1939.

The scope and intensity of the trade depression by 1933, its influence having spread to other commodities such as coffee and sugar of which the Netherlands Indies were large producers, was sufficiently great finally to persuade the Netherlands Indies government of the desirability of cooperating with other major rubber producers in the regulation of exports. Understandably, however, the Netherlands authorities recoiled from the task of attempting to apply measures that would require strict control over the production and export of rubber from immense territories in which rubber areas had never been surveyed, individual ownership never registered and where often it was difficult even to identify rubber trees amongst the secondary forest in abandoned cultivation clearings. Until 1936, restriction in the Netherlands territories was affected only by the rough tool of a varying export tax.

In Malaya, as elsewhere, a clear division was made between estate rubber and small-holding rubber in the allocation of quotas. It was generally agreed that rubber production by

Malayan small-holders was greatly under-assessed—in 1933, for example, rubber small-holding exports constituted 47·8 per cent. of total net rubber exports from Malaya, yet under the agreement, in 1935, small-holders as a group were given only 36·8 per cent. of Malaya's total basic export quota.[12] The new planting and re-planting provisions of the agreement also discriminated against the smallholder. New planting was almost completely banned, whilst between 1934 and 1938, replanting was permitted up to a maximum of 20 per cent. of planted area. Bauer claimed it was technically impossible for a smallholder to replant such a percentage of his typically small acreage, and that anyway he could rarely afford to forego the income from the replaced trees.[13] Silcock[14] has

TABLE 5

MALAYAN RUBBER ACREAGE AND PRODUCTION
COMPARED WITH WORLD PRODUCTION, 1922, 1930 AND 1940

	Acreage ('000 acres) Malaya	Production ('000 tons)		Malayan Production as Percentage World Production
		Malaya	World	
1922	2,328	212·4	402·0	52·8
1930	3,049	452·0	825·0	54·8
1940	3,464	547·2	1,417·0	38·6

Source: Lim Chong Yah.

demonstrated that even during the Great Depression, the Malay peasant was financially better off, or could get more rice and of better quality, if he grew rubber for exchange rather than rice, and Bauer has illustrated the fact that the small-holder was certainly the lowest-cost producer of rubber even when estates had cut their costs to the absolute minimum.[15] There was no general tendency by smallholders to replace rubber by another crop, although occasionally a smallholder cut out a portion of his poorest rubber in order to grow food-stuffs for his own needs.[16]

There seems less doubt in the case of the rubber industry, especially its smallholding sector, even than in that of the tin industry that, at least during the 1930s, it was prevented from deriving full benefit from its low cost advantages—

a conclusion well supported by the generally acknowledged fact that when the agreement went into operation in 1934, the world economy was already improving. Between 1930 and 1940, the acreage of rubber in Malaya increased by only 15 per cent., compared with 30 per cent. between 1922 and 1930, and Malayan production grew by 21 per cent. compared with a world increase of over 70 per cent. during the same period (Table 5).

The Malayan export economy between the wars was dominated by the tin and rubber industries, but it is worth noting that during the 1930s a new export crop, palm oil, consistently increased its contribution to the country's export trade. Between 1930 and 1939, Malayan palm oil production had expanded from 3,300 tons to 57,400 tons and the country's contribution to total world output from 1 per cent. to over 11 per cent., despite generally low prices during the decade. The commercial planting of oil palms began, in Selangor, in 1917 and in terms of acreage grew rapidly and steadily until 1930, after which the rate of planting slackened. However, the volume of output increased during the next decade as trees reached their bearing age of four years and matured to their period of highest productivity between about ten and thirty years. The export of palm oil was not subject to international control, as were rubber and tin, and Malaya's contribution to world production was therefore essentially a function of the rising yield from trees planted mainly in the 1920s. The distribution of these plantings—which were entirely on estates as a consequence of the size of investment necessary in processing facilities—was closely related to the distribution of rubber in order to take advantage of the existing infrastructure, but the active encouragement to the industry given by the governments of the Federated Malay States and of Johore, put those states in an initially advantageous position.

The various analyses of the Malayan export industries between the two world wars illustrate quite clearly that the purpose behind the restrictions to which the free operation of the open economy was subjected was the maintenance of a price level at which the more highly capitalized producers could operate and thus maintain both the momentum of the economy and government revenues, to both of which they were the principal contributors. The protagonists of the restriction schemes claim that, had the schemes not existed, the effects of the inter-war depressions on the Malayan economy would have been much worse than they were, but it is difficult not to believe (though probably impossible to prove) that in both tin and rubber production, Malayan producers would have expanded their share of the shrinking market. It may be argued that, in world terms, the deliberate restriction of the development of a pattern of specialization based entirely on cost advantage, that was one obvious result of the tin and rubber control schemes, was desirable in that it prevented too great a concentration of production in limited localized areas to the greater disadvantage of the less economic. This after all was a major argument in support of the growing world-wide protectionism of the period. Malaya's problem was, however, that it was denied not only the full fruits of its comparative advantages in raw material production but also any advantages of alternative developments that protectionism might have offered.

Patterns of Trade Between the Wars

In 1913 the combined trade of Singapore and Penang, which accounted for the bulk of Malayan trade, was valued at $846 million, of which nearly 70 per cent. was handled by the larger port. The pattern of this trade for each individual port is examined in greater detail in Chapter 6, but in general terms it can be stated that characteristic of both was an emphasis on trade with the Malayan hinterland on the one hand and with the United Kingdom and British possessions on the other. The entrepot role, which had been a major function of the Straits ports in the early decades of their trading history, although remaining significant, had to an important extent been replaced by that of serving as a link between the export-oriented economy of mainland Malaya and the industrial economy of north-western Europe (especially Britain) and the U.S.A.

The increasing dependence of the Malayan economy on its export sector is demonstrated by the relationship between the value of the country's tin and rubber exports, and the value of total export income. Throughout the period of price fluctuations in the 1920s and 1930s the proportional contribution of the two commodities never fell below 41.4 per cent.—and that was in the year of rock bottom rubber prices—their average contribution was 59 per cent. in the 1920s and 61 per cent. in the 1930s (up to 1937).

The value of import trade, in its turn, was primarily determined by the value of the raw material exports since a considerable proportion of general imports—mining equipment,

TABLE 6

MALAYA—VALUE OF TIN AND RUBBER EXPORTS
AS PERCENTAGES OF TOTAL EXPORT INCOME, 1920–1937

Year	Per cent.	Year	Per cent.
1920	45·2	1929	66·2
1921	39·0	1930	55·4
1922	50·0	1931	50·3
1923	59·7	1932	41·4
1924	60·5	1933	56·3
1925	72·3	1934	69·3
1926	71·0	1935	65·9
1927	68·3	1936	70·7
1928	61·2	1937	75·6

Source: Lim Chong Yah.

rough goods such as cement or corrugated iron, and luxuries—was intended for the estates and mines of the mainland. Indeed, for a period in the early 1920s there was a suspension of all building works by mines, plantations and government departments, except for those of an essential nature, whilst estate requirements were taken only in small quantities and when needed. Even when better prices ruled for rubber, dealers continued to trade conservatively showing no inclination to purchase beyond their immediate requirements. A local domestic market in Malaya with a purchasing power unrelated to the tin and rubber industries, which could perhaps have acted as a stabilizing influence on the economy simply did not exist. Even the demand for sundry and piece goods, particularly cottons, which were provided by what was known as the 'bazaar trade', largely originated from the Tamil and Chinese labourers employed by the plantations and mines, whilst much of the spending power of the Malay community was earned by their rubber smallholdings. Even the value of the entrepot trade was sharply affected by the earning power of tin and rubber since these commodities were significant elements in the imports from Thailand and Sumatra.

Whilst there can be little doubt that the very considerable fluctuations in the value of trade passing through the Straits

TABLE 7

STRAITS PORTS—PERCENTAGE OF TRADE BY VALUE WITH THE U.S.A.,
1913–1938

	1913	1914	1915	1916	1917	1918	1919
IMPORTS	1·4	1·3	1·7	2·1	n.a.	2·5	3·6
EXPORTS	12·1	12·3	24·4	27·6	n.a.	35·2	35·6

	1920	1921	1922	1923	1924	1925	1926
IMPORTS	4·5	4·5	2·8	2·3	2·6	2·2	2·3
EXPORTS	33·0	20·3	33·4	35·6	35·5	44·1	40·0

	1927	1928	1929	1930	1931	1932	1933
IMPORTS	3·2	3·2	3·6	3·3	2·5	1·8	1·4
EXPORTS	44·0	42·0	42·7	34·7	33·0	19·7	31·4

	1934	1935	1936	1937	1938
IMPORTS	1·7	1·9	1·8	2·3	3·0
EXPORTS	33·2	36·6	46·3	44·1	29·7

Source: Calculated from figures in Colonial Annual Reports.

ports in the interwar years were of greatest significance to the Malayan economy, a gradual re-orientation of trading relationships was slowly becoming apparent which, in a very real way, bore considerable responsibility for these fluctuations in value. Not only was it true that the Malayan economy had come essentially to be dependent on the export of two raw materials but, from the end of the First World War, it had become heavily dependent on one market—namely the U.S.A.—for the absorption of these export commodities. In 1913, the U.S.A. had taken 12 per cent. by value of the exports from the Straits ports; by the end of the war this had risen to 35 per cent. and, except for the immediate postwar depression years of 1920 and 1921, the importance of the U.S.

market increased almost annually until it was taking a peak of nearly 43 per cent. by 1929 (see Table 7). Thereafter its share reflected faithfully the various phases of the Great Depression, thereby transmitting to Malaya the economic vicissitudes through which the industrial economy of the U.S.A. itself was passing.* Even in 1932 the U.S.A. absorbed 67 per cent. of the rubber exports and 42 per cent. of the tin exports from the Straits ports.

If the United Kingdom had been replaced by the U.S.A. as Malaya's principal export market by the end of the First World War, she was beginning to face competition as the leading source of imports for the Malayan market from other directions. It was observed, even as early as 1913, that imports from European sources (both Britain and the Continent) of items such as cotton piece goods, linen cloth, hardware, ironware and cooking utensils were decreasing, and that imports from Japan, Hong Kong, China and South-east Asia were growing.[17] Especially noticeable during the 1920s was the extent to which Japan was emerging as a supplier of imports and also as a shipping nation. In terms of tonnage recorded at the Straits ports, Japanese shipping showed a generally consistent increase from the years of the First World War onwards. Japanese tonnage occupied fourth place (after Britain, Germany and the Netherlands) in 1913, but practically equalled, and in some years actually exceeded, Dutch tonnage in second place throughout the 1920s.

Japan's entry into the Malayan market was particularly important with regard to cotton piece goods, though also of significance in low priced heavy goods such as cement. 1925— a year in which the Stevenson scheme had brought about a substantial improvement in rubber prices—was a record trade year for the Straits ports, exceeding the previous best (1920) by 30 per cent. The value of the import trade from Japan, however, increased by over 80 per cent., cotton piece goods being mainly responsible. In 1927, when the value of trade in all commodities (except tin) had declined in total, that in cement and dyed cotton piece goods from Japan increased, and by 1933, 68 per cent. of the cottons entering

---

* Outside the U.S.A. rubber consumption was, in fact, well maintained during the depression.

the Straits ports were of Japanese origin. As Table 8 clearly illustrates, the principal exporter to suffer by this competition was the United Kingdom.

TABLE 8

BRITISH MALAYA—PERCENTAGE OF IMPORTS OF COTTON PIECE GOODS
BY QUANTITY FROM MAJOR SUPPLIERS, 1925–1933

	1925	1926	1927	1928	1929	1930	1931	1932	1933
UNITED KINGDOM	58	54	52	52	52	27	22	26	
JAPAN	18	21	23	18	21	48	50	57	68
OTHERS	24	25	25	30	27	25	28	17	

Source: Colonial Annual Reports for Straits Settlements.

The growing competition in the Malayan market, especially for lower priced goods such as cotton piece goods, that was facing United Kingdom exports from Japan and, though to a much smaller extent, from other Asian producers such as India and Hong Kong, caused the emergence of opposition to the free trade policy of the Straits ports from the very British merchant houses who had benefited so much from it in the past. This opposition was voiced, for example, by the Penang Chamber of Commerce in 1934 in a bitter speech by a committee member who spoke of Japanese trading as a 'deadly menace which (was) threatening the British import trade (of the) colony with extinction'.[18]

In 1934, legislation was enacted with retrospective effect to 7th May to regulate and control by means of quotas the introduction into the colony, for Malayan consumption, of cotton and rayon piece goods manufactured in foreign countries.[19] To safeguard the entrepot trade of Penang and Singapore, re-export depots, or bonded warehouses, were established. These restrictions continued throughout the 1930s and included an extension in 1938 to cover certain made-up cotton and artificial silk piece goods. A considerable decrease in the import of cotton and rayon piece goods was the predictable outcome of the quotas.

The official attitude towards the various economic controls affecting the Malayan economy by the mid-1930s as expressed by the Straits Settlements annual report, was that free trading was essentially maintained:

Notwithstanding these restrictions . . . and the continued operation of the tin and rubber control schemes, it can be said that on the whole the Colony's tradition of free trade was maintained. Apart from excise duties on liquors, tobacco and petroleum imposed solely for revenue purposes, there are no import duties in the Straits Settlements, and commerce and passenger traffic flow with a freedom that in these days is remarkable.[20]

The freedom of 'passenger traffic flow' had in fact been impaired in 1930, before which year immigration had been practically free, but in which year a quota system was applied to the immigration of male labourers from China, with the object of reducing unemployment, raising the standard of labour and improving the sex ratio. The 1932 Aliens Ordinance further extended control to all immigrants of other than

TABLE 9

BRITISH MALAYA—SURPLUS OR DEFICIT OF MIGRANTS, 1929–1940

1929	1930	1931	1932	1933	1934
+130,121	−33,741	−187,529	−162,978	−38,449	+14,2089

1935	1936	1937	1938	1939	1940
+125,206	+82,809	+267,206	+31,038	−2,712	−8,299

Source: Colonial Annual Reports.
    N.B. Lim considers Chinese immigrational statistics to Malaya to be 'ridiculously inaccurate'.[21]

British or British protected nationality. A net loss of population was recorded in each of 1930, 1931, 1932 and 1933, mainly of Chinese and South Indians, as a combined result of the immigration restrictions and of the discharge of labourers from estates and mines. A reversal of this situation was first apparent in late 1933. An amendment to the Aliens Ordinance, which permitted bona fide employers to import labour outside the quota from 1934, and the beginnings of economic recovery contributed to the surplus that is apparent from 1934 (Table 9). After 1938, the restriction policy was extended to cover alien females as well, thus ending the considerable flow of Chinese females into Malaya between 1933 and 1938 which had helped to even out the Malayan

Chinese sex ratio (and which later was to step up the Malayan Chinese reproduction rate).

Until the end of the First World War, the attitude of the colonial government towards the growth of the Malayan economy was expressed in the belief 'that free trade, accompanied by government provision of essential services, would in some undefined way increase the wealth of the businesses in Malaya and its government revenue. The interests of labourers were considered not in terms of maximizing their income, but of insuring freedom of contract, honest migration conditions and healthy surroundings'.[22]

Nevertheless, as a consequence of the economic circumstances that followed the war, the government was forced to intervene in the economy in a variety of ways. It has not been the purpose of this chapter to offer a critique of these interventions *per se*, but primarily to observe their effects on the pattern of specialization in the Malayan economy. It seems apparent, however, that most intervention was motivated by a desire to maintain the viability of the European commercial sector rather than to ensure the most effective use of resources within the group of territories as a whole that made up British Malaya. The rubber industry exercised political influence through trading and estate owning interests; the political influence of the tin industry, through a concentration of control in agencies and smelters, was exerted mainly in the interest of maintaining capital values, and not only in Malaya; the trading companies, shipping agents and secretarial companies had very close links with the rubber and tin interests. The government's attitude to Malay rubber smallholders and to immigrant labourers was such that it did not regard them primarily as economic agents, while official policy towards rice production was one of encouraging higher productivity and eliminating specific abuses within the general framework of subsistence agriculture and opposing the spread of commercial attitudes amongst rice farmers.[23]

The necessary outcomes of the political pressures that existed and of the general attitude towards the non-European sector of the economy were the various restrictions under which the economy operated in the 1920s and 1930s From the evidence that is available it appears that the specialization that had begun to appear by the First World War, and which was based, as has been seen, on certain very real advantages, was prevented, at least partially, from further development in the supposed interests of that sector that was European controlled This partial prevention of the extension of specialization was, however, on negative grounds—there was no firm intent to develop alternative economic activities, either to broaden the export base or to provide alternative opportunities for the employment of capital and, especially, labour within Malaya The increase in output of the oil-palm industry in the 1930s was fortuitous and quite unrelated to any deliberate diversification—indeed in the 1930s palm oil and palm kernel oil prices themselves were low and did not encourage extensive planting The restriction of imports of foreign manufactured cottons by quota was entirely on the grounds of protecting imperial, essentially British, made cottons, and no effort was made to establish a textile industry in Malaya itself The principal effect, apart from temporarily preserving the British trade, must have been to raise the cost of cotton textiles to the average Malayan, with no positive benefits to him. During the period of depressed export industries and stagnant international trade, some efforts were admittedly made, both by western and by Chinese interests, to establish manufacturing industries in Malaya. Among them were the Bata shoe factories opened at Klang in 1937 and at Singapore in 1939 with labour trained by foremen from the company's Indian factories. Two Chinese firms of rubber shoe manufacturers also began production at Klang. Efforts by British-American Tobacco to maintain a factory in Singapore in the early 1930s were defeated, however, by competition from cheap imports.[24]

The Malayan economy, in the period under review in this chapter, may be seen as falling between two possible and alternative lines of development. On the one hand, its role as a colonial, export-oriented economy suffered from control over its freedom to expand output of those commodities in the production of which it had greatest advantage. On the other, the fact that it was governed as part of a much wider trading empire rather than as an independent unit made impossible the development of a protected industrial sector

K

as was happening, in response to much the same economic difficulties, in Australia, South Africa and Argentina for example. The geographical response to this situation consisted

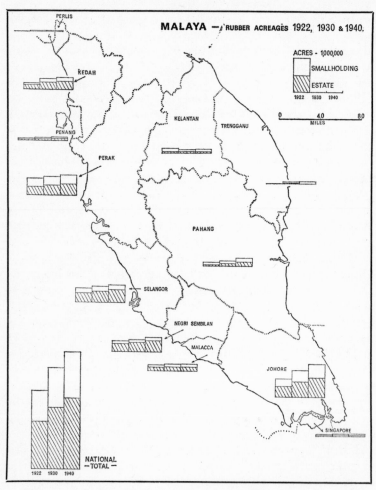

Figure 14. Malaya—Rubber Acreages 1922, 1930 and 1940

essentially of an increase in the acreage devoted to export crops, mainly rubber, though as Table 5 indicated, this was a much smaller proportionate expansion than took place in the world as a whole, and was concentrated essentially in those states already dominant in the rubber growing industry (Figure 14), and of the more intensive working, as new and bigger dredges were introduced, of the major tin-fields of the Kinta Valley and central Selangor.

There was some development of the infrastructure, particularly during the 1920s when government revenue was less affected by low tin and rubber prices than in the 1930s. The railway network was extended by the construction of the line north from Prai to Padang Besar on the Thai frontier in 1918 (thus drawing Kedah into the rubber belt), and from Gemas to Kuala Lipis in 1920 and thence to Tumpat (Kota Bharu) by 1931. The railway also crossed the Johore Strait on a causeway to Singapore in 1923. In 1931, the Federated Malay States Railway had a budget deficit for the first time and it was not until 1959 (in an era of large iron ore movement by rail) that it carried a freight tonnage equal to or greater than that of 1929. The period up to 1928 also witnessed the completion of a direct road link from Johore Bahru to the Thai border, a growing network in the west coast states and, in the 1930s, development in the east coast states and Johore, chiefly in areas not served by the railway. As a relatively labour-intensive activity, road building appeared to be less affected by the depression. Electricity, stimulated by the mechanization of the tin industry and by the demands of the main urban centres, was available in most of the west coast towns by 1927, and in a few east coast centres by 1931. Major steam and hydro-electric stations came on stream at Malim Nawar and Chenderoh in Perak in 1928 and 1929.

The interwar period saw a continued increase in urbanization in Malaya*, though a slower rate was recorded in the intercensal decade 1921–1931 than had been recorded between 1911 and 1921. The increase in tertiary activity and consequent employment opportunities, better health services in the urban than in the rural areas, and periods of unemployment in the mining and plantation areas all contributed to the relatively faster population growth of the urban centres.

At the commencement of the Pacific War in 1942, the

* The percentage of urban population (in gazetted areas of 10,000 population and over) to total population in peninsular Malaya was 10·7 per cent. in 1911, 14·0 per cent. in 1921 and 15·1 per cent. in 1931. Figures calculated on a state basis are given in Table 24.

economy of Malaya was still characteristically colonial. It remained dependent on a very limited range of export commodities and on the services provided, both for the domestic export trade and to some extent for the export trade of neighbouring regions, by the trading ports of Penang and Singapore. Compared with many, indeed with most, territories in the tropical world Malaya was a relatively prosperous country, with a high standard of administration and a basic pattern of social services, and there can be no doubt that these were the direct product of its export economy. Nevertheless its economic base differed little from what it had been nearly a third of a century earlier and seemed to offer little scope for any major economic advance.

REFERENCES

1   Penang Chamber of Commerce, 'Report for 1913', Penang, 1914
2   *Ibid.*, 'Report for 1918', Penang, 1919
3   Lim Chong Yah, *Economic Development of Modern Malaya*, Kuala Lumpur, Oxford University Press, 1967, p. 42
4   Knorr, K. E., *Tin Under Control*, California, Stanford University Press, 1945, p. 79
5   Lim, *op. cit.*, p. 59
6   Knorr, *op. cit.*, p. 229
7   Lim, *op. cit.*, pp. 59–60
8   Silcock, T. H., 'The Economy of Malaya. Relevance of the Competitive Laissez-Faire Model', in Hoover, C. B. (ed.), *Economic Systems of the Commonwealth*, Durham, N. C., Duke University Commonwealth Studies Centre Series, No. 16, 1962, pp. 341–42
9   Courtenay, P. P., *Plantation Agriculture*, London, G. Bell & Sons Ltd., 1965, p. 151
10 Rowe, J. W. F., 'Studies in the Control of Raw Material Supplies, No. 2. Rubber', London, Royal Economic Society, 1931, p. 18
11 *for example*, McFadyean, Sir A., *The History of Rubber Regulation 1934–43*, London, Allen & Unwin Ltd., 1944
    Knorr, K. E., *World Rubber and its Regulation*, California, Stanford University Press, 1945
    Bauer, R. T., *The Rubber Industry: A Study in Competition and Monopoly*, London, Longmans Green & Co., 1948
12 Lim, *op. cit.*, p. 81
13 Bauer, R. T., 'The Working of Rubber Regulation', *Econ. J.*, 1946
14 Silcock, T. H., *The Economy of Malaya*, Singapore, Donald Moore, 1956, p. 18
15 Bauer, R. T., *The Rubber Industry*, op. cit., p. 59
16 Straits Settlements, 'Colonial Annual Report for 1932', p. 16
17 Ibid., 'Colonial Annual Report for 1913', p. 8
18 Penang Chamber of Commerce, 'Report for 1934', Penang, 1935

19 Straits Settlements Government Gazette Extraordinary, 20th June 1934, 'The Importation of Textiles (Quotas) Ordinance, 1934'
20 Straits Settlements, 'Colonial Annual Report for 1935', p. 43
21 Lim, *op. cit.*, p. 187f.
22 Silcock, T. H., 'The Economy of Malaya. Relevance of the Competitive Laissez-Faire Model', *op. cit.*, pp. 336–7
23 *Ibid.*, *op. cit.*, pp. 339, 344
24 Allen, G. C. and Donnithorne, A. G., *Western Enterprise in Indonesia and Malaya*, London, Allen & Unwin Ltd., 1957, pp. 261–2

CHAPTER 5

Industrialization in Malaya

In Chapter 3 an attempt was made to show how the nature and pattern of economic development in Malaya reflected certain advantages possessed by the peninsula, and how these were able effectively to influence its economic geography as a consequence of the free economy and free trade environment within which economic activities were carried on. The outcome of economic development within this environment was a sophisticated adjustment of production in the commercial sector to physical conditions, and the concentration of the activities of this sector on a limited range of raw material exports and on an associated trading economy that leant very heavily upon them. The need in the 1920s and 1930s to reduce the freedom of operation of the economy, for example by the restricted export of tin and rubber and by the imposition of quotas on textile imports, was symptomatic of the changing economic circumstances that emerged after the First World War. Following the Second World War, in an era of political and economic nationalism, rapidly growing populations and the universal call for the economic advancement of the under-developed world, these circumstances were to begin considerably to modify the economic geography of Malaya.

Malaya emerged from the Second World War with her economy disrupted by three and a half years of Japanese occupation and by the destruction wrought by the hostilities that had preceded it. There was widespread unemployment and destitution, and a major task of economic reconstruction to be undertaken. The rehabilitation of the tin mines and rubber plantations, and the re-establishment of international trade links were the prime objectives in the commercial sector, and by 1949 the foundations of the economy had been restored to at least their pre-war level, with tin and rubber production exceeding the output of the late 1930s (see Table 10) and shipping similarly recovered to its pre-war volume. Despite the outbreak of the Communist armed insurrection (the 'emergency') in 1948 and the economic and financial problems

TABLE 10

MALAYA—TIN & RUBBER PRODUCTION, 1938–1948

	Tin-in-concentrate (long tons)*	Rubber ('000 long tons)†
1938	43,375	359·5
1939	47,416	360·1
1940	83,000	547·2
1941	79,400	
1942	15,748	
1946	8,432	396·7
1947	27,026	646·4
1948	44,815	698·2
1949	55,203	671·5

Sources:
* International Tin Council—Statistical Supplement, 1965.
† Lim Chong Yah, p. 328–9.

that it created, economic recovery continued, and by 1950 Malaya was in a position to turn from her pre-occupation with reconstruction to the problems of further economic expansion.[1]

From this point onwards, despite the fact that in very many ways, physically, historically and economically, Malaya is a unit, with Singapore closely related by history and function to Penang, and by commerce to the peninsular mainland, it becomes necessary to consider Singapore separately from the rest of Malaya. This necessity is the outcome of the political division in 1948 of what conveniently may be termed 'British Malaya' into the Federation of Malaya—made up of the former Federated Malay States, Unfederated Malay States, Penang (including Province Wellesley) and Malacca—and the island state of Singapore. The background to this political dichotomy has been examined elsewhere*, but the

* e.g. by C. A. Fisher in 'Malaysia—a Study in the Political Geography of Decolonization' in Fisher, C.A. (ed.), Essays in Political Geography, London, Methuen, 1968.

TABLE 11

FEDERATION OF MALAYA: POPULATION (BY STATE AND COMMUNITY*) 1947

	Total-All Communities	Malaysians†	Chinese	Indians	Europeans	Eurasians	Other Communities
Total Federation of Malaya	4,908,086	2,427,834	1,884,534	530,638	9,607	10,061	45,412
Penang	446,321	136,163	247,366	57,157	1,239	2,412	1,984
Malacca	239,356	120,327	96,144	19,718	308	1,978	881
Perak	953,938	360,361	444,509	140,176	2,267	1,182	5,173
Selangor	710,788	187,324	362,710	145,184	2,785	2,816	9,969
Negri Sembilan	267,668	110,560	114,406	38,082	761	880	2,979
Pahang	250,178	135,772	97,329	14,744	788	79	1,466
Johore	738,251	323,680	354,770	55,044	881	478	3,398
Kedah	554,441	377,075	115,928	51,347	298	161	9,632
Kelantan	448,572	412,918	22,938	4,940	114	25	7,637
Trengganu	225,996	207,874	15,864	1,761	60	14	423
Perlis	70,490	55,185	11,788	1,684	8	7	1,818
Unlocated	2,087	325	782	801	98	29	52

* The term 'community' to describe the Malays, Chinese, etc. was suggested by the Report on the 1947 census to replace the inaccurate (in this context) term 'race' which is still in popular, official and unofficial, use.

† Includes immigrant Indonesians and aborigines.

Source: 1947 Census

division appears largely to have been the outcome of the unwillingness of the Malays to risk the political domination of an independent Malaya by people of recent immigrant origin who already dominated the country economically. Political separation did not, of course, produce complete commercial separation, but it did create a situation in which two distinct and independent nations* evolved their own approaches to variants of the same basic problem of economic development, and these have had interesting geographical consequences.

The Changing Economic Geography of Peninsular Malaya† since 1950

Following its political separation from Singapore in 1948, the Federation of Malaya inherited an economy that was certainly more varied than that of the island city-state but one whose commercial sector was still dominated by the export-oriented tin and rubber industries and which in a political, though not of course an economic, sense had lost its major port and commercial centre. It was a nation whose population, at the 1947 count, numbered 4.9 million (see Table 11) and whose high growth rate of 2·4 per cent. in 1947, was to increase to 2·6 per cent. in 1950 and to 3·2 per cent. in 1953. The bulk of this population, especially the non-Malay immigrant section, was concentrated in the west coast states from Penang to Johore, where—as has been seen—had developed the principal commercial activities of the country. Only in Kedah and Perlis on the west coast, and in the east coast states, where there existed a significant economy based on wet rice cultivation and fishing, did Malays outnumber the immigrant communities.[2]

The cultural diversity of the Federation's population created a whole host of problems of its own, of course, and many of these were considerably aggravated by the fact that, in general, the Malays were the poorest and economically least sophisticated community, amongst whom capital and entrepreneurial ability were very scarce, though politically

* The Federation of Malaya became an independent nation in 1957. Singapore was given internal self-government in 1959 as the State of Singapore, joined with the Federation of Malaya, Sarawak and North Borneo (Sabah) in the fully independent Federation of Malaysia in 1963, and then left the Federation to become the fully independent Republic of Singapore in 1965.

† See definitions, appendix 1.

they were powerful. Economic development therefore had the added burden of attempting to improve the relative position of one important community whilst aiming at raising the living standard of the whole, and rapidly growing, population. Every assistance was to be given to rural development, but in the interests of balanced growth as well as, most importantly, of maintaining the earning power of the export sector—the major prop of the economy—commercial and industrial development had to be encouraged, and the more rapidly this sector grew, the more rapidly was likely to grow the economic imbalance between the Malays and the rest.[3]

In June 1950, a Draft Development Plan for the Federation of Malaya was published. This dealt specifically with the development of social services, of national resources and utilities, and of trade and industry. In the sections on economic development, certain assumptions were made regarding long term planning. These were, first, that Malaya in the past had been too dependent on a limited range of products; secondly, that the emphasis of development should be on promoting those types of economic activity, whether primary or concerned with industrial production, in which Malaya, by reason of its climate, soil, geographical situation, and the technical abilities of its inhabitants is best fitted to engage; thirdly, that Malaya should aim at producing more of the food that it consumes; fourthly, that as far as possible there should be even development throughout the country; and, fifthly, that development should be planned to increase and not to diminish the total natural wealth of the country.[4]

It was recognized that these considerations were to some extent contradictory but the clear intention was that economic development should not take place at the expense of social justice, but at the same time the very real contribution that the traditional export sector could make to the country's prosperity was not ignored. Whilst development was to be on as broad a front as possible, with the provision of drainage and irrigation works and research into the intensification of yields in the padi growing areas, with attempts to diversify the production of food crops by the expansion of fruit and vegetable growing and with research into the fishing industry, the draft plan stated clearly that it was apparent that with a rising standard of living and an expanding population there cannot be much hope of reducing substantially the very large quantities of imported food; on the contrary they are likely to become even greater in the future. There is only one way of paying for these imports of food . . . and that is by increasing the quantity and the value of exports, i.e. rubber, tin, palm oil.[5]

Malaya had no alternative but to remain a trading nation and, this having been accepted, considerable encouragement was given to the traditional export industries. The rubber industry, which in 1950 (admittedly a year of high prices due to the Korean War) earned 60·9 per cent. of the Federation's total export income of 4,020 million Malayan dollars[6] (£469 million), received much official encouragement and support, especially by means of replanting grants, in order to raise both quality and yields. This was realized to be especially necessary in view of the growing competition from synthetic rubber, against which natural rubber's only real weapon was a lower priced product of equivalent or better quality. Partly as a result of frequent complaints by estate interests of over-taxation and of an actual decline in estate replanting acreages in 1953 and 1954, a government mission was appointed to look into the questions of taxation of the rubber industry and the need for replanting. As a result of its report[7], certain changes were made in taxation and replanting grant arrangements, and considerable stimulation to replanting by both plantations and smallholdings was provided by financial inducements. After 1954 the acreage of replanted rubber increased substantially, much of it consisting of new high yielding material, whilst other developments—mainly of an operational nature—aimed at improving efficiency and thereby reducing the unit cost of natural rubber.*

The contribution of the tin-mining industry to employment, overseas earnings and government revenue was also realized. Although since the mid-1930s tin had regularly contributed

* For example, daily tapping tasks have been increased and commonly consist of about 600 trees, and experience is showing that the rubber tree can stand greater frequency of tapping than was originally thought. The traditional yoked buckets in which tappers carried latex to the collecting stations increasingly are being replaced by carriers on bicycles or even motor cycles. With new planting techniques trees are brought to maturity in 4½–5 years instead of the previously accepted 6–7 years.[8]

a much smaller percentage than rubber to the total export income (11·6 per cent. in 1950[9]), Malaya's comparative advantage in its production is probably greater than that which she has in the production of rubber, and whilst, in

TABLE 12

MALAYA—RUBBER ACREAGE REPLANTED ON MALAYAN ESTATES AND SMALLHOLDINGS, AVERAGE ANNUAL RUBBER PRICE AND WORLD SYNTHETIC RUBBER PRODUCTION, 1938–1962

| | Rubber Acreage Replanted ('000 acres) | | | Average S'pore Price | World Synthetic Production |
	Estate	Smallholding	Total	(M $ per picul)	('000 tons)
1938	25·5	n.a.	25·5	24·06	6·0
1939	36·2	11·0	47·2	31·00	23·7
1940	49·0	14·0	63·0	37·55	42·4
1941	34·0	n.a.	34·0	38·56	77·5
1946	6·7	n.a.	6·7		806·6
1947	24·8	4·4	29·2	37·31	539·3
1948	45·5	2·0	47·5	42·15	532·2
1949	52·8	2·4	55·2	38·19	440·3
1950	44·0	3·5	47·5	108·18	534·6
1951	58·2	3·8	62·0	169·55	908·4
1952	51·6	4·2	55·8	96·07	877·8
1953	29·8	29·5	59·3	67·44	935·6
1954	39·1	22·6	61·7	67·30	716·4
1955	57·6	25·3	82·9	114·16	1,085·3
1956	78·4	46·5	124·9	96·76	1,211·0
1957	76·3	49·8	126·1	88·75	1,262·7
1958	64·8	59·7	124·5	80·25	1,243·4
1959	68·2	69·1	137·3	101·56	1,632·5
1960	75·2	69·5	144·7	108·08	1,880·0
1961	70·5	57·3	127·8	83·54	1,975·0
1962	63·1	96·2	132·3	78·20	2,240·0

Sources: Acreage replanted from Lim Chong Yah, Economic Development of Modern Malaya, Appendix 49.
Prices and synthetic production from International Rubber Study Group, 'Rubber Statistical Bulletin'.

some uses, tin has had to face competition from aluminium, its distinctive properties and elemental nature make it less susceptible than rubber to substitution. Emphasis on the exploitation of a 'wasting asset', especially when, as is frequently true of tin, land with alternative agricultural uses is despoiled, is often criticised as short-sighted. It has been shown, however, that the yield per acre from tin mining is so vastly superior to that achieved by rubber growing that if, at 1963 prices, one year's government revenue alone from one acre of tin bearing land were invested at $5\frac{1}{2}$ per cent. its yield would equal nearly 60 per cent. of the total annual income of the same acre under rubber, and four times the annual government revenue from the rubber.[10] The opinion has been expressed that the value of tin-bearing land is such that tin-mining has a clear claim to first priority in land development policy.[11]

In order to help maintain the earning power of the tin-

TABLE 13

MALAYA, INDONESIA AND BURMA—PRODUCTION OF TIN-IN-CONCENTRATE AND SINGAPORE TIN PRICES, 1960–1967

	Malaya	Indonesia (long tons)	Burma	Avge. Straits Price Ex-Works (M $ per picul)
1960	51,979	22,596	950	393·68
1961	56,028	18,574	951	446·85
1962	58,603	17,310	1,041	447·79
1963	59,947	12,947	914	455·40
1964	60,004	16,345	568	619·42
1965	63,670	14,699	464	702·80
1966	68,886	12,526	370	645·23
1967	72,121	13,601	259	600·10

Source: International Tin Council.

mining sector, the Malayan Federal Government has been a firm upholder of the International Tin Agreements negotiated since the Second World War, despite the temporarily adverse effects of tin export control during the period 1957–60.[12] Individual state governments have become increasingly willing to permit both tin mining in the Malay Reservations (though requiring the participation of Malays in the enterprises), and off-shore exploration by the large mining companies. Between the ending of restricted exports under the International Agreement in 1960 and the re-introduction of control in 1968, Malayan annual tin output increased from 51,979 long tons to 71,121 long tons. Much of this expansion was made possible by the high world prices ruling during the period,

but the generally favourable political environment in which
the industry operated must be given due credit. A telling
comparison may be made with Burmese and Indonesian
production which declined substantially in the same period
of high prices (Table 13).

The dangers of excessive reliance on a very small number
of export commodities, especially rubber and tin whose prices
have a well-known history of great fluctuations, was clearly

TABLE 14

MALAYA—PRODUCTION AND EXPORT OF IRON ORE, BAUXITE AND
ILMENITE CONCENTRATE, 1957–1969

	IRON ORE		BAUXITE		ILMENITE CONCEN-TRATE
	Production (long tons)	Exports (long tons)	Production (long tons)	Exports (long tons)	Exports (long tons)
1957	2,972,359	2,919,737	325,629	340,623	91,734
1958	2,795,261	2,591,382	262,364	246,605	74,827
1959	3,760,684	3,772,329	381,747	363,808	72,851
1960	5,640,258	5,500,173	451,958	447,999	118,242
1961	6,733,520	6,435,054	409,881	284,356	106,975
1962	6,507,302	6,441,112	349,419	314,857	101,657
1963	7,264,543	6,581,785	444,047	450,463	147,014
1964	6,479,070	6,316,968	463,829	547,945	129,263
1965	6,852,037	6,634,198	843,172	670,894	121,566
1966	5,762,440	5,680,691	940,447	1,007,157	116,386
1967	5,349,780	5,245,852	885,389	852,298	89,372
1968	5,085,332	5,086,812	786,042	776,993	123,838
1969	5,151,022	5,219,435	1,056,068	862,953	126,893

Source: Monthly Statistical Bulletin of West Malaysia.

understood. Whilst the very real benefits to be obtained from
the efficient exploitation of these resources was fully appreciated,
they could not be relied upon alone to provide the reliable
economic growth that the independent Federation of Malaya
needed. Diversification of raw material exports was essential
and, as was coming rapidly to be recognized in most parts
of the developing world, so was a degree of industrialization.
Apart from tin, the Malayan peninsula possesses a variety of
other minerals, especially bauxite, gold, iron ore, ilmenite,

tungsten ores and manganese ores. Deposits of most of these minerals have been worked for many years but have contributed only a small amount to the country's income. The major exception is iron ore which has been worked since about 1921 in Johore, Trengganu, Kelantan and Perak, and the output of which expanded very considerably following the Second World War and which reached a peak in 1963. This expansion has been made possible by the growing demands of the Japanese steel industry which has been the major customer and in recent years by the establishment of Malaya's own iron and steel industry at Prai (see, p. 174).

Amongst her agricultural exports, Malaya has included copra, palm oil, pineapples, tea and cocoa, the latter two on a very small scale, and all completely over-shadowed by rubber. Possibilities for expansion on a large scale seem limited to palm oil, however, and since 1957 there has been a considerable development of palm oil production to the extent that in some areas it is replacing rubber. Between 1958 and 1965 the planted area rose by 72 per cent. and the output of palm oil by 94 per cent. Rising palm oil prices in recent years have increased the net income yielded per acre to well above that earned by rubber, whilst its earlier maturing and somewhat lower labour requirements add to its economic attractions. Economic disruption in the world's previously major producing countries—the Congo and Indonesia—has given Malaya a favourable competitive position, and re-planting subsidies to estates, and, since 1962, to smallholders, for the replacement of rubber by oil-palm wherever soils are suitable have been provided by the Federal Government. Smallholder participation in the expanding oil-palm industry is being made possible mainly through the Federal Land Development Authority which, especially in its major scheme in central Pahang (the Jengka Triangle Project), is aiming to establish individual holdings around a small nucleus estate with nurseries and factories.[13]

The developments since the Second World War in commodity production and exports, though contrasting with the relative neglect suffered by similar activities in some of Malaya's neighbours, in themselves represent no major change in the nature of the Malayan economy, and most likely would have taken place under the mainly free-trading colonial economy of pre-war days. Geographically they have had little influence on the landscape beyond the increase in mining operations in a limited number of areas,* and the replacing

TABLE 15

MALAYA—PRODUCTION OF PALM OIL, PALM KERNELS, TEA, FRESH PINEAPPLES AND COPRA, 1957–1969

	Palm Oil (long tons)	Palm Kernels (long tons)	Tea ('000 lbs)	Fresh Pineapples (long tons)	Copra* (long tons)
1957	58,507	14,781	5,247	n.a.	35,843
1958	69,671	18,273	4,878	n.a.	34,820
1959	71,541	19,294	5,359	145,295	33,079
1960	90,343	23,672	5,595	150,557	32,309
1961	93,348	24,227	5,809	161,239	33,841
1962	106,462	27,844	6,259	191,596	33,214
1963	123,649	30,135	6,020	190,552	32,219
1964	120,106	30,001	6,853	208,169	26,670
1965	146,333	34,426	7,388	254,294	30,721
1966	183,394	42,669	7,597	254,088	27,684
1967	213,402	48,318	6,823	275,284	27,379
1968	260,725	58,715	7,645	255,326	28,040
1969	320,755	73,691	7,690	255,733	22,876

* Estate Production
Source: Monthly Statistical Bulletin of West Malaysia.

of rubber trees by oil palms on some estates. It is in the field of industrialization that both the economy and the economic geography of peninsular Malaya have begun to show major changes since 1950 and these have been possibly only as a result of the abandonment of the free trade policy in order to permit the deliberate encouragement of industry by the government.

Industrial Development since 1950—the Development Plans

The Draft Development Plan of 1950 commented briefly on the question of secondary industry in the Federation of Malaya,

* For example at Berjuntai, in Selangor, where the Selangor River feeds swampland between Rawang and the coast, and where land had to be filled and built up for the location of the first mining camp.[14]

and whilst tending largely to dismiss the possibilities of heavy industry in the country, it considered the potential for the

TABLE 16

PENINSULAR MALAYA—WORKERS ENGAGED IN SECONDARY INDUSTRIES, 1947

('000)

1. HANDICRAFTS

	Total	46·2	(32·3%)

2. PROCESSING

Rubber milling, packing, etc.		16·0	
Tin smelting		0·4	
Sawmilling etc.		7·9	
Rice, coconut, palm oil milling, etc.		9·5	
Fish curing and other		2·6	
	Total	36·4	(25·4%)

3. FOOD, DRINK AND TOBACCO

	Total	18·2	(12·7%)

4. ENGINEERING

Railway workshops		3·0	
Dockyards, etc.		1·5	
Motor vehicle workshops etc.		8·4	
Electrical installation and repair work		1·2	
Foundries, forges etc.		8·9	
	Total	23·0	(16·1%)

5. OTHER MANUFACTURING

Bricks, tiles etc.		2·4	
Soap		0·6	
Metal containers etc.		0·7	
Rubber and other footwear		3·4	
Other rubber goods		2·3	
Furniture etc.		3·8	
Newspapers, printing and photography		3·9	
Miscellaneous		2·3	
	Total	19·4	(13·6%)
	GRAND TOTAL	143·2	(100%)

Source: International Bank for Reconstruction and Development, *The Economic Development of Malaya*, Kuala Lumpur, 1955, pp. 301–2.

extension and improvement of the processing of raw materials, the establishment of light manufacturing industries to make, for

L

the home market, goods which would otherwise have to be imported, and for cottage industries. In relation to the development of light manufacturing industry, the plan drew attention to the concept of industrial estates as provided in many countries by local authorities or semi-public corporations and considered it highly probable that such estates would be necessary if light industries were to develop satisfactorily in Malaya.

In 1955 was published the report of the International Bank for Reconstruction and Development which had been invited by the governments of the Federation of Malaya, the Crown Colony of Singapore and the United Kingdom to undertake a survey of the Malayan economy and to make recommendations for practical measures to further economic and social development.[15] The Bank considered that Malaya had to, and undoubtedly would, continue to broaden its base of secondary manufacturing. The 'Population by Industry' and 'Population by Occupation' tables of the 1947 Census of Population had shown that 5 per cent. of the total gainfully occupied population of the Federation of Malaya were employed in manufacturing industry, but with few exceptions these industries were of a type which had a decisive margin of 'natural' protection in terms of location, and typically were associated directly or indirectly with Malaya's role as a primary producer and trader. (Table 16). The stage of development existing in 1947 had been achieved almost entirely without the aid of tariff protection or other governmental assistance, but with the exception of certain engineering trades which barely existed before the First World War (e.g. motor vehicle repair), the pattern of industrial activity was very similar to that reported from the Straits ports in 1911 (compare Tables 3 and 16). Although the International Bank Report considered that secondary industry had contributed substantially to the growth in real income between 1949 and 1953,[16] much of it in small scale establishments in the Federation and Singapore, a comparison of the occupation structure of the 1957 census with that of 1947 showed little progress in industrialization in Malaya.[17] In the intercensal period the number of workers in the manufacturing sector rose only by 7·5 per cent. compared with a 13.3 per cent. growth of the economically active population and a 105 per cent. growth in urbanization.*

As part of its 1954 election manifesto, the Alliance Party had declared its intention of assisting the economic growth of the country, *inter alia*, by encouraging industrial development, and a Working Party, appointed in May 1956 to assist the government in formulating an appropriate policy, reported eight months later.[18] The Working Party based its case for encouraging industrial development in the Federation on the fact that the economy was unduly dependent on the fortunes of its two major export industries, rubber and tin, and that opportunities had to be found for employment of the rapidly growing population, whose rate of increase at about 3 per cent. per annum was amongst the highest in the world. It drew attention to the significant fact that increasing numbers of the population, probably nearly one half, were now centred in or near urban areas, and that it was necessary to strengthen and if possible broaden the base of the economy, if living standards were not to become depressed and the standards of the social services to be maintained, more particularly if there were to be no marked further expansion of the primary industries. The Working Party came to the inescapable conclusion, however, that if industrial development were to provide employment for the urban populations of the future, a great deal of private capital would be required and that its attraction on the necessary scale was not likely to be easy without substantial government-inspired inducements. In general it considered

> that if any extensive industrial development is to take place in the Federation, except in fields where there are over-whelming natural advantages, active Government assistance in various directions will be necessary both to stimulate the establishment of industry, and in appropriate cases to protect it.[19]

The First Five Year Plan for the Federation of Malaya, called the General Plan of Development, was adopted in

---

* An urban area is defined as an administrative area with a population greater than 1,000. This definition would, in fact, include most 'new villages', and much of the increase in urbanization during the period in question was caused by the Emergency, as well as by increased government economic activity, especially in the tertiary sector.

October 1956 for the period ending 31st December, 1960. During the period of the plan, the total population of the Federation increased from about six to about seven millions, and the total labour force by about 310,000. Investment, both public and private, far exceeded the levels achieved before 1956, (actual public investment being nearly twice as great as in the earlier period) and the output of the economy more than kept pace with the population growth.[20] The main increase in private investment during the years of the plan took place in the manufacturing field. Measured in terms of horse power, the number of machines and other installations in manufacturing establishments more than doubled between 1955 and 1959, and a sample survey conducted in 1958 indicated that gross fixed investment in manufacturing in that year amounted to M $85 million or about 14 per cent. of total investment. Total employment in the manufacturing sector rose by about 12,000 (about 9 per cent.) during the Plan period.[21]

There was clearly a growing awareness among entrepreneurs of the market potential of the Federation for manufactured goods, and the industrial policy of the government provided considerable incentives to private investors. The Pioneer Industry policy, inaugurated in 1958, exempted from income tax profits of enterprises that qualified as 'pioneer' for periods between two and five years according to their scale of investment,* gave consideration to justified requests for the duty free import of certain necessary industrial inputs, and also made possible the granting of tariff protection for infant industries. The Pioneer Industry policy proved effective in encouraging increased investment in industry and was aided by the establishment of industrial estates in the major urban centres of the west coast states. The most successful of these was at Petaling Jaya, in the Klang Valley about six miles south-west of Kuala Lumpur (Figure 25).†

The Second Five Year Plan, adopted in January 1961 for the period 1961–65, was far more ambitious than the First Plan but broadly it represented a continuation of the policies

---

* Since income tax on industrial profits was 45 per cent., this was a considerable inducement.

† A more detailed study of Petaling Jaya, and also of the industrial estates in Penang and Singapore, is made in Chapter 6.

previously established. The Second Plan, *inter alia*, re-emphasized the importance of manufacturing to the Federation's long-run development and re-affirmed the government's intention to rely on private initiative, 'but at the same time to encourage the growth of private industry through every reasonable means of assistance, consistent with the general interest'.[22] The preservation of a sound and stable monetary climate, free from the restrictions, controls and uncertainties that accompany financial instability and inflation, was considered the basic contribution that government could make, and this was reinforced by continued financial support to Malayan Industrial Development Finance Ltd.,* an organization established in 1960 to provide credit on reasonable terms for sound industrial ventures.

The Second Plan also provided for the establishment of additional industrial estates and set up a trust fund of $7.5 million to enable loans to be made to the States for this purpose. The Petaling Jaya estate was rapidly filled up and work on the first phase of a second Selangor estate at Batu Tiga, between Petaling Jaya and Klang, began in 1965. The significance of this location to the urban and industrial geography of central Malaya is examined more fully in Chapter 6, but it is apparent that it will contribute to the even more rapid growth of the Port Swettenham-Kuala Lumpur axis. Outside Selangor, estates were established in Penang, Perak, Negri Sembilan and Johore—of which those at Butterworth, Johore Bahru and Ipoh were most successful in attracting development.

Public investment during the Second Five Year Plan aimed especially at improving the national infrastructure for industrial growth.[23] The Plan in its original form called for M $2,150 million of public expenditure for development purposes but revisions by 1963 had raised the target to M $2,930 million, and of this revised total 45.5 per cent. was allocated to the transport, communications and public utilities sectors. The

* MIDFL was established in March 1960 with part of its share capital suscribed by the Federal Government and the remainder by private investors, both local and foreign. Reorganization and a great increase in its resources, with assistance from the International Bank for Reconstruction and Development, were recommended by staff members of that institution who visited Malaya in 1962. The aggregate potential resources of MIDFL were $250 million in 1965.

TABLE 17

PENINSULAR MALAYA—ALLOCATION OF PUBLIC INVESTMENT IN MAJOR SECTORS OF INFRASTRUCTURE DURING THE FIRST AND SECOND FIVE-YEAR PLANS

SECTOR	Approximate Actual Expenditure 1956-60 (M$ million)	Percent of total	Original Plan Target 1961-65 (M$ million)	Percent of total	Revised Plan Target 1961-65 (M$ million)	Percent of total
TRANSPORT	206·5	21·2	362·0	17·3	510·0	19·6
Roads and bridges	95·2	9·8	190·0	9·1	336·1	12·9
Railways	71·4	7·3	65·0	3·1	50·2	1·9
Ports	37·0	3·8	55·0	2·6	64·0	2·5
Civil Aviation	2·9	0·3	52·0	2·5	59·7	2·3
COMMUNICATIONS	51·6	5·3	72·9	3·5	129·2	5·0
Telecommunications	47·4	4·9	50·0	2·4	84·5	3·2
Broadcasting	2·7	0·3	5·0	0·2	14·9	0·6
Posts	1·5	0·1	17·9	0·9	12·9	0·5
UTILITIES	238·6	24·6	402·0	19·2	545·7	20·9
Electricity	142·0	14·6	254·0	12·1	341·5	13·1
Water	80·6	8·3	140·0	6·7	196·2	7·5
Sewerage	16·0	1·7	8·0	0·4	8·0	0·3

Source: Interim Review of Development in Malaya under the Second Five-Year Plan.

main share of expenditure on transport facilities was allocated to roads and the proportion of total public investment devoted to them was raised from 9·1 per cent. to 12.9 per cent. when the plan was revised. It was recognized that roads constituted the principal transport system in Malaya and that their traffic bearing capacity needed to be expanded in line with the overall expansion of the economy. Particular emphasis was put on the improvement of the main west coast road (Route 1) and on providing a major road link connecting the east and west coasts. The main feature of the railway programme of expenditure was continued dieselization.

Planned expenditure on ports was concentrated on the expansion of facilities at Port Swettenham, especially on the North Klang Straits project, and on the construction of deepwater berths at Butterworth, the mainland part of the port of Penang, which was to be expected to increase its share of the handling of Penang's trade at the expense of Georgetown.

Investment in electric power capacity aimed at keeping up with an anticipated 30 per cent. increase in power consumption by 1965. The revised plan increased the allocation of investment to electricity from the much enlarged budget by 1 per cent., from 12·1 per cent. to 13·1 per cent., and the amount of power generated in 1965 was in fact 79 per cent. greater than that generated in 1960. Over this period consumption by industrial and commercial users had risen from 24·7 per cent to 33·3 per cent. Much of the increased power was produced by the Cameron Highlands Hydro-Electric Scheme which was completed in June 1963,[24] and by the thermal Sultan Ismail Power Station in Johore Bahru opened in the same year.

Real gross domestic product grew at an average annual rate of 6·3 per cent. in peninsular Malaya during the period of the Second Five Year Plan, despite both a generally poor export performance and the political and military 'confrontation' with Indonesia that took place subsequent to the formation of the Malaysian Federation in 1963. This compared with an average annual figure of slightly less than 5 per cent. for the developing nations as a whole and was particularly rapid by Asian standards. It also represented a marked acceleration from the 4 per cent. per annum growth rate achieved during the period of the First Plan. Real income grew slightly less than gross domestic product since the steady decline in rubber prices more than offset the sharp rise in the price of tin whilst import prices remained relatively stable. Despite continued population increase over the period, however, per capita real income showed an annual growth of over 2 per cent.

The striking characteristic of the performance of the economy in the 1961–65 period, according to the review published as part of the First Malaysia Plan,[25] was that, in contrast with other periods of expansion in recent history, rapid growth occurred despite a stagnant level of export earnings and a

TABLE 18

PENINSULAR MALAYA—DOMESTIC PRODUCTION AS PERCENTAGE OF
TOTAL CONSUMPTION, SELECTED INDUSTRIAL PRODUCTS, 1960 AND 1965

	1960	1965
Cigarettes	60	90
Manufactured Tobacco	69	75
Biscuits	93	108*
Soap	106*	120*
Bicycle Inner Tubes	97	125*
Cement	89	108*

* Net exporter.
Source: First Malaysia Plan.

sluggish rate of expansion in export volumes. The impetus for the expansion of output was a rapid rise of domestic demand characterized by a significant shift in the composition of output away from production for export and towards production for the domestic market. In large part this shift could be traced to the rapid rise in domestic investment between 1960 and 1965. This occurred in both the private and the public sectors, the dynamic components of private investment being non-residential construction, and investment in manufacturing, forestry, transport, commerce and other service industries. In part the growth of private investment was a reaction to the increased need for plant and equipment to keep pace with the general growth of the economy over the period, but it also reflected the considerable investment undertaken in the process of import substitution (see Table 18).

Employment during the period of the Second Plan increased at approximately the planned rate although the distribution of employment turned out to be somewhat different from that projected in 1960 (see Table 19). Unemployment remained at 6 per cent. of the labour force, however, and a high proportion of young urban workers remained in that group.

TABLE 19

PENINSULAR MALAYA—EMPLOYMENT GROWTH, 1960–1965*

(in '000s)

Sector	1960	1965		Annual Growth Rate (%)
		Target	Actual	
Agriculture	1,277	1,417	1,388	1·7
Mining and Manufacturing	196	235	234	3·6
Construction, Transport and Utilities	150	219	210	7·0
Government Services	200	236	257	5·1
Other Trade and Services	351	393	429	4·1
TOTAL EMPLOYMENT	2,174	2,500	2,518	3·0
Unemployed	138		160	
Total Labour Force	2312		2678	
Unemployment	6·0%		6·0%	

Source: First Malaysia Plan.

* More precise indicators available since the Plan was published suggest unemployment was higher in 1965 than indicated by Table 19 and was probably 6·3 per cent.

During the course of the Second Five Year Plan, in 1963, the Federation of Malaya was joined politically with Singapore and with the British Borneo states of Sarawak and North Borneo (Sabah) to form the new federal nation known as the Federation of Malaysia. Apart from the new federal link with the Borneo territories, which, as a consequence of their lower level of development than peninsular Malaya in most sectors, social, political and economic, promised to be an additional responsibility for the more developed West Malaysia,* the major factor likely to have been of considerable significance to the

* As the former Federation of Malaya was now termed, see definitions, appendix 1.

economy and to the economic geography of the former federation was its political integration with Singapore. In 1963, the International Bank for Reconstruction and Development submitted a report on the economic aspects of Malaysia (the Rueff Report)[26] in which it stated its conviction of the advantages of a Malaysian Common Market for industrialization, which sector it believed would in the long run benefit most from the political merger. A rather different point of view was expressed in 1965 by E. L. Wheelwright[27] who, arguing in terms of cumulative advantage, claimed that the equalization of industrial incentives throughout Malaysia (recommended by the Rueff Report) would lead to a concentration of industrial enterprise in Singapore at the expense of the rest of Malaysia. In the event, the withdrawal of Singapore from the federation in 1965 occurred too soon for either forecast to have proved itself, and, although the separation was to create potential economic problems for Singapore (see below), the situation with regard to industrial development problems in peninsular Malaya remained basically what it had been before 1963.

The Second Five Year Plan was followed by the First Malaysia Plan, 1966–70,[28] which included the Borneo territories as well as West Malaysia. Like the previous plans the First Malaysia Plan consisted of a programme of public investment for the five year period and an outline of policies to be followed to help the private sector make its 'assigned contribution to development'.[29] The plan was also formulated as the First phase of a 20-year Perspective Plan which laid out, in general terms, a series of essential goals for the future. Specific goals relating to per capita income growth, full employment, income redistribution, social and community services, economic infrastructure, and population and family planning were set as targets to be reached by 1985. The need for economic diversification was re-iterated as a basic principle of the development strategy for those long-term objectives and the role of industrialization was again stressed.

Calculations made in connection with the plan suggested that national output would rise at an average annual rate of about 5 per cent. and that since it was anticipated that the output of all export commodities combined would rise at only 2·4 per cent., it was concluded that over-all growth would be heavily dependent on increases in production for the local market. It was expected that the highest growth rates of

TABLE 20

PENINSULAR MALAYA (WEST MALAYSIA)—GROWTH TARGETS OF
FIRST MALAYSIA PLAN

A. GROSS DOMESTIC PRODUCT BY SECTOR OF ORIGIN, 1965 AND 1970
TARGET

($ millions)

Sector	1965	1970 Target	Annual Growth Rate Target (%)
Agriculture, forestry and fishing	2,005	2,435	4·0
Mining and quarrying	600	475	4·6
Manufacturing	665	1,070	10·0
Construction	360	530	8·0
Electricity, water and sanitary services	125	200	10·0
Ownership of dwellings	305	370	4·0
Wholesale and retail trade	1,100	1,370	4·5
Public administration and defence	425	515	4·0
Other services	1,230	1,645	6·0
GROSS DOMESTIC PRODUCT AT FACTOR COST	6,815	8,516	4·8

B. EMPLOYMENT BY SECTOR, 1965 AND 1970 TARGET
(thousands)

Sector	1965	1970 Target	Net Increase 1966–70 Target (%)
Agriculture, forestry and fishing	1,388	1,553	11·9
Manufacturing	173	209	20·8
Mining and quarrying	61	61	—
Construction, utilities and transport	210	252	20·0
Public administration and defence	257	312	21·4
Other services	429	508	18·4
TOTAL	2,518	2,895	15·0

Source: First Malaysia Plan.

physical production would be achieved by manufacturing, rubber planting, construction and some service industries. The creation of nearly 380,000 new jobs was anticipated in West

Malaysia if the outline growth targets (see Table 20) were achieved, of which 36,000 would be in manufacturing. The

TABLE 21

PENINSULAR MALAYA (WEST MALAYSIA)—
SECTORAL ALLOCATION OF PUBLIC DEVELOPMENT EXPENDITURE
FOR 1966–1970 ($millions)

Sector	Planned expenditure 1966–1970	Percentage of total (rounded)
AGRICULTURE AND RURAL DEVELOPMENT	900·2	24
MINING	1·3	0·03
INDUSTRIAL DEVELOPMENT	110·3	3
Malaysian Industrial Development Finance Ltd. (MIDFL)	16·0	
Industrial Estates	14·0	
National Institute of Scientific and Industrial Research	5·0	
Standards Institute	0·1	
National Productivity Centre	0·2	
Federal Industrial Development Authority (F.I.D.A.)	5·0	
Majlis Amanah Ra'ayat (M.A.R.A.)	70·0	
TRANSPORT	365·3	10
Roads	255·5	
Railways	20·0	
Civil Aviation	9·0	
Ports	80·8	
COMMUNICATIONS	156·6	4
UTILITIES	695·0	19
Electricity	545·0	
Water	150·0	
SOCIAL SERVICES	797·4	21
ADMINISTRATION	87·9	2
DEFENCE AND SECURITY	599·6	16
TOTAL	3,713·6	100·0

Source: First Malaysia Plan.

achievement of the employment target would bring about a fall in the rate of unemployment from the estimated 6.0 per cent. to 5·2 per cent. by 1970.

Between 1960 and 1965 the contribution of the manufacturing sector to gross domestic product at constant factor cost in West

Malaysia rose from 8·7 per cent. to 10·8 per cent. As indicated in Table 20A, the First Malaysia Plan incorporated a target rate of increase in manufacturing output of 10 per cent. p.a. over the plan period. In general, the role of government remained, as before, the promotion and facilitation of industrial growth by means of the maintenance of a sound and stable financial and monetary climate, the encouragement of private savings for investment, the provision of favourable incentives for private industrial investment, the continued development of the infrastructure of the economy, the development of the educational system to provide appropriately qualified man-power, and the encouragement of broadly-based participation in industrial development. This last point concerned a deliberate attempt by means of the Majlis Amanah Ra'ayat (MARA)* and the Bank Bumiputra† to assist the Malay com-munity to participate more effectively in industrial development.

Planned expenditure on the infrastructure was concerned particularly with transport facilities and with electricity and water supply. The road development plan, which was allocated the lion's share of planned expenditure on transport facilities, aimed to extend communication roads, so that important population centres in the north-east and in the central west coast areas would have more direct access to important com-mercial centres, as well as to improve existing trunk roads and to develop or to extend rural roads where necessary. The biggest single new road construction project was the Northern East-West Highway connecting Kota Bharu and Butterworth via Grik. This route, when completed during the Second Malaysia Plan, will link the most densely populated area on the east coast of Malaya with the major market and industrial areas of Penang and Perak. Its significance is more fully discussed in Chapter 6. Expenditure on railways was mainly to continue the dieselization programme, and for the completion of the extension from Prai across the Prai River estuary to Butter-worth. The new deep water berths at Butterworth, new berths

* Although government policy is to leave industrial development largely to the private sector, an exception to the rule relates to some of the activities of MARA (lit. People's Trust Board). In certain circumstances and to achieve particular objectives, MARA establishes and controls—by itself or jointly with private investors—industrial ventures which meet predetermined criteria.

† Bumiputra—sons of the soil—is a recent term employed as a synonym for the Malay community.

in the old port area of Port Swettenham, and land reclamation and new berth construction at North Klang Straits accounted for the bulk of the financial allocation for port development. In mid-1967 a Malaysian Transport Survey was commenced with the assistance of the United Nations Development Programme and the World Bank to assure the development of a co-ordinated transport system that will serve national objectives over the long term.

Whereas between 1955 and 1965 the demand for electricity had been dominated by the tin mining industry, and in 1965 industrial users consumed only 16·2 per cent. of the total power supplied, industrial expansion was expected to contribute substantially to the growth of power demand during the First Malaysia Plan period, with major demands expected in the Kuala Lumpur-Port Swettenham and the Butterworth areas. Electricity generation projects included in the plan were therefore for new thermal stations at Prai and Port Dickson, for extensions to the Johore Bahru thermal station and for hydro-electric schemes at Batang Padang, Bentong, Raub and the Upper Perak River. A sum of $137 million was allocated to transmission and distribution facilities especially to the creation of an efficient and flexible Western Network system that linked Alor Star (Kedah) to Kluang (central Johore) in one national grid by 1967. A mid-term review of the First Malaysia Plan, to cover the period 1966–68, was published in 1969.[30] It reported that, by contrast with expectations and with the experience of the preceding five years, the primary source of growth in the volume of output for the period 1966–68 was production for export which had grown at 7·6 per cent. p.a., over five times the projected rate, whilst production for domestic use had grown at only 5·8 per cent. p.a., compared with the plan's projection of 8 per cent. p.a. In terms of prices, however, export receipts had increased by only 1·4 per cent. p.a. whilst the value of production for domestic use had grown at the planned 8 per cent. p.a.

Manufacturing recorded a high 10·7 per cent. p.a., growth rate between 1965 and 1967 as import substitution activities continued and as efforts to export manufactured goods intensified. Nevertheless, growth was slower than it had been during the previous five years, owing particularly to a general slack in the economy in 1967 and early 1968 as the result of low rubber prices—a circumstance that served as a reminder of the continuing significance of the rubber industry to the whole economy. By 1967, manufacturing was accounting for over 11 per cent. of the gross domestic product.

One of the most disappointing aspects of the trend of the economy up to 1967 had been its failure significantly to cope with the unemployment problem. The availability of more precise indicators since the Plan was published suggested that unemployment had been higher in 1965 than previously believed (see footnote to table 19, p. 157) and that there was little chance that the employment growth rate projected in the Plan had been achieved by 1967. The growth in output of the manufacturing sector had been associated more with enhanced productivity than with increased employment of labour and a familiar problem was beginning to emerge, namely that the efficiency of industry, necessary if it was to make a real contribution to the wealth of the nation and to succeed in the increasingly important export markets, was less likely to be achieved by the large scale employment of labour than by the use of more sophisticated production and management techniques. 11,000 new jobs had been created in industry between 1965 and 1967, but if the 1970 Plan target was to be fulfilled, a further 25,000 were needed.

During the course of the First Malaysia Plan, government began attempts to co-ordinate industrial development more on a national scale than previously had been the case. In 1967, there was established the Federal Industrial Development Authority (FIDA), the principal function of which was to co-ordinate and strengthen the country's industrial development programme and to share, with the national Economic Planning Unit, the over-all approach to industrial growth. Despite the continuation of a generally free-market economy, the FIDA is to give greater attention to the development of investment incentives specifically designed to assist firms and industries that are labour intensive, that utilize domestic raw materials (especially agricultural raw materials), that manufacture capital or intermediate goods for which extensive markets already exist or are in prospect, or that manufacture for export. The 1968 Investment Incentives Act extended the maximum period of tax relief for a pioneer industry from five to eight years if it produced a priority product, incorporated a specified amount of local material in its product or, especially significant from a geographical point of view, if it was located in a designated development area. The Act also granted tax credit to non-pioneer firms which met the same conditions, and provided certain export incentives.

A more co-ordinated policy with regard to industrial estate development was envisaged, with federal assistance to the states (the appropriate authorities for such development) for the establishment of additional industrial areas being provided only after projects have been justified by thorough feasibility studies. Eight industrial estates had been established in West Malaysia by 1968—at Petaling Jaya and Batu Tiga (Selangor), Mak Mandin (Penang), Kamunting, and Tasek (Perak), Senawang (Negri Sembilan), Larkin and Tampoi (Johore)—and four more were under construction by 1970, at Prai and Bayan Lepas (Penang), Menglembu (Perak) and Tanah Puteh (Pahang). Only some 36 per cent. of the total available area had been occupied, and the mid-term Review commented that 'several of the industrial estates (had) . . . been launched with insufficient regard to probable demand for the facilities provided'.[31]

Public development expenditure for industrial development was revised upwards for the last two years of the Plan period to increase the originally planned total of $114·5 million to $133·9 million for the five years. The major part of the increased expenditure was allocated to MARA and to the industrial estates.

A major new development in national planning undertaken in the latter stages of the First Malaysia Plan was the preparation of comprehensive area development plans based on surveys of available resources and needs. Preparations for the Penang Master Plan were well advanced in 1968 and similar studies of Pahang, Trengganu, Johore and Malacca (as well as of Sarawak in East Malaysia) were planned to commence in 1969–70. The influence of such regional development plans on the location of all economic activity, not merely of manufacturing, could be considerable in the medium and long term.

*The Nature & Location of Industrial Development
in Peninsular Malaya*

It has already been observed (see p. 150) that the majority
of the Federation of Malaya's secondary industries in the
late 1940s and the 1950s, as in pre-war years, were associated
directly or indirectly with the country's position as a primary
producer and trader, and usually consisted of activities for
which there was some advantage of location in relation to the
services that they provided. Table 16 (p. 149), which tabulates
the number of workers in secondary industries in 1947, indicates
a marked emphasis on processing industries, the manufacture
of food, drink and tobacco, engineering activities oriented
towards the repair and maintenance of transport equipment
and a variety of other manufacturing of a universally localized
type. The expansion of manufacturing activity into a more
diversified field, which was necessary if industrial growth
was to make a significant contribution to the national economy,
was likely to involve competition with the products of the
industrial powers of Europe, America and Japan. Consequently
those goods that were most likely to be able successfully to
survive such competition were clearly the ones on which
attention was focused. The International Bank Report of
1955 considered that Malayan industrial development, in
the future as in the past, needed to take the form of fairly
small advances along a very wide front, chiefly for the home
market and for neighbouring export markets and that, in
that context, the outlook was reasonably promising.[32] An
analysis of the industries that have been established on the
major industrial estates indicates that considerable development of such import-substitution activities has certainly
occurred.

It must be emphasized that industrial development in
Malaya has taken place within a free enterprise economy,
within which, to date, the government has seen its role, on
the whole, as one of establishing and maintaining a political
and financial atmosphere conducive to the attraction of
private capital as well as of providing the necessary infrastructure of transport and communications facilities, and of power
and water supply. There is no direct government investment

M

in industry (except in Malayawata Steel, see below) and the granting of pioneer status or of tariff protection, which may be seen as favouring particular types of industry, becomes effective only when applications for such favourable treatment

TABLE 22

MAK MANDIN INDUSTRIAL ESTATE (PENANG)—
CLASSIFICATION OF FACTORY LOTS AS AT END OF 1967

Section or Division Code	Malayan Industrial Classification*	No. of Lots
30	Food and fodder manufacturing industries	10
33	Manufacture of textile, rope, twine and nets	5
34	Manufacture of footwear, other wearing apparel and made-up textile goods	1
37	Manufacture of paper products	2
40	Manufacture of rubber products	1
41	Manufacture of chemicals and chemical products	5
44	Basic metal industries	1
45	Manufacture of metal products except machinery and transport products	4
46	General engineering including manufacture of machinery and transport equipment	1
48	Manufacture and repair of electrical machinery and appliances	1
8	Transport, storage and communication	3
	TOTAL	34

* This classification generally follows the Revised International Standard Industrial Classification of All Economic Activities except that the Malaysian system has a separate division to include both the agricultural and manufacturing operations connected with the major agricultural crops which, by necessity or custom, are generally processed to some extent, but where there is no consistency as to whether this processing is done by the agricultural establishment or by a separate establishment under different ownership and at a different location.

are made, these decisions cannot be responsible for *initiating* particular developments. Neither the federal nor the individual state government has the power to direct industry to particular areas, though the choice of locations for industrial estates is a state matter, and the federal government may designate certain districts as 'development areas' within which pioneer status can be extended for up to three years longer than is generally possible elsewhere. (see p. 152).

Stimulated by the pioneer industry policy and by the

TABLE 23

PETALING JAYA INDUSTRIAL ESTATE (SELANGOR)—
CLASSIFICATION OF FACTORY LOTS AS AT END OF 1966

Section or Division Code	Malaysian Industrial Classification	No. of Lots	No. of Pioneer Establishments
30	Food and fodder manufacturing industries	30	5
31	Beverage industries	5	—
32	Tobacco manufactures	5	—
33	Manufacture of textile, rope, twine and nets	3	—
34	Manufacture of footwear, other wearing apparel and made-up textile goods	3	—
35	Manufacture of wood, except furniture and wooden clogs	13	—
36	Manufacture of furniture and fixtures	11	—
37	Manufacture of paper products	3	1
38	Printing and publishing and allied industries	14	—
40	Manufacture of rubber products	8	1
41	Manufacture of chemicals and chemical products	29	16
43	Manufacture of non-metallic mineral products	19	5
44	Basic metal industries	9	1
45	Manufacture of metal products except machinery and transport products	14	7
46	General engineering including manufacture of machinery and transport equipment	32	2
48	Manufacture and repair of electrical machinery and appliances	11	4
49	Miscellaneous manufactures	1	—
5	Building and construction	4	—
6	Electricity, gas and water	4	—
7	Commerce	4	—
8	Transport, storage and communication	7	—
9	Services	13	—
	Unclassified (insufficient data)	22	—
	TOTAL	264	42

construction of industrial estates, which, apart from their guarantee of the provision of essential services, can offer the intending industrialist an immediate land title (a facility not always available in the context of Asian systems of land tenure), private investment has been attracted to activities that have held out promise of fairly rapid profitability and to locations economically favoured.* Tables 22 and 23 attempt a classification of the industries to which lots have been allocated on the Petaling Jaya and Mak Mandin estates. Although mere numbers of establishments fail to give any realistic assessment of the contribution of each group to the economy in terms of labour employed or value added, the tables do illustrate the broad areas of manufacturing to which investment has been attracted. The types of manufacturing favoured by pioneer status also become apparent.

As might reasonably be expected, there is considerable emphasis on the food, beverages and tobacco industries (19 per cent. of the manufacturing establishments at Petaling Jaya and 32 per cent. of these at Mak Mandin are included in these categories), some of which are new industries and some, especially milk product factories, are operating under pioneer status, whilst others are extensions of existing industries. Noticeable, however, especially at Petaling Jaya, are the relatively large numbers of industries in the rubber, chemicals and chemical products divisions (divisions 40 and 41), and in the metal, machinery, engineering and electrical equipment divisions (divisions 44, 45, 46, 48). Pioneer industries are particularly numerous in the former divisions, being concerned with the manufacture of paints and varnishes, pharmaceuticals, cosmetic and toiletry products, plastic and rubber goods—including Malaya's largest tyre factory opened in 1963. Divisions 44, 45, 46 and 48 industries at Petaling Jaya also have a number operating under pioneer certificates, these including the manufacture of bolts and nuts, steel pipes, cables, metal containers, air conditioning plant, television

---

* About 75 per cent. of the capital invested in recent industrial development in Malaya has been foreign, its principal sources being Britain, the United States, Japan, Hong Kong and Taiwan. In a number of cases well known world brands of goods are now being produced in Malaya principally to serve the local market e.g. Dunlop tyres and rubber goods, Brylcreem, Colgate-Palmolive, Johnson & Johnson. Local capital is raised from a broad spectrum of the population, and share issues are rapidly taken up locally.

receivers, batteries, lamps and tubes. Included in this category, too, though not pioneer, are a number of motor assembly
works.

An interesting comparison that emerges between the

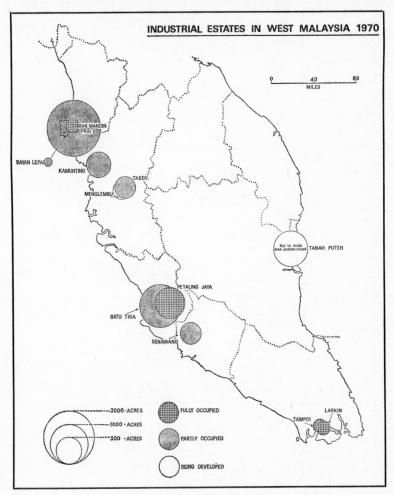

Figure 15. West Malaysia—Industrial Estates

industrial divisions represented at Petaling Jaya and those
at Mak Mandin is the much higher proportion of food and
beverage and of textile and wearing apparel industries on the

TABLE 24

PENINSULAR MALAYA: URBAN POPULATION (GAZETTED AREAS 10,000 POPULATION AND OVER) BY STATES, 1957

STATE	Total Population 1957 ('000s)	Urban Population 1957 ('000s)	Percentage of Urban to Total				
			1911	1921	1931	1947	1957
Federation of Malaya	6,278·8	1,666·3	10·7	14·0	15·1	15·9	26·5
Johore	926·9	202·4	—	10·1	10·9	15·4	21·8
Kedah	702·0	93·4	—	3·4	4·3	8·2	13·3
Kelantan	505·5	49·4	4·4	3·5	4·1	5·1	9·8
Malacca	291·2	69·8	17·0	20·0	20·4	22·8	24·0
Negri Sembilan	364·5	64·0	—	9·7	9·2	13·2	17·8
Pahang	313·1	69·6	—	—	—	—	22·2
Penang	572·1	324·5	37·3	41·8	47·7	52·9	56·7
Perak	1,221·4	305·3	11·0	13·3	14·4	17·1	25·0
Perlis	90·0	—	—	—	—	—	—
Selangor	1,012·9	435·2	15·9	23·0	24·8	32·7	43·0
Trengganu	278·3	52·8	9·1	8·1	7·8	11·9	19·0

Source: 1957 Population Census of the Federation of Malaya. Report No. 14, Table 2.2.

Penang estate, and the far smaller proportion of chemical and related products and of fabricated metal products. This would appear to be related to the smaller national market for these more sophisticated manufactures (many of which it has been noted are produced at Petaling Jaya under pioneer certificates) and their consequent preference for location near the major market of central Malaya.*

The significance of the established centres of population of the west coast states for the location of the industrial estates is very marked (Figure 15). Not only are the existing facilities of these centres available to serve the estates but the increasing urbanization of the Malayan population that has been apparent since at least 1921, but which was particularly great between 1947 and 1957, makes the main towns and cities the country's principal markets and sources of labour, especially young labour, seeking employment. The largest concentrations of population are clearly in Selangor and Penang (see Table 24), in which states the country's two largest cities, Kuala Lumpur and Georgetown, are located, followed by Perak and Malacca. The marked preference of industry for location in Selangor, particularly at Petaling Jaya and Batu Tiga, reflects the choice of the most economic location by concerns whose activities are less influenced by raw material sources than by the availability of a readily accessible market and an adaptable and increasingly skilled labour force. The resulting concentration of industry in the main urban centres of Malaya may be criticized on the grounds that the economic gulf between the already more developed urban areas and the backward areas, particularly of the east coast, will become wider and that, since there is already a high degree of correlation between economic status and ethnic group, the country's social and political difficulties will be exacerbated. It may well be argued, however, that in a situation where concessions and stimuli are necessary to initiate industrial development in the first place, a policy seeking to encourage such developments in other than the most economic locations would add an additional unwarranted burden to manufacturing. Other policies than directing manufacturing industry to the backward rural areas would seem preferable as means of tackling

---

* An analysis of industrial concentration is attempted in appendix 2.

their economic and social problems. It is interesting to note that the one industrial estate planned for the east coast of Malaya is proposed for Kuantan, a town of over 50,000 people only 150 miles from Kuala Lumpur, with which a direct road link exists. The criticism of unco-ordinated industrial estate development voiced by the Mid-term Review of the First Malaysia Plan (see p. 164) and the relatively limited success of some of the estates (notably some of those located in Perak and Negri Sembilan) suggests, however, that in some states enthusiasm for industrial estate development as a panacea for economic problems has outrun economic realities.

Although a considerable proportion of peninsular Malaya's recent industrial development has taken place on the industrial estates, it would be wrong to conclude that all new developments have been confined to them or indeed that most have been pioneer. Apart from the special cases of the iron and steel works and oil refineries (discussed in more detail below) a number of large establishments have been located in Penang and Selangor other than on the industrial estates, and one of the responsibilities of MARA is the encouragement of small scale industrial enterprises in rural areas.

In Penang, for example, a sugar refinery and large pipe works have been constructed on the south bank of the Prai river, adjacent to, though not as part of, the Prai industrial estate (Figure 19), and at Klang, near Port Swettenham (Figure 27), Malaya's third tin smelting works was opened in 1964. This smelter, operated by a joint Japanese-Malaysian company, Oriental Tin Smelters Ltd., began producing at a rate of 500 tons per month, and in 1969 had reached 800 tons with plans announced to further increase capacity to over 1000 tons per month. At the end of 1969, however, operations at the plant were suspended indefinitely owing to a doubtful ability to maintain sufficient production for economic operation, in some ways a not surprising development in view of the considerable recent increase in tin smelting capacity in South-east Asia.[33] The reasons behind the establishment of the new smelter were a little obscure, but may have been related to Japan's desire to safeguard her raw material supplies by having some control over their production. The smelter was supplying about 500 tons of tin metal per month to Japan[34] before its closure.

There is evidence to suggest that, in the middle and late 1960s, peninsular Malaya was approaching the end of its import-substitution phase of industrialization and was seeking to move into the second, and more difficult, phase of industrial growth—i.e. into industries the scale of whose operations are too great to operate efficiently to serve a home market of only ten million people and which therefore must seek export openings, and into basic industries to replace the imports of, for example, steel that have been demanded in increasing quantities by the secondary industries.

A number of major new projects implemented by 1965— including three cement factories, two oil refineries, a tyre factory, a cigarette factory, a sugar refinery and an aluminium rolling mill—had sufficient capacity to provide for an exportable surplus after satisfying domestic demand,[35] and betweeen 1960 and 1966 the value of capital and intermediate goods production appeared to be rising as fast as the production of consumer goods. This was interpreted by the Mid-term Review of the First Malaysia Plan as indicating that the nation's industrialization was being based not solely on import substitution within the consumer goods area but on a wide range of manufacturing activities, including production for export.[36] Table 18 (p. 156) shows peninsular Malaya as a net exporter of biscuits, soap, bicycle inner tubes and cement by 1965, and it was reported in 1969 that the country was virtually self-sufficient in the local assembly of motor-cycles and motor-scooters.[37] Government policy, as stated in 1969, that will permit the retention of 51 per cent. or more of the equity in new industrial projects in Malaysia by foreign investors only if the projects are export-oriented, can dispense with tariff protection, are highly labour intensive or turn out products with a large content of local raw materials, is indicative of the recognition of the decline in relative importance of import-substitution activities.

The first of a group of newly established, highly capitalized basic industries to be established in peninsular Malaya were two petroleum refineries at Port Dickson on the coast of Negri Sembilan, operated by Esso Standard and by Shell.

The availability of deep water for the berthing of tankers at a site reasonably central to the principal West Malaysian market favoured Port Dickson as a location for the refineries. Since establishment, capacity has been increased and there are plans for further expansion. Drawing crude from the Middle East, the Port Dickson refineries produce a range of petroleum fractions, from liquefied petroleum gas to asphalt, which are marketed in West Malaysia, Singapore and East Malaysia. One major consumer is the National Electricity Board's large thermal power station at Port Dickson. Associated with the Esso Standard refinery is an ammonia plant, completed in late 1966.

The Esso Standard refinery and ammonia plant together represent a capital investment exceeding $72 million. The refinery alone employs over 200 people, and its output meets more than half Malaysia's domestic requirements for petroleum products. Esso Standard operated initially under a five-year pioneer certificate. The construction of the refineries at Port Dickson, and the subsequent location of the N.E.B's $91 million thermal power station almost alongside, make the Negri Sembilan coast the nation's principal centre of fuel and power production. In conjunction with the secondary industrial development at Seremban, to which the port is connected by what was the Sungei Ujong railway (see p. 89,) the Seremban-Port Dickson axis may be viewed as an embryo third industrial region in West Malaysia.

Although neither the Draft Development Plan of 1950 nor the International Bank report of 1955 considered heavy industry a likely development in Malaya, mainly on the grounds of an absence of coking coal, discussions were taking place by 1960 on plans for the establishment of a steel mill in Malaya. Negotiations were undertaken with the Yawata Steel Co. of Japan and, in 1967, a joint Malayan-Japanese iron and steel works, Malayawata Steel Ltd., was opened at Prai—the first integrated iron and steel plant in South-east Asia. The site at Prai was selected on the grounds of ready accessibility to raw materials, to the growing secondary industries of Butterworth, which would be amongst the mill's customers, and to transport facilities and tide-water. An adequate water supply, utilizing sea water from the Prai River estuary wherever possible, was a further advantage of the site. Malayawata draws its iron ore, a high grade haematite, from deposits in Kedah and Perak, ferro-alloys from India and Japan, its limestone flux from Ipoh, and makes use of charcoal fuel. The charcoal, of high quality, is prepared from rubber tree wood (available as a consequence of rubber replanting operations) at seven 'kiln centres' located in Penang, Perak and Kedah. If and when this supply of rubber wood is exhausted, there are plans to make use of jungle timber.

In 1969, Malayawata employed nearly one thousand people at the steelworks, many of them with skills in handling steel acquired over many years' experience in the ship repair yards and related employment. The blast furnace was producing about 200 tons of pig iron per day and the rolling mill turning out 5,000 to 7,000 tons of finished products per month, mainly round bars and angled bars. Plans exist for a second blast furnace by 1971 and for expansion into a wider range of rolling mill products such as wire rods. In its early years of establishment and growth, Malayawata Steel has been granted various incentives and protection. It has been granted the full five-year period of pioneer status with the situation then subject to review, tariff protection on cast pig iron, round bars, wire rods, flat bars and angle bars, ingots and billets, whilst quotas on imports have also been imposed. The company was facing competition in its rolled products from rolling mills in Kuala Lumpur, which were working with imported steel billets, and the degree of preferential treatment given to Malayawata is some indication of the problems facing the establishment of basic industry in Malaya.

In 1968, the Asian Industrial Development Commission of ECAFE recommended that the Malayawata plant should be expanded to form the nucleus of a large steelworks with a broad range of products, including tin plate. Malaysia Gold and Tin Dredging Ltd., another joint Malaysian/Japanese venture, began construction of a tin plate works, adjacent to Malayawata Steel, in 1970, with the expectation of commissioning by the end of 1972 with an annual output of 500,000 tons. Malayawata will provide strip steel for the plant which will operate with United States and British technical assistance.

The concentration of industrial activity in what might be described as the traditionally favoured economic centres of Malaya and the relatively disappointing achievement of manufacturing, so far, in reducing the urban unemployment rate despite its success in other regards have already received comment. The planning of industrial estates to undertake further import substitution activities in locations that are inherently uneconomic, though likely to tempt state governments, is unlikely to prove the most effective means of combatting unemployment in rural and smaller urban areas, and emphasis on agricultural development and processing and on small scale industry seems most appropriate. The Majlis Amanah Ra'ayat (MARA) is particularly charged with handling the problems of industrial development outside the major urban focuses. 'Backyard industries' to take assembly or allied work to the villages is one suggested development which might disseminate industrial-type employment opportunities more widely but which would still most likely favour areas within reach of major industrial and urban centres. Improvements in the infrastructure, however, particularly by projects such as the east-west highway, could well increase the competitiveness of currently remote areas and enable them to participate economically in industrial development.

The Changing Economic Geography of Singapore since 1950

Singapore's economic problems in the years following the end of the Second World War have had much in common with those of peninsular Malaya, including the need to provide employment for a rapidly growing labour force in a post-war situation of very changed political and economic conditions. There were, however, very significant differences that made the need for economic readjustment and modification even more essential for the survival of Singapore than for that of the peninsula. These differences were the consequence of Singapore's position as a semi- and then fully-independent city-state with no raw materials, apart from the skills and ingenuity of its population, and with a traditional emphasis on entrepot trade.

As in peninsular Malaya, there was a rapid recovery of the foundations of the economy to the immediately pre-war situation. Singapore harbour had been bombed but not damaged to any great extent, though it was blocked by wrecks and debris and had not been dredged during the years of occupation, and despite problems of manning, slow turn-rounds in many of the smaller ports of South-east Asia and steadily increasing running expenses, shipping companies were able to revive the trade of the port. The chairman of the Straits Steamship Company, whose business had been an essential part of Singapore's economic life since 1890, claimed in 1947, for example, that

> despite the severe losses incurred during the war and the serious handicaps imposed upon all commercial enterprises since the war, we have regained, with extra-ordinary rapidity, a position closely approximating our pre-war standing'.[38]

There was, however, very little prospect that Singapore would be able to revert to the economic pattern of pre-war years. Most authors who touch on the economy of Singapore attribute the port's phenomenal growth and commercial prosperity to its combination of location and free port tradition. C. A. Fisher says Singapore's

> superb geographical position and its commodious and sheltered anchorage, combined with the enlightened free-port system introduced by Raffles, enabled it within a few years to become the greatest entrepot in the whole of South-east Asia,[39]

whilst N. S. Ginsburg states

> what has kept Singapore the largest port in South-east Asia is its status as a free port and its strategic location at the western entrance to the South China Sea and the Pacific Ocean basin.[40]

Singapore's location and free port status were most advantageous, as Chapter 3 indicated, when it was able freely to act as an entrepot and when it was able, almost uniquely, to provide commercial and financial services for a very wide area of South-east Asia. As early as the 1870s, Singapore was losing trade with the French and Dutch-controlled territories of the region but was compensated for this loss by the very considerable economic development of its Malayan hinterland. Singapore's freedom to trade was further restricted by the ever-tightening national controls over trade during the depression years of the 1920s and 30s, and in 1940 E. H. G. Dobby wrote that it stood 'as a free port to a hinterland and a world that restrict(ed) liberty of trade movements'.[41]

In the years following the Second World War, entrepot trade in its traditional form was subject to even greater threats from the economic nationalism that was developing in South-east Asia. With the political separation of Singapore from what became the Malayan Union in 1946 and the Federation of Malaya in 1948, followed by the national independence of the latter territory in 1957, Singapore faced the likely loss of at least some of its trade from what had been its national hinterland, as well as the very considerable loss of business with Indonesia which resulted from that country's policy of direct trading and by-passing of the Malayan entrepot ports. The economic policy that was pursued by the Federation of Malaya after independence, as discussed earlier in this chapter, especially its deliberate attempts to promote industrialization by the use, *inter alia*, of protective tariffs, reduced the free movement of goods into the country by way of Singapore, and the emergence of the Kuala Lumpur-Port Swettenham axis as the prime industrial focus of the Federation greatly increased the competitive role of Port Swettenham.

This very apparent weakening of Singapore's traditional economic function was accompanied by a population growth rate averaging 4.3 per cent. per annum that raised the number of people that the island had to support, from 947,000 in 1947 to 1,446,000 in 1957, an increasing number of whom were at the younger end of the age range. Furthermore, whereas in pre-war years a proportion of the population consisted of transients who could be expected to arrive or depart whenever prosperity attracted or depression repelled,* a large proportion of the post-war population was locally born and a majority of the remainder was permanently domiciled in Singapore and expected to find its means of livelihood there. An analysis of the economic characteristics of the population of Singapore,[43] based on the 1967 census, indicated that about one half of the population over ten years of age was economically active,

---

* There were, for example, net losses of migrant population in 1932, 1938 and 1940 and only a very small net gain in 1933.[42]

and that 72 per cent. of this economically active population was employed in the tertiary sector.* It was also apparent that the economically active population consisted largely of juveniles and young adults (54 per cent. were under 35 years of age and 75 per cent. under 45), a situation with serious implications for the unemployment problem, since only a very small proportion of the unemployed could expect to find work as a result of old persons retiring. At the time of the census, 5 per cent. of the economically active population was reported as unemployed but it is almost certainly true that the census under-estimated the full extent of unemployment, especially amongst the illiterate section of the population.

It was becoming very apparent in the 1950s, to use the words of Allen and Donnithorne,[44] that 'the era which Raffles saw in long perspective was drawing to its close' and that although Singapore was likely to remain an important entrepot, it was essential that it should develop alternative employment possibilities. In 1954, the Singapore Improvement Ordinance required the Singapore Improvement Trust to carry out a diagnostic survey of the use of land in the colony and to submit a report of the survey to the government, together with a master plan. The Master Plan[45] was published in 1955 and was accompanied by a series of study group and working party reports. The Industrial Resources Study Group concluded that

> the expansion of manufacturing industry would in the long run be best for the Colony from all points of view. The recommendations of this report are therefore directed mainly towards the development of this type of industry and if our recommendations are put into effect, we consider

---

* Compared with 47 per cent. in the U.K., 45 per cent. in Australia, 22 per cent. in Japan and 12 per cent. in Thailand at approximately the same period. Employment in the tertiary sector in Singapore in 1957 broke down as follows:

Industry	% employed
Electricity, gas, water and sanitary services	1·7
Commerce and finance	36·1
Transport, storage and communication	15·0
Personal services	17·7
Defence services	12·5
Other services	17·1
TOTAL	100·0
Persons ('000)	336·7

that more employment opportunities would become available than if present trends were allowed to continue.[46]

The Study Group's recommendations included the granting by government of certain taxation privileges to industry, the creation of an industrial finance corporation and of an industrial research and advisory organization, and the establishment of industrial estates.

The Study Group's conclusions were in accord with those reached by other students of Singapore's economy and problems, such as D. W. Fryer who, writing of the great seaports of South-east Asia in general in 1953, forecast that 'it may well be that the great cities' brightest future lies in an increase in the range and pace of industrialization'.[47] As others have pointed out, however, realistic and practical programmes of industrialization could not alone solve Singapore's problems. The state needed a balanced programme of expansion of trade and industry (and agriculture where possible) and effective industrialization had to avoid being offset by serious dislocations in other sectors of the economy such as the entrepot trade. Trading links, indeed, needed to be developed in order to maintain and expand markets both for traditional exports from Singapore and also for the products of those new industries that became efficient enough to break into overseas markets.[48]

In 1960, the Singapore government sought the assistance of a United Nations Industrial Survey Mission which visited the island in late 1960 and early 1961, and in June 1961 proposed a development plan for Singapore. The Mission's report (The Winsemius Report)[49] was a guide to industrialization in Singapore, providing both a general outline for potential industrial growth and specifically showing the need for the creation of factory space for 39,000 workers during 1961–65.

The State of Singapore Development Plan for 1961–64,[50] which was extended until 1965, recognized both the continuing importance of the entrepot trade and the need for emphasis on industrialization to provide employment opportunities for the growing population. It was noted that the 1957 census had shown that manufacturing already gave employment to almost as many persons as entrepot trade, if not more, and contributed more to the national income. The emphasis, however, was on the familiar products of foodstuffs, garments and footwear, wood products, paper products and printing and general engineering and electrical products. As in peninsular Malaya, any expansion of industrial development was likely to involve a move into fields of manufacturing where competition was to be expected from the established industrial powers whose goods traditionally had ready entry into the free port of Singapore.

Despite the island's obvious lack of most raw materials for industrial development and the problems of competition that would have to be met if Singapore's free port status was to be retained, and this was considered essential if the entrepot trade was to continue, prospects for the expansion of manufacturing were generally good. The high level of education of the youthful population* and the training facilities that were being developed were creating a labour force adaptable to any significant industrial development. Many of the services and amenities created for servicing the entrepot trade—a very good port, financial institutions, good power and water supply and good communication services—could equally be called upon and expanded to serve manufacturing industry. Singapore's central position and deep water anchorages gave the city considerable advantages as a location for industries which would need to depend on export markets in the region and on imported raw materials, whilst the home market, though not large in numbers, had the highest per capita national income in southern Asia. There was a considerable amount of local capital which could probably be channelled into industrial development. Such capital was largely accumulated as the result of trading activities, however, was accustomed to short period risks and quick profits, and was believed not easily adaptable to industrial investment without deliberate measures of inducement by government.

* The general literacy rate for the population as a whole in 1957 was 523 per thousand. The general literacy rate for persons 15 years of age and over had improved compared with earlier censuses. The general literacy rate for those 15 years and over was 496 per thousand in 1957, 465 per thousand in 1947 and 363 per thousand in 1931. The improvement was mainly for those with ages between 15 and 44.[51]

N

The main objective of the Development Plan, therefore, was to expand the resources at the disposal of the government and other public authorities in such a way that they would contribute to increasing employment opportunities for those who would be entering the labour market each year. Although the plan presumed greater efforts on the part of the government and public authorities towards economic development, the efforts were to be confined to limited fields. The plan did not envisage the government becoming the initiator of all industrial development or even the main industrial entrepreneur. It was recognized that a very great deal of future industrialization would have to be left to private enterprise, both local and foreign, and the government's major task was to create the conditions that would attract substantial private capital towards industrialization.

A total sum of $871·02 million* was allocated initially for development during the period of the plan and apportioned to main groups of projects as follows:

	$Million	%
Economic Development	507·95	58·32
Social Development	349·88	40·17
Public Administration	13·19	1·51
TOTAL	871·02	100·00

Over 66 per cent. of the sum allocated to economic development was for industry and commerce, and 23 per cent. for transport and communications. The largest single item was $100 million, phased over the four years, for the Economic Development Board which was to become the instrument of the government's direct participation in industrial activity. Table 25 illustrates the capital expenditure estimates for economic development for the period of the first plan, 1961–64.

The Economic Development Board, established as a statutory body in 1961, was based to some extent on the experience gained by the Singapore Industrial Promotion Board, a small statutory organization that had been set up

* Final expenditure for the extended plan period 1961–65 was $936 million—62·3 per cent. of which was for economic development, 36·1 per cent. for social development and 1·6 per cent. for public administration.

TABLE 25

SINGAPORE—DEVELOPMENT PLAN CAPITAL EXPENDITURE ESTIMATES ON ECONOMIC DEVELOPMENT, 1961–1964

(in $ millions)

	1961	1962	1963	1964	Total
1. LAND & AGRICULTURAL DEVELOPMENT					
TOTAL: Land & Agricultural Development	10·90	16·19	13·47	12·71	53·27
2. INDUSTRY & COMMERCE					
Economic Development Board	40·00	20·00	20·00	20·00	100·00
Kallang Project	0·50	4·50	20·00	15·00	40·00
Jurong Project	1·00	14·00	15·00	15·00	45·00
Land Acquisition for Industrialization & other development costs for Industrialization	5·60				5·60
Electricity	19·40	11·80	24·42	22·88	78·50
Water	9·10	14·45	16·73	13·95	54·23
Gas	1·76	4·72	3·70	3·85	14·03
TOTAL: Industry & Commerce	77·36	69·47	99·85	90·68	337·36
3. TRANSPORT & COMMUNICATIONS					
East Wharf Development	6·70	6·00			12·70
Improvement of Singapore River	2·00	3·70	5·00	5·00	15·70
Roads	3·90	9·30	8·10	8·30	29·60
Others	18·18	16·14	13·48	11·52	59·32
TOTAL: Transport & Communications	30·78	35·14	26·58	24·82	117·32
TOTAL: ECONOMIC DEVELOPMENT	119·04	120·80	139·90	128·21	507·95

Source: State of Singapore, Development Plan 1961–64. Table 3.1.

with a nominal capital of $1 million in 1957 but whose activities had been limited to making small loans to a handful of small industrial operators. The Economic Development Board was

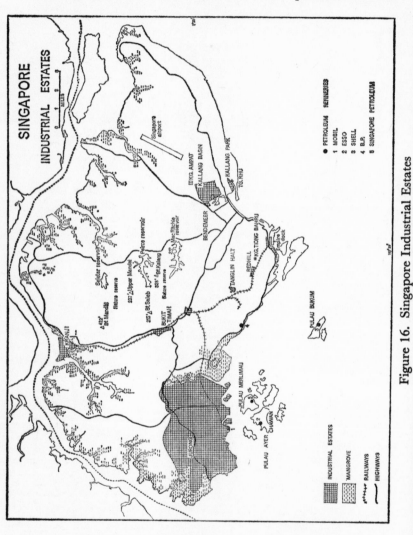

Figure 16. Singapore Industrial Estates

given much larger capital resources and far greater powers. It was empowered to make loans on favourable terms to such industrial projects as would result in advantages to the general programme of industrialization, to participate in industrial projects planned by the Board or by private enterprise by subscribing to their share capital, to undertake the physical development of industrial estates and to provide a wide range of services for potential and actual investors.

The maximum assistance that government could provide was reinforced by a variety of liberal incentives. These included tax exemption for up to five years for companies declared pioneer, tax exemption on income increased as a result of additional investment in productive equipment, accelerated depreciation of productive equipment, tax exemption on interest on foreign loans, on royalties, fees etc., tariff protection for selected industries, duty-free import of equipment and raw materials, preferential government buying of local products and free repatriation of profits and capital. The granting of tariff protection for selected industries was, of course, a major modification of the traditional free-port status of Singapore and represents a very significant step in the economic evolution of the island. In order to maintain the port's entrepot role, however, free trade zones were established.

The principal modifications to the landscape of Singapore that were to be brought about by the planned industrialization of the island were those associated with the establishment of industrial estates. Although certain localities in Singapore had already developed as primarily industrial in character, the pattern of development had been haphazard. The intention of the plan for industrial estates was to ensure, through the medium of various schemes and by a conscious effort to group industries into particular areas, that the future location of industry in Singapore would be more satisfactory than it had been in the past. The existence of several thousand functioning industries already in Singapore and a wide range of industrial skills and experience made possible the development not only of a number of small estates but also of one large industrial town. The small estates represented the re-development of a number of localities in the city (Figure 16) as at Redhill, Tanglin Halt, Bendemeer Road, Kampong Tiong Bahru and Kampong Ampat. In some of these estates flatted factories of five to seven storeys came to be constructed in addition to

TABLE 26

Singapore—Stage of Implementation of Firms that had Acquired Sites in Jurong Industrial Estate at 31st December, 1966

INDUSTRY GROUP	No. of firms that have acquired sites	Firms commencing production before 1966	Firms commencing production in 1966	Total number of firms in production in 1966	STAGE OF IMPLEMENTATION OF OTHER JURONG FIRMS					Firms to commence production in 1967
					No. of firms with building under construction	No. of firms which have completed construction	No. of firms which have ordered machinery	No. of firms which have installed machinery	Total No. of firms in implementing stage	
Food and Beverages	9	3	1	4	—	—	2	3	5	5
Textiles, Garments and Leather	11	8	1	9	—	—	2	—	2	1
Wood and Paper Products	9	4	3	7	1	—	1	1	2	1
Rubber Products	3	1	1	2	—	—	—	1	1	—
Chemicals and Chemical Products	17	6	3	9	4	—	1	3	8	2
Petroleum and Petroleum Products	3	—	1	1	2	—	—	—	2	1
Non-Metallic Mineral Products	6	2	3	5	—	—	1	—	1	1
Metals and Engineering	26	14	3	17	3	—	2	4	9	3
Electrical Products	6	3	1	4	—	—	1	1	2	2
Miscellaneous	16	4	4	8	4	—	1	3	8	4
TOTAL	106	45	21	66	14	—	11	15	40	20

Source: E.D.B., Annual Report, 1966.

conventional single and double storey buildings. In the Bendemeer Road Industrial Estate, for example, some 200,000 square feet of factory space had been allocated by the end of 1967 to 23 industrial concerns and five 7-storey flatted factories were proposed, were under construction or were completed. Medium-sized industrial estates were established at Kranji (Woodlands) and at Kallang. This latter estate was sited on a partly reclaimed area of tidal swamp at the confluence of the Kallang and Whampoa rivers behind the narrow estuary of the Kallang River. Fringed by temporary residential settlements and several saw mills and other industrial premises it was ideally situated for access by sea and river and is in the process of complete redevelopment.*

The major industrial development in Singapore, however, is taking place at Jurong. The Master Plan of 1955 had shown a new town at Bulim in the west of the island, and in 1956 it was suggested that an area adjacent to Damar Laut in the south-west should be utilized for industry by cutting the hills to fill swampland. In 1957 the Master Plan team extended the Bulim town to the coast, and in 1958 development was recommended.[52] In 1960 an outline plan was drawn up for the development of an industrial estate at Jurong, between Bulim and the coast and a Japanese survey team visited Singapore in November and December 1960 to prepare a report on the planning and design of Jurong as a new town. The United Nations Mission Report (Winsemius Report) of 1961 confirmed the choice of Jurong as Singapore's main industrial centre.†

It was expected that the formation of the Malaysian federation in 1963 would lend impetus to Singapore's industrialization programme as the island anticipated its role as the major industrial centre in the federal nation of 12 million people. The separation of Singapore from the rest of Malaysia after only two years, and the disruption caused by the 'confrontation' with Indonesia prevented this role from developing, however, and the growth of Jurong slackened. Industries that had hoped to locate at Jurong went elsewhere or scaled

---

* Development at Kallang is expected ultimately to provide jobs for 100,000 people.
† A detailed description of Jurong is included in Chapter 6.

TABLE 27

SINGAPORE—DISTRIBUTION OF EMPLOYMENT IN ALL FIRMS THAT HAD ACQUIRED SITES IN JURONG INDUSTRIAL ESTATE BY INDUSTRY GROUP AND BY OCCUPATION AS AT 31ST DECEMBER, 1966

OCCUPATION GROUP

INDUSTRY GROUP	Managerial and Supervisory	Clerical and Sales	Technical	Skilled and Semi-skilled	Unskilled	Others	Total	Estimated Total at full production
Food and Beverages	30	63	25	101	124	14	357	1023
Textiles, Garments and Leather	32	37	93	382	355	156	1054	3590
Wood and Paper Products	45	97	45	206	947	55	1395	1941
Rubber Products	56	57	21	225	21	77	457	538
Chemicals and Chemical Products	35	67	47	87	229	13	478	996
Petroleum and Petroleum Products	12	7	34	103	—	—	156	160
Non-metallic Mineral Products	10	31	15	60	107	85	308	789
Metals and Engineering	206	217	81	1230	408	185	2328	3471
Electrical Products	8	22	30	145	52	25	282	709
Miscellaneous	21	31	34	85	102	8	281	594
TOTAL	455	630	425	2624	2345	617	7096	13,810

Source: E.D.B. Annual Report, 1966.

down their projects. Nevertheless, by the end of 1966, 106 firms had acquired sites in Jurong industrial estate, 66 were in production and 40 implementing production. Of the 40 firms, 14 had begun construction work, 11 had ordered machinery and 15 had installed machinery.[53] There was marked emphasis on metal and engineering products, and chemicals and chemical products (Table 27), whilst employment totalled just over 7,000, a figure estimated to rise to 13,810 by the time all the existing firms were at full production.

The separation of Singapore from Malaysia in 1965 made the island, for the first time in its history, a fully independent sovereign state—the Republic of Singapore. The political separation occurred at a time when the level of trade was depressed as a consequence of the confrontation with Indonesia and was followed at the end of 1967 by the British government's decision to withdraw the 20,000 British servicemen from Singapore by 1971. This decision was to affect a total of 42,000 locally employed civilians and personnel as well as drastically to reduce the gross national product that benefited from some £60 million per annum of British government expenditure on the military base as well as from servicemen's expenditure on the island. The need for Singapore's industrialization programme to succeed was even more essential at a time when the island's domestic market was slashed to a mere two million by the separation.

In the five-year period from 1961 to 1966, the number of manufacturing establishments with ten or more workers (excluding rubber processing) doubled and the manufacturing output increased at an annual rate of 21 per cent.[54] The main sources of growth were the chemical and petroleum industry, food and beverage industry, basic metals, and the metal products and machinery industry. Faced with the full responsibility for the economic survival of the island state, and encouraged by the confidence of foreign investors from the United States, Europe, Japan, Hong Kong* and Taiwan especially, the Singapore government pursued vigorous policies to reinforce the attractions of the republic for manufacturers.

* Considerable panic capital from Hong Kong flooded into Singapore in 1967 bringing with it vital trade and banking connections. As the colony recovered from its political troubles, investment from Hong Kong fell, but interest in Singapore remained at a substantial level.

The Second Five Year Development Plan (1966–70) placed particular emphasis on the building up of the industrial base largely with export markets in view. Provision was made for expenditure amounting to $1,730 million in the first instance, and this was revised upward to $1,928 million. Of this revised total 67·2 per cent. was allocated to economic development, 26·8 per cent. to social development and 6 per cent. to public administration.

New labour legislation to rationalize employer/employee relationships, with a view to attracting new investment and to increasing the efficiency of Singapore's trading and industrial enterprises, was enacted in 1968. This removed excess fringe benefits and asserted certain management rights, especially in regard to hiring, dismissing, promoting and transferring labour.*

In 1968, three new institutions were set up—two of them growing out of the Economic Development Board—further to strengthen the industrialization programme. The Development Bank of Singapore was formed to take over the financing functions of the Economic Development Board. In addition to financing purely manufacturing undertakings, its scope extends to include tourist and estate projects (especially in connection with the urban renewal programme) and the Bank took over the entire loan portfolio previously held by the Economic Development Board. The Development Bank was established with a total paid-up capital of $100 million.

The ownership and management of the industrial estate in Jurong and of six other industrial estates, at Kallang, Tiong Bahru, Kampong Ampat, Tanglin Halt, Kallang Park and Tanjong Rhu, was transferred from the E.D.B. to a newly established Jurong Town Corporation. At the end of October 1968 this responsibility covered 293 factories in production, giving employment to more than 21,000 persons, and the ownership of many flats and shophouses in Jurong.

The International Trading Company (INTRACO) was incorporated in November 1968, with an authorized share capital of $50 million, to be owned jointly by the government, the Development Bank and the private sector with holdings of 20 million issued shares in a 6 : 3·8 : 10·2 ratio. Intraco's

---

* As well as increasing contributions, both by employers and employees, to the Central Provident Fund.

special responsibility is the promotion of Singapore's export trade and clearly it has a difficult and crucial role to play in assisting the economic progress of the Republic. One of its major fields of activity is in conducting trade with Communist countries on behalf of the Singapore government.

Improvements in the infrastructure undertaken to assist the economic growth of Singapore include the construction of a new power station at Jurong to meet an increased demand for electricity, which will raise the total installed capacity by 1974 to a level more than four times as great as that of 1961, road programmes and port developments. Apart from major developments in the port of Singapore, discussed more fully in Chapter 6, a new port is under construction at Jurong where 8,000 feet of wharves and various facilities for the mechanical handling of bulk cargo have been developed.

Although it is clearly not possible at such an early stage to assess the success or otherwise of Singapore's efforts to convert itself from a major trading port with limited industry to a major industrial as well as trading centre with considerable emphasis on the export of its own manufactured goods, indications at the end of the 1960s were that industrialization was catching hold and exports growing. Large international companies, mostly American, were becoming aware increasingly of the advantages that Singapore offers to investors, and the establishment of branch plants of such concerns may be seen to have many advantages for Singapore, including the provision of skilled entrepreneurs and often the availability of well-established advertising and distributive networks throughout South-east Asia.[55]

By 1968 several industries were already making significant contributions to Singapore's domestic exports. The petroleum industry, footwear, apparel and leather industries, electrical machinery industries, and rubber products and wood and cork industries were the principal export-oriented manufacturing groups and markets were being developed not only in southern Asia but in Africa and in western and eastern Europe. The textile industry is largely export-oriented but its prospects are influenced very much by the quota restrictions of developed countries, and its success may well depend on its ability to diversify into non-quota articles and to develop and expand into new markets. The expansion of the shipbuilding and ship-repairing industry, a significant contributor to foreign exchange earnings, would appear to have good prospects as the number and tonnage of vessels calling at Singapore increase. The large shipyards of the Port of Singapore, which took over the Singapore naval dockyard and labour force for commercial use, and of Jurong dominate this section of the economy.

The need to develop 'outward looking' industrialization is of more immediate importance to Singapore than it is to West Malaysia, not only because of the limited home market for import-substitute commodities but also because there is little employment alternative for Singapore's predominantly urban labour force other than in making and trading goods that can be sold overseas. Overseas markets for typical import-substitute goods, beverages, foodstuffs, tobacco etc. are very limited since these are the very goods that possible trading partners are themselves developing behind protective tariffs.

The basis of Singapore's efforts to develop a more sophisticated industrial structure with export markets in view is the Singapore steel industry, consisting of two steel mills located at Jurong and Woodlands (Kranji). National Iron and Steel Mills Ltd., was established in 1961 on the recommendation of a United Nations team which concluded that a mill to make 50,000–60,000 tons of finished steel from local scrap would be both economic and profitable in Singapore. Production began at Jurong in 1964 and mild steel bars and wire rods are turned out by two electric furnaces, with a third to be in use in 1970. Plans were announced in 1969 to develop National Iron and Steel as a fully integrated iron and steel works importing ore from Australia and Malaysia with the intention of making Singapore the steel centre of South-east Asia.

The Malayan Iron and Steel Mills Ltd. at Woodlands was incorporated in 1962 and similarly produces mild steel bars. The establishment of the two steel mills has encouraged the growth of the metal fabrication industry, making goods such as steel pipes and tubes, galvanized sheets, wire mesh, wire nails, nuts and bolts, bicycles and parts, office equipment, water tanks and cables whilst items such as diesel engines, motor vehicle components, machine tools, pumps, compressors and power presses are considered feasible.

A copper mill, also located at Jurong, commenced production in 1970 to manufacture all types of copper wire, copper tubes and other copper, brass and bronze products, making use of reclaimed raw material especially from the local ship-breaking industry, which, located alongside National Iron and Steel, already provides scrap for the steel mill. The copper mill will make Singapore self sufficient in copper and copper alloy products with a surplus for export. Further evidence of increasing sophistication of Singapore's manufacturing industry is provided by the growth of the electronics industry. By 1969 fourteen electronics plants were in operation, employing about 5,000 workers, 80 per cent. of whom were girls. These companies assemble or manufacture a variety of components, including integrated circuits, transistors, transformers, diodes, digital heads and capacitors. Additional plants, branches of American concerns, are being established for the manufacture of radio chassis, electron tubes and other electronic equipment which, like the existing products, will be export oriented, with Hong Kong and Taiwan as important markets.

REFERENCES

1 International Bank for Reconstruction and Development, 'The Economic Development of Malaya', Singapore, Government Printer, 1955, p. 13
2 McTaggart, W. D., 'The Distribution of Ethnic Groups in Malaya 1947–57', *J. Trop. Geogr.*, 26, 1968
3 Fisk, E. K., 'Special Development Problems of a Plural Society: The Malayan Example', *Econ. Rec.*, 1962
4 Federation of Malaya, 'Draft Development Plan', Kuala Lumpur, 1950, p. 22
5 *Ibid.*, p. 134–5
6 Lim Chong Yah, *Economic Development of Modern Malaya*, Kuala Lumpur, Oxford University Press, 1967, Appendix 4.1, p. 325
7 Mudie, R. F. (Chairman), 'Report of the Mission of Enquiry into the Malayan Rubber Industry', Kuala Lumpur, Government Printer, 1954
8 Correspondence with Manager, Dunlop Plantations Ltd.
9 Lim Chong Yah, *loc. cit.*
10 O'Reilly, J. M. H., 'An Assessment of the Malayan Tin Mining Industry in the Twentieth Century', *J. Trop. Geogr.*, 17, 1963
11 Alexander, J. B., 'The Evolution of Land Suitability Maps in the Federation of Malaya', *J. Trop. Geogr.*, 18, 1964

12 Courtenay, P. P., 'International Tin Restriction and its Effects on the Malayan Tin Mining Industry', *Geogr.*, 46, 1961
13 Jackson, J. C., 'Oil Palm: Malaya's Post-Independence Boom Crop', *Geogr.*, 52, 1967
14 *Tin*, March 1961, pp. 61–62
15 International Bank, *op. cit.*
16 International Bank, *op. cit.*, p. 15
17 Lim, *op. cit.*, pp. 216–7
18 Federation of Malaya, 'Report of the Working Party on the Encouragement of Industrial Development in the Federation of Malaya', Kuala Lumpur, Government Printer, 1957
19 *Ibid.*, p. 7
20 Federation of Malaya, 'Second Five Year Plan 1961–65', Kuala Lumpur, Government Printer, 1961, p. 1
21 *Ibid.*, p. 3, 4
22 Federation of Malaya, 'Second Five Year Plan', *op. cit.*, p. 19
23 Ward, M. W., 'A Review of Problems and Achievements in the Economic Development of Modern Malaya', *Econ. Geogr.*, 44, 1968
24 Burns, R. S., 'The Cameron Highlands Hydro-Electric Power Scheme', *Geogr.*, 51, 1966
25 Federation of Malaysia, 'First Malaysia Plan, 1966–1970', Kuala Lumpur, Government Printer, 1965, pp. 18–40
26 International Bank for Reconstruction and Development, 'Report on the Economic Aspects of Malaysia', Kuala Lumpur, Government Printer, 1963
27 Wheelwright, E. L., *Industrialization in Malaysia*, Melbourne University Press, 1965, pp. 138–9
28 Federation of Malaysia, *op. cit.*
29 *Ibid.*, p. 10
30 Federation of Malaysia, 'Mid-Term Review of the First Malaysia Plan 1966–70', Kuala Lumpur, Government Printer, 1969
31 *Ibid.*, p. 82
32 International Bank, *op. cit.*, p. 306
33 Courtenay, P. P., 'Changing Patterns in the Tin Mining and Smelting Industry of South-east Asia', *J. Trop. Geogr.*, 25, 1967
34 *Tin Int.*, 42, September, 1969, p. 233
35 Federation of Malaysia, 'First Malaysia Plan', *op. cit.*, p. 125
36 Federation of Malaysia, 'Mid-Term Review of the First Malaysia Plan', *op. cit.*, p. 64
37 *The Straits Times*, 27th October, 1969
38 Tregonning, K. G., *Home Port Singapore. A History of Straits Steamship Company Limited, 1890–1965*, Singapore, Oxford University Press, 1967, p. 230
39 Fisher, C. A., *South-east Asia*, London, Methuen & Co. Ltd., 1964, pp. 594–5
40 Ginsburg, N. S., 'The Great City in South-east Asia', *Am. J. Sociol.*, 40, 1955
41 Dobby, E. H. G., 'Singapore—Town and Country', *Geogr. Rev.*, 30, 1940
42 Colony of Singapore, 'Master Plan. Reports of Study Groups and Working Parties', Singapore, Government Printer, 1955, p. 18
43 Saw Swee Hock and R. Ma, 'The Economic Characteristics of the Population of Singapore, 1957', *Mal. Econ. Rev.*, 5, 1960

44 Allen, G. C. and Donnithorne, A., *Western Enterprise in Indonesia and Malaya*, London, Allen & Unwin Ltd., 1957, p. 255

45 Colony of Singapore, 'Master Plan. Report of a Survey', Singapore, Government Printer, 1955

46 Colony of Singapore, 'Master Plan. Reports of Study Groups etc.' *ibid.*, p. 64

47 Fryer, D. W., 'The Million City' in South-east Asia', *Geogr. Rev.*, 43, 1953

48 Lim Tay Boh, *The Development of Singapore's Economy*, Singapore, Donald Moore, 1960

49 United Nations, 'Report of Industrial Survey Mission to Singapore', 1961

50 State of Singapore, 'Development Plan 1961–1964', Singapore, Government Printer, 1961

51 Chua, S. C., 'Report on the Census of Population 1957', Singapore, Government Printer, 1964, p. 76

52 Economic Development Board, Singapore, Industrial Facilities Division, 'Development of Jurong New Town—1960–1967', Singapore, 1967, p, 10

53 Economic Development Board, 'Annual Report, 1966', Singapore, 1967, appendix III (A), p. 67

54 Economic Development Board, 'Annual Report, 1967', Singapore, 1968

55 Bottomley, A., 'The Role of Branch Plants in the Industrialization of Singapore', *Mal. Econ. Rev.*, 7, 1962

CHAPTER 6

The Major Urban Concentrations of Malaya

Successive censuses of Malaya, both of peninsular Malaya and of Singapore, have given evidence of the extent to which three principal urban complexes have been attracting population in larger numbers than most other areas of the region (Table 28)* Two of these complexes, Georgetown–Butterworth–Prai, in the north-western Malaysian state of Penang, and Singapore, have grown from the two early British foundations of 1786 and 1819 and owe their pre-eminence to the commercial growth based initially upon their free-port status and reinforced in recent years by industrial diversification. The third, Kuala Lumpur–Port Swettenham, has its origin in the tin-mining expansion of the 1850s, its significance re-inforced by the selection of Kuala Lumpur as the administrative centre first of the Federated Malay States in 1896 and then of the whole Malayan Federation in 1948, and its economic base much strengthened by industrial development since the 1950s. The railway port of Port Swettenham, destined to become, as ocean outlet for Kuala Lumpur, the major peninsular port, may be seen as the successor to the third historic Straits port of Malacca, which proved both inadequate and poorly situated to serve a central Malayan hinterland. The far richer tin deposits of the Klang and its tributary valleys shifted the focus of economic activity northwards from the immediate ambit of Malacca early in the nineteenth century development of the region, and the port was far less developed than either

* Though it should be noted that they have rarely recorded the largest *rate* of population growth, which, in most intercensal periods, has been achieved by rather smaller urban centres e.g. between the 1947 and 1957 censuses the highest growth rate for an urban centre was that for Kluang, Johore (349 per cent.). The next highest, however, was that for Butterworth (230 per cent.).[1]

Penang or Singapore to be able to retain its function as an outlet by virtue of existing facilities.

The purpose of this chapter is to examine the economic

TABLE 28

POPULATION OF MAJOR URBAN CONCENTRATIONS
OF MALAYA, 1911–1957
(in thousands)

	1911	1921	1931	1947	1957
GEORGETOWN[a]	101·2	123·1	149·4	189·1	299·8
BUTTERWORTH[b]	3·9	4·1	13·5	21·3	42·5
Total Georgetown-Butterworth	105·1	127·2	162·9	210·4	277·4
Percentage of Total Malayan Population	3·98	3·82	3·75	3·60	3·88
KUALA LUMPUR	46·7	80·4	111·4	176·0	316·2
PETALING JAYA	—	—	—	—	16·6
KLANG[c]	7·7	11·7	20·9	33·5	75·6
Total Kuala Lumpur-PJ-Klang	57·4	92·1	132·3	209·5	408·4
Percentage of Total Malayan Population	2·17	2·77	3·04	3·58	5·29
SINGAPORE	303·3	418·4	557·7	938·1	1,445·9
Percentage of Total Malayan Population	11·47	12·57	12·83	16·04	18·71
TOTAL MALAYAN POPULATION	2,643·3	3,328·4	4,347·7	5,848·1	7,725·9

N.B. Population data for the total urban areas in each case are difficult, if not impossible, to obtain especially for the earlier census years. Figures for peninsular Malaya quoted here are for municipalities, town councils, new villages etc. with a population of 10,000 or over. Totals are therefore almost certainly under-estimates of the size of the urban concentrations. Figures for Singapore, on the other hand, are for the island and are therefore an over-estimate of the size of the urban concentration.

(a) Includes Ayer Itam in 1957.
(b) Butterworth incorporates Prai.
(c) Klang incorporates Port Swettenham.

Sources: 1957 Population Census of the Federation of Malaya. Report on the Census of Population 1957 (Singapore).

geography of these three urban complexes, to consider the response of each unique place to the changing economic environment as described in the three preceding chapters and to attempt to assess the relationship and contribution of each to the economic development of the Malayan region as a whole.

I. GEORGETOWN–BUTTERWORTH–PRAI

Trade & Industry in the Colonial Period

The settlement of Georgetown, established on Penang* island by Francis Light in 1786, has developed into the major port and industrial centre of north Malaya which is the second largest urban concentration in the Malaysian Federation. The colony was first established on a low sandy point at the north-eastern tip of the island where two small streams of 'remarkably fine water'[2] flowed into the sheltered roads where Light's small fleet of ships was anchored. The island, 108 square miles in extent, is essentially a granite massif, rising to 2,722' at its highest point, and forms part of the so-called 'Kedah-Singgora Range', the westernmost of the series of folded structures that characterize the physical geography of the Malay peninsula.[3] Deposition of both land-derived and marine sediments has built up narrow alluvial plains in the west and south-east of the island (Figure 17) and a probable sequence of beach ridges[4] contributed to the construction of the alluvial headland selected as the site of the East India Company's settlement.

Early Georgetown, serving as a port of call for Indiamen and country traders and as a collecting centre for the native produce especially of the Straits region, occupied an approximately rectangular area fronting onto the southern shore of the headland, where deeper water approached closer inshore. The first detailed analysis of the town's population, Braddell's

---

* The name Penang (Malay *Pulau Pinang*—the arecanut island) has always been preferred both to the official colonial name for the island, Prince of Wales Island, and to that of the city, Georgetown. Since the formation of the Federation of Malaya in 1948, Penang has been the official name of the state that replaced the former Straits Settlement of Prince of Wales Island and Province Wellesley. The Malay name, *Tanjong* (cape or promontory), is in popular use amongst Malays as an alternative name for the city.

Throughout this chapter the term Penang is used in its present day political sense i.e. it refers to the whole former colony and present state and thus includes both the island and Province Wellesley.

figures for 1812,[5] gave a total of 26,000* which included 7,500 Chinese, 9,800 Malays and 7,100 Indians. Chinese worked as carpenters, masons, smiths, traders, shopkeepers and planters; Indians were employed as shopkeepers and

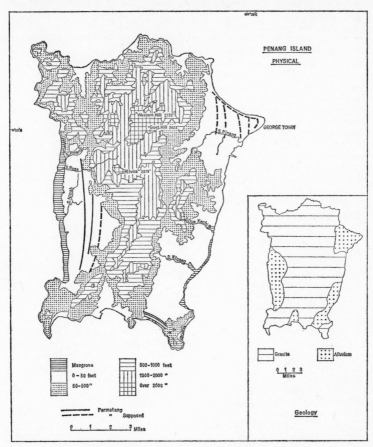

Figure 17. Penang—Physical Features

labourers, whilst Malays were occupied principally in agriculture, growing rice, sugar and fruit to the west of the town. In 1800, the area of the colony was considerably enlarged by the acquisition of a 280 square mile strip of territory on the mainland (Province Wellesley) in order to establish control

* Figures are rounded.

over both sides of the harbour and to provide further supplies of foodstuffs for the growing port. Province Wellesley was not included in population counts of the colony, however, until 1833.

For the greater part of the nineteenth century Georgetown functioned as an entrepot for a region that included north-

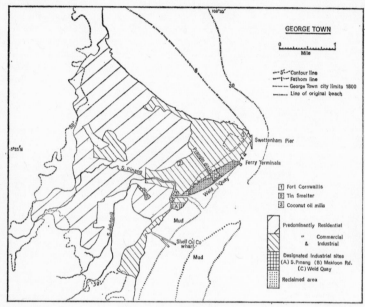

Figure 18. Georgetown

western Malaya, northern Sumatra, the Kra isthmus of southern Thailand and the Tenasserim coast of Burma. Chinese and native traders brought Straits produce, including rice and tin, to the port, and distributed manufactured products in the native states. British trading companies conducted business between Georgetown and overseas areas, particularly with Europe.

The Colony grew slowly, and as immigrant Chinese relentlessly increased their proportion of Georgetown's population, it acquired many of the characteristics of a southern Chinese city, especially the distinctive two or more storeyed 'shophouse' with its regular fifteen foot unit of street frontage and frequent joint function as shop or workshop and home. The right of free loading and discharging over the beaches of Georgetown dated from the earliest days of the settlement and until 1870, the port's landing facilities remained limited to a small number of *ghauts* or stone jetties along the water-front which developed as extensions of the streets that ran inland from the shore. Reclamation of the areas between the ghauts, assisted by natural silting, and the construction of offices and warehouses upon the land so reclaimed had, however, extended the shoreline some five hundred feet seaward,[6] and the line of the original beach, now Beach Street, had become the hub of the port with most of the warehouses at its northern end.

The relatively leisurely growth of Georgetown between about 1820 and 1870 reflected its position as something of a quiet colonial backwater and commercial dependency of Singapore. Most imported European manufacturers reached Georgetown from Singapore once the younger settlement had established itself as the major entrepot in the Malayan region, and much trade between the two ports was speculative as prices rose or fell at each. The merchant houses that were being set up in the Straits settlements immediately preceding and following the end of the East India Company's monopoly in 1834 were almost entirely established in Singapore, with Georgetown branches founded as subsidiaries.

The opening of the Suez Canal in 1869 and the development of the Larut and Kinta tinfields in the 1870s and 1880s, especially after the establishment of British political control in Perak in 1874, greatly increased the economic significance of Georgetown, and the growing volume of trade handled by the port each year from 1870 onwards soon made obvious the inadequate nature of the landing facilities. A quay running the length of the shore linking up the ends of the ghauts, Weld Quay, was constructed in 1882, but, since it was unsuitable for craft other than lighters, ships of all sizes continued to anchor in the Roads and discharge into lighters, as coasters, for the most part, still do. The need of larger vessels for deep water facilities led, after much agitation and planning, to the construction by the Settlement government of a deep water berth at the tip of the headland. Known as Swettenham Pier, the berth was in use by 1904 and later

extended. A ferry link was established between Georgetown
and a mainland terminal at Butterworth in 1893, and in 1903
a rail ferry joined Georgetown to the terminus of the new
F.M.S. railway at Prai.

The new landing facilities and the transport links with the
mainland reflected the settlement's growing importance as an
outlet for the raw material exports of the developing tinfields

TABLE 29

PENANG—SHIPPING & TRADE, 1878–1906

	Vessels Cleared With Cargo[a]		Value of Trade		
	Number	Tonnage	Imports ($'000)	Exports ($'000)	Total ($'000)
1878	1,543	791,196	20,862·6	23,009·1	43,871·8
1881	1,570	919,921	20,495·7[b]	16,005·3	36,501·1
1886	2,433	1,260,304	41,194·3	40,212·5	81,406·8
1891	2,949	1,738,447	40,341·7	41,436·2	81,777·9
1895	2,707	1,713,559	45,965·9	43,644·8	89,610·7
1901	2,450	2,386,841	63,716·7	62,636·4	126,353·2
1906	2,324	2,868,459	94,546·1[c]	90,709·2	185,255·3
1911	2,888	3,803,328	131,189·2	118,451·0	249,640·2

(a) excluding native craft.
(b) dollar valued at 3s. 9d. stg.
(c) dollar valued at 2s. 4d. stg.

Source: Straits Settlements Blue Books.

and plantations of the north-western region of the peninsula,
especially of Perak. Figures showing the value of trade handled
annually by the settlement from 1878 until the years immediately preceding the First World War suggest a marked
growth (Table 29) but are difficult to compare over the period
because of the variations in value of the diverse silver dollars
in use in the Straits before the introduction of the standardized
Straits dollar in 1904.* Total volume of trade is also difficult

* The dollar replaced the rupee, previously the official currency for all purposes,
in 1867, and dollars coined in Hong Kong, Mexico, Peru, Bolivia and Spain
were all legal currency. The American trade dollar and Japanese yen were also
recognized after 1874. In 1890 the Mexican dollar was recognized as standard
but declines in the price of silver led to the reduction of exports of coin from Mexico
and to a shortage of currency. For a while a British dollar was minted at Bombay
but the price of silver continued to depreciate. In 1902 a commission was set
up to investigate the whole question of Straits currency and following its report
in 1904, the Hong Kong and Mexican dollars were demonetized and a new Straits
dollar, fixed at 2s. 4d. sterling, was introduced.[7]

to assess because of the different units in which commodities were recorded (e.g. cotton goods in 'pieces', yarn by length, tin metal by weight). Perhaps the best measure of trade is the annual tonnage of vessels cleared with cargo, and this figure increased almost fivefold between 1878 and 1911 (Table 29).

The gradual re-orientation of the trade of Georgetown in this period is apparent from Table 30, which illustrates the percentage of the port's trade that was conducted with

TABLE 30

GEORGETOWN—PERCENTAGE OF TRADE WITH
VARIOUS REGIONS, 1878–1911

	1878	1881	1886	1891	1895	1901	1906	1911
Malay Peninsula	4	7	13	19	22	23	21	28
Other Straits Settlements	7	12	6	8	9	4	3	5
Siam	8	<1	6	5	5	3	8	4
Netherlands Indies	27	15	19	14	13	12	8	6
Other Foreign Countries	11	18	16	11	16	15	19	16
Other British Colonies	23	33	24	28	23	26	22	19
United Kingdom	20	15	16	15	14	17	19	24

Source: Straits Settlements Blue Books.

particular regions at approximately five year intervals. The growing significance of the Malayan peninsula is very apparent —it accounted for only four per cent. of Georgetown's trade in 1878 but for twenty-eight per cent. in 1911—as is the decline in relative importance of the Netherlands Indies (primarily Sumatra). The proportion of Georgetown's trade with the other Straits Settlements (especially Singapore) also shows a a small but probably significant decline as the port established more independent trading links. A substantial proportion of the trade with 'other British colonies' consisted of rice imports especially from British Burma.

Between the censuses of 1871 and 1881, the number of persons returned as employed in the commercial sector doubled, while the total population of the island increased by fifty per cent. In the same intercensal period the proportion returned as 'industrial' grew only fractionally faster than the total population, and trades classified as 'industrial' were mainly of a craft nature, such as boot-makers, carpenters, farriers, jewellers, potters, sawyers, tailors, tanners, weavers and wood and ivory-carvers, whilst a considerable number were fishermen and labourers.* In the 1890s, however, major contributions to Georgetown's industrial status were made by the establishment of processing industries in the city as well as by the expansion of small workshops and manufactories. In 1897 a tin smelting works using imported anthracite as fuel was constructed in the city. The site chosen for the smelter was on the southern edge of the urban area in the valley of the small Penang River, where, owing presumably to the low-lying and rather swampy ground, no other building had taken place. A second tin smelter was built by the Straits Trading Company on the mainland coast at Butterworth in 1902. Georgetown's first large oil mill, to process copra supplied both by the mainland and by the entrepot trade, was established on the western edge of the city also at this period. A general, though in many ways rather unsatisfactory, summary of the manufactories in Georgetown in 1911, classified by numbers of premises, is given in Table 3 (p. 110).

The expanding rubber industry of the mainland had less influence on the industrial development of Georgetown than had the tin industry. Unlike the smelting of tin, the processing of raw rubber did not require highly capitalized plant. The initial coagulation of the latex by the addition of a weak acid and its subsequent rolling into sheets was largely carried out on the plantations themselves, whilst other processes such as the milling of scrap could be peformed in any conveniently local centre. Georgetown, therefore, did not develop as a particularly major centre of rubber processing though at least one milling factory was established in the colony to cope with local rubber† and with scrap from Sumatra. The port's position at the terminus of the west coast railway, which ran through the centre of the developing rubber belt of west Malaya, was ideal for the export of production of the

---

* Comparable classifications of occupations to these of 1871 and 1881 unortunately are not recorded by the Blue Books for the censuses of 1891, 1901 and 1911.

† There were 4994 acres of rubber in Penang island in 1911 and 14,725 acres in Province Wellesley.[8]

plantations, however, and the agency houses were quick to see the value of the rubber trade. Not only did they undertake the auctioning of rubber and handle its grading, packing

TABLE 31

PENANG—VALUE OF TRADE, 1915–1940
(in $ millions)

Year	Imports	Exports	Total
1915	115·0	103·0	218·0
1916	135·8	124·4	260·2
1917	155·3	155·3	310·6
1918	183·2	167·2	350·4
1919	205·4	186·4	391·8
1920	297·6	241·7	539·3
1921	121·4	101·7	223·1
1922	142·7	131·4	274·1
1923	205·1	199·1	404·2
1924	230·3	222·5	452·8
1925	326·0	307·2	633·2
1926	347·3	320·9	668·2
1927	320·4	290·6	611·0
1928	278·6	260·1	538·7
1929	154·3	202·3	356·6
1930	104·5	140·0	244·5
1931	70·2	93·7	163·9
1932	56·5	62·2	118·7
1933	61·0	72·6	133·6
1934	79·1	109·1	188·2
1935	84·2	124·2	208·4
1936	96·0	149·1	245·1
1937	135·0	209·5	344·5
1938	105·3	124·5	229·8
1939	127·0	158·2	285·2
1940	150·0	257·7	407·7

Source: Annual Reports, Penang Chamber of Commerce.

and despatch, but in may cases invested in plantations themselves.

The value of Penang's trade during the economically unstable years of the 1920s and 1930s fluctuated both widely and wildly (Table 31), being caught up irrevocably with the violent price changes suffered by tin and rubber—it is a barely credible fact that the value of the port's trade in 1932 was the lowest in the century, and can be compared only with the years at the end of the nineteenth century before any rubber had crossed its quays.

Of considerable interest and significance during the inter-war years, apart from the overwhelming effects on value imposed by world economic conditions, were gradual changes in the origin of Penang's import trade. Particularly noticeable from about 1933 onwards is the increasing volume of Japanese shipping arriving at Penang and the growing amount of goods of Asian origin reaching the port. These included bulky commodities such as cement and galvanized iron and especially low-priced cottons from India, Hong Kong and Japan. Table 32 illustrates the rapidity with which Japan established herself

TABLE 32

PENANG—IMPORTS OF COTTONS (PLAIN, DYED & PRINTED)
(in yards), 1932–1934

Source	1932	1933	1934
Japan	77,882	622,707	3,193,000
Hong Kong	49,490	64,400	14,400
China	2,362,261	1,543,485	1,077,934
Others	11,746,431	8,443,163	5,831,141
TOTAL	14,236,064	10,673,755	10,116,475

Source: Report of the Penang Chamber of Commerce for 1934.

as a leading exporter of cotton goods to Penang. In a period of generally declining business, Japanese cotton imports were soaring both relatively and absolutely. Indian textiles were also competing strongly in Penang, their quality constantly improving and their prices cheaper than anything Europe could offer.

Throughout the economic fluctuations of the 1920s and 1930s, and despite the limited employment opportunities outside the trading sector, Georgetown's population increased at a steady rate averaging over two per cent. per annum between the censuses of 1921 and 1931. An interesting aspect of the population structure of Penang during this period was the considerable advance towards levelling out the discrepancy between the numbers of males and females in the colony. The ratio of 650 females per 1,000 males in 1921, had increased to 797 per 1,000 by 1931, a fact resulting from the increasingly older established nature of the immigrant communities and to a growing willingness amongst Chinese to settle permanently, bringing their womenfolk from China, as the pioneering atmosphere of Malaya was passing.

It is probably true to say that, by the end of the First World War, Penang was almost entirely dependent economically on the mainland. Rubber, tin and—to a much less extent— tapioca were the staples of its trade, and the great bulk of these products came from the Malay states. Improved transport links with this hinterland were therefore urgently needed. The railway, so important in linking Penang with the Perak tinfields, had reached Prai from the south in 1903 and, following the peace settlement of 1909 with Siam, which placed Kedah under British settlement, rail construction began northwards from the junction at Bukit Mertajam. The line, single track metre gauge, reached Alor Star, the Kedah capital, in 1915 and by 1918 had crossed the border at Padang Besar to join up with the Royal Siam State Railway at Haadyai. The principal significance of this new railway connection was to stimulate plantation development in Kedah and southern Thailand, and rubber was to become the most important commodity reaching Penang from Thailand by land. Whilst the expansion of Penang's railway links with the peninsula was a live topic, there was some agitation for a direct transmontane line to the east coast states. The Chairman of the Penang Chamber of Commerce is on record in 1916 as saying that 'before Kelantan can be economically developed rail communication must be provided to Penang'.[9] There was little support for such a view, and when Kelantan did get its railway link (in 1931) it was with Singapore via Kuala Lipis and Gemas. It was not until the First Malaysia Plan (see p. 161 and below, p. 220) that a firm plan to link Kelantan with Penang, by road, was drawn up.

The ferry links between Georgetown and the mainland were improved in 1925, but the waterfront facilities in the port remained practically unchanged despite the increasing volume of trade. Recommendations to reclaim the foreshore of Weld Quay, made in 1907 and again in 1928, went unheeded, as did proposals to dredge the Penang River used for deliveries to oil mills, rice mills and the warehouses of salt importers. Some development took place on the mainland, however. In 1920 construction of wharves was begun at Prai, and in 1924 a slip-way was built at Bagan Dalam, Butterworth, for the maintenance and repair of the port's small craft, ferries and lighters. In the same year, the Straits Steamship Company acquired foreshore rights for the dockyard frontage at Sungei Nyok, on the Prai estuary, where a modernization programme was initiated and the building of specially designed coasters (the '75-tonners') undertaken. Further proposals to provide deep water accommodation along the Prai estuary were made during the 1930s, but generally met with opposition from the trading houses in Georgetown. Like the transport link with Kelantan, this development had to await the changed economic and political atmosphere of the post-war years.

When Penang was taken by the Japanese in 1942, its basic function was little different from what it had been before the First World War. Despite the economic difficulties that plagued the Malayan export economy between the wars, there had been no attempt to reduce the dependence of the colonial economy on its raw material exports. The economic geography of Penang was still that of a colonial trading link with overwhelming emphasis on the handling and processing of raw material exports and of a multitude of mainly consumer goods imports, and with a small manufacturing sector producing a limited range of commodities for the local market. Admittedly the number of industrial establishments had increased as the size of the port had grown, the volume of copra milled and exported as coconut oil rather than as raw copra increased considerably, for example, but the industrial base remained limited and, with the exception of the Straits Trading Company's tin smelter at Butterworth and a power station at Prai, the economic activity of the colony was located entirely in Georgetown.

The Changing Economic Geography of Penang since the Second World War

As discussed in Chapter 5 in relation to Malaya as a whole, the political and economic changes that followed the Second World War had a profound effect on Penang and produced considerable changes in its economic geography. In the immediate post-war years, Penang, in common with the rest of Malaya, was concerned with the rehabilitation or re-establishment of its traditional economic pursuits, and its success in rebuilding its trading activity is illustrated by Table 33. Since a large proportion of Penang's export trade was, and remains, accounted for by the tin and rubber output of the mainland, the successful recovery and development of those

TABLE 33

PENANG—VALUE OF FOREIGN TRADE, 1947–1959
(in $ millions)

	Imports	Exports	Total
1947	206·3	300·4	506·7
1948	280·2	416·8	697·0
1949	297·7	425·4	723·1
1950	438·5	990·2	1,428·7
1951	691·7	1,421·2	2,112·9
1952	571·0	870·2	1,441·2
1953	464·1	617·0	1,081·1
1954	442·3	655·6	1,097·9
1955	522·8	883·4	1,406·2
1956	597·6	944·2	1,541·8
1957	599·6	867·0	1,466·6
1958	547·7	734·7	1,282·4
1959	530·6	985·3	1,515·9

Source: Federation of Malaya Department of Statistics.

industries was a very important contribution to the recovery of the port's trade, whilst the boom associated with the Korean War period of 1950–53 raised the value of these raw material exports to record levels.

During the 1950s, however, the changed political and economic environment within which the port operated began to influence both the pattern and volume of its trade, whilst the new national emphasis on industrialization as one means to diversify the Malayan economy and to provide more employment opportunities for the fast growing population also had profound effects on Penang.

Perhaps the most striking change in the nature of Penang's trade has been the decline in its entrepot activities. The distinction between entrepot trade and direct trade is deeply rooted in Penang and, although perhaps difficult clearly to differentiate logically, the two categories are understood to refer to trade with Sumatra, Thailand and Burma on the one hand, and with mainland Malaya and the rest of the world on the other.* As illustrated by Table 30, Penang's trade with Malaya and with the rest of the world was expanding at the expense of trade with other South-east Asian markets as early as the turn of the century as the resources of the mainland were developed, and by the 1950s trade with Sumatra, Thailand and

TABLE 34

VALUE OF TRADE OF PENANG WITH INDONESIA,
THAILAND & BURMA, AND ENTREPOT TRADE AS
PERCENTAGE OF TOTAL FOREIGN TRADE, 1961–1969
(in $ thousands)

	Trade with Indonesia	Trade with Thailand	Trade with Burma	Entrepot Trade as percentage of total Foreign Trade
1961	153,990	145,562	22,637	17·6
1962	172,748	152,882	25,960	19·0
1963	106,215	148,770	26,956	15·3
1964	3,311	186,547	15,704	11·5
1965	682	202,378	7,125	10·8
1966	906	110,680	3,990	6·3
1967	15,715	67,184	4,663	4·9
1968	150,440	68,271	3,867	1·1
1969	145,236	55,041	4,441	0·9

Source: Department of Statistics.

Burma was averaging only between about 15 per cent. and 20 per cent., by value, of Penang's total foreign trade. Imports from these entrepot partners consisted largely of raw materials, especially tin, rubber and copra, and exports, much smaller in value and volume, of manufactured goods and foodstuffs.

Since 1960, the entrepot trade has declined drastically both in absolute value and as a percentage of Penang's total trade (Table 34). The principal cause underlying this decline is the economic nationalism of the port's entrepot partners whose aims of developing their own national ports and trading links as well as their own import-substitution industries are reducing

* This distinction is made in the trade statistics and is the basis of the official definition of entrepot trade in Penang.

the trade conducted on their behalf by Penang. Trade with Sumatra, suffering in the late 1950s and early 1960s by increasing Indonesian government regulation especially over the traditional barter trade, all but ceased during the period of military confrontation between Malaysia and Indonesia in the mid-1960s and, although recovering, is unlikely to regain its

TABLE 35

PENANG—VALUE OF TOTAL TRADE AND FREIGHT
TONNAGE OF GENERAL CARGO (excluding coal and
bulk petroleum) HANDLED, 1960–1969

	Value of Total Trade ($ millions)	General Cargo Handled (freight tonnage)
1960	1,880·4	3,232,117
1961	1,830·2	3,821,838
1962	1,841·3	3,511,911
1963	1,839·2	2,947,000
1964	1,793·7	2,745,204
1965	1,931·3	2,952,971
1966	1,816·2	2,525,221
1967	1,760·6	2,504,028
1968	2,028·7	2,086,789
1969	2,350·4	2,243,373

previous levels. Trade with Thailand, much of which consisted of tin ore and concentrates destined for the Penang smelters, was drastically reduced when Thailand began operating its own tin smelter at Phuket in mid-1965 and prohibited the further export of tin ore.[10]

Trade with Burma, a relatively insignificant entrepot partner in post-war years, is strictly controlled by the Burmese government and is likely to continue to decline as the nation develops its own trading facilities and industries. The depressed state of the tin industry in Burma, despite expansion elsewhere in South-east Asia, further limits trade with Penang.

Whilst the volume and value of Penang's entrepot trade have declined so markedly during the 1960s, its direct trade i.e. trade between Malaya (including that originating on Penang island itself) and the rest of the world other than Indonesia, Thailand and Burma, has not expanded in value to compensate for the loss and, except for a few years in the

TABLE 36

PENANG—STRUCTURE OF IMPORT TRADE, 1960-1969

Commodity Groups		Percentage of Trade in Commodity Groups (by value)									
		1960	1961	1962	1963	1964	1965	1966	1967	1968	1969
0, 1	Foods etc.	28·5	28·8	23·5	28·2	35·0	32·2	29·7	26·7	23·9	24·1
2, 3, 4	Crude Materials, Fuels, Oils	38·9	32·5	37·9	30·6	21·4	20·8	11·5	13·7	28·5	30·1
5, 6, 7, 8	Manufactures	31·6	31·6	37·9	40·5	42·9	46·3	57·7	55·4	44·4	43·1
9	Others	0·9	0·7	0·7	0·6	0·6	0·7	1·1	4·3	3·0	2·7

early 1960s when there were large shipments of iron ore from Prai to Japan, even the volume of trade has shown a tendency to decline (Table 35). This situtation is related to the limited economic development within Penang and its hinterland during the early and mid-1960s but especially to the growing competition within that hinterland, particularly its southern part, from Port Swettenham. Between 1961 and 1969 the percentage of West Malaysian foreign trade handled by Penang declined from 38 per cent. to 34 per cent.*

The developments at Port Swettenham are discussed below, but it may be noted here that improvements to communications in central Malaya, the expansion of facilities at Port Swettenham and the transfer of headquarters of many commercial firms from Singapore to Kuala Lumpur after independence are all contributing to the expansion of Port Swettenham's trade area at the expense of Penang.[11] Construction of the tin smelter at Klang, although its output was small compared with that of the two works in Penang†, drew some tin trade from Selangor which previously moved north to Penang.

The declining entrepot trade and the vigorous competition from Port Swettenham for the trade of at least part of Penang's Malayan hinterland are difficulties specific to Penang that are additional to the national economic problems associated with population growth and the need for diversification. Attempts to cope with both the specific and general problems are having a profound effect on the economic geography of Penang and include the improvement of port facilities, the development of manufacturing industry and the enlargement of the port's hinterland by the establishment of road communication with the east coast.

The increasing significance of mainland Malaya as the principal source and destination of Penang's trade since the beginning of the century has already been noted, and it has been seen (Table 34) that by the late 1960s over 95

---

* There were, however, significant changes in the nature of the imports handled by the port over the period as import-substitution industries became established on the mainland: particularly noticeable, as Table 36 indicates, were declines in crude materials and increases in manufactures, especially producer goods, on the import list.

† This smelter, opened in 1964, closed in 1969, see p. 172.

P

per cent. of the total foreign trade of the port consisted of direct trade, the whole of which, with the exception of a small amount of rubber and copra grown on the island, originated from the mainland. This situation leads to an exceptional amount of double handling, adds substantially to the costs of shipment and is not sound in principle.[12] The existence of commercial and processing facilities on the island and, in general, the opposition of the commercial interests of Georgetown largely had been successful before the Second

TABLE 37

CARGO HANDLED OVER PRAI WHARF, 1954–1959
(in long tons)

	Imports	Exports	Total
1954	193,477	202,670	396,147
1955	222,764	191,672	414,436
1956	232,352	394,357	626,709
1957	195,521	448,257	643,778
1958	149,389	442,455	591,844
1959	155,144	984,552	1,139,696

Source: Penang Chamber of Commerce, Annual Report, 1959.

World War in limiting the development of port facilities on the mainland. The first plan for deep water wharves on the mainland at Butterworth was drawn up in the late 1920s, but it was not until the great increase in the handling of bulk latex and iron ore over the Prai Wharf in the 1950s and the over-taxing of existing port facilities during the Korean War that the necessity for additional facilities was brought prominently to notice (Table 37).

The project for mainland wharves was examined in great detail by the Federal Ports Committee in 1952 and the conclusion reached that no immediate necessity existed for deep water wharves at Butterworth and an alternative proposal recommended that such wharves should be constructed at Prai in view of the location there of the railway terminal. The relative merits of Prai and the Butterworth site at Bagan Luar were the subjects of reports by consulting engineers in 1955 who concluded that, on grounds of cheapness and of efficiency of layout, the Bagan Luar site was to be preferred.

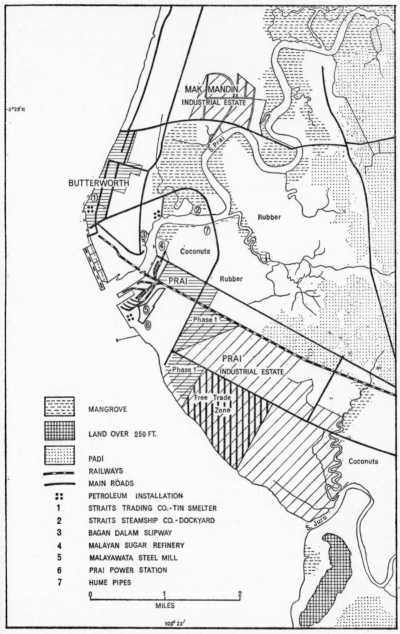

Figure 19. Butterworth—Prai

The decision to extend the railway across the Prai River to Butterworth nullified much of the argument, based on rail access, in favour of Prai. The Penang Port Commission's recommendation for the construction of deep water wharves between the ferry terminal at Butterworth and the north bank of the Prai River (Figure 19) which involved the filling and reclamation of about 150 acres of mangrove swamp and sea bed, was accepted by the Federal Government for the period 1961–70. The wharf project was originally designed to provide six conventional cargo berths and associated storage facilities, but the recent advances in the field of containerization led to substantial changes in plan and the decision to complete three conventional berths and two container berths with ancillary facilities. The completion of the project in 1970 made Butterworth the first port in South-east Asia capable of handling containerized cargo.[13]

The construction of the new wharves at Bagan Luar is a major step in the movement of the economic centre of gravity of Penang from Georgetown to Butterworth/Prai, and cargo handled by these wharves will be additional to that already passing through the bulk latex and iron ore facilities at Prai, the petroleum wharves and storage depots at Butterworth and Prai, the Straits Trading Co's tin smelter and jetties at Butterworth and the various privately owned jetties and godowns along the Prai River unless the use of these latter is replaced by the use of the new wharves. It seems likely that the provision of deep water facilities, adequate storage space (especially compared with the crowded Georgetown water-front) and the elimination of the ferry crossing necessary for any mainland trade handled at Georgetown will outweigh the advantages of traditional usage and the existence of banking and commercial facilities possessed by the island. The time will surely come, anyway, when shipping offices, insurance companies and similar commercial undertakings will do business on the mainland side of the channel.

Industrial development in Penang is also favouring the mainland. Early industrial development at Butterworth was clearly related to local raw material supplies—the tin smelter, rice mills and saw mills—but since independence there has been a marked tendency for new industrial undertakings to choose to locate on the mainland rather than on the island, especially since the establishment of the Mak Mandin industrial estate in 1961. The marked preference for the mainland by industry may be seen to date from 1953 when a range of import duties was imposed by the federal government on commodities entering the Malayan customs area, which does not include Penang island. Manufacturers on the mainland who aimed to serve the domestic market, as did most industries

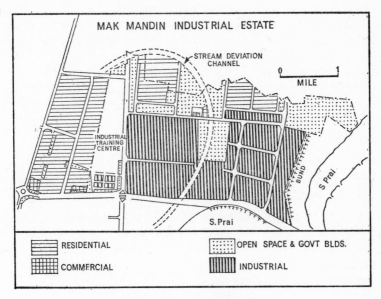

Figure 20. Mak Mandin

in the early import-substitution phase of industrial growth, clearly had an advantage over competitors in Georgetown, whose finished products faced not only ferry charges but import duty on entering the mainland, whereas mainland manufacturers were often able to obtain customs exemption on imported raw materials. There seems little doubt that the maintenance of Penang island's free port status has been a major factor responsible for limiting industrial development in Georgetown despite the local labour supply, immediate local market and the provision and planned development of three small industrial sites at Sungei Pinang, Makloon Road and Weld Quay and another at Bayan Lepas.

Apart from the advantages of being within the protective walls of the customs area, the mainland has other obvious ones for the location of industry, including plentiful potential sites and direct land communication with the national market. When the Penang State Government selected the site for the state's first industrial complex in 1961, it was necessarily on the mainland, and an area of 652 acres to the east of Butterworth, adjoining a number of already existing industrial establishments, was chosen. Bounded to the south and east by the Prai River (Figure 20), much of the land was low-lying and traversed by the Mak Mandin stream which gave the estate its name. Filling costs consequently formed a large portion of the development costs and, even with filling, factories on the estate need to be constructed on piles.[14] By the end of 1967, 34 factory lots had been allocated, eight factories were completed and five more were under construction. An interesting element of the industrial development at Mak Mandin is the construction of industrial terrace buildings for small scale industries, a modern adaptation of the traditional blocks of Chinese shop-houses.

A second area, formerly plantation land and swamp, is being developed for industrial purposes between the railway and the Juru River south of Prai. Here a 2,500 acre Prai industrial complex is planned and sites on phase 1 were available for occupation by 1968. Between 500 and 700 acres of this area lying between the railway and the coast are designated as a free trade zone, presumably in anticipation of the inclusion of Penang island within the customs area at some future date (see p. 221).

The nature of the industry being attracted to the Butterworth estate was analysed in Chapter 5 (see pp. 166–168), where it was noted that emphasis was on a narrower range of import-substitution goods than was true of the industrial estates of central Malaya. Nevertheless, the establishment of the Malayawata iron and steel works and the beginning of the neighbouring tinplate works at Prai put Penang in the fore-front of second phase industrialization in Malaysia. Provided these industries can prove fully viable when operating without the special considerations they currently receive, Penang, with its expanding harbour facilities and existing trading links, is well suited for industrial development aiming at

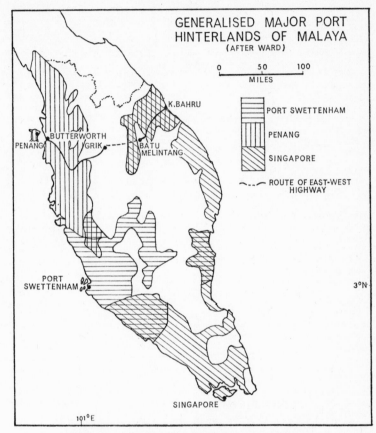

Figure 21. Major Port Hinterlands of Malaya

export markets. Future industrial distribution in West Malaysia may well show a contrast between central Malaya, with its major national market serving as a continuing attraction for import-substitution industries, especially those whose capacity is such that one or two plants can meet the whole of the national demand, and north-west Malaya, whose raw materials and trading links, favour it for export-oriented manufacturing.

The relatively limited local market for goods manufactured in Penang is a function both of its position peripheral to West Malaysia and of the historically developed transport links which limit the economic distribution of its goods to the north-west coast. The establishment of direct land communication with the north-east coast would not only extend Penang's hinterland for trading purposes but also increase the market area for its manufactures. This doubly advantageous role that such a link would play accounts for the strong support in Penang for the east-west highway that is planned to link Butterworth with Kota Bharu by way of Grik and Batu Melintang (Figure 21). Such a highway will do more than strengthen Penang's trade and industry—as indeed is intended—since it will provide accessible markets and tide water for the products of Kelantan and may well be expected to stimulate agricultural output especially of rubber, oil palm and rice, in the north-east. It is also highly probable that new tin bearing land will be opened up in north Perak thanks to the highway. Industrially, however, Penang is likely to be the major beneficiary, unless manufacturing in the north-east is to be doubly protected, since goods from the established north-west will have ready access to the small market of Kelantan.

The very considerable changes in the economic functions of Penang, which, although apparent in pre-war years, have become most marked since about 1950, raise the question of the relevance of the continuing free port status of the island. As analysed in Chapter 3, freedom of trade was a basic factor in the growth of the colonial economy and contributed a very great deal to the economic development of Malaya, at least until the First World War. The disadvantages of some aspects of the open economy became apparent between the wars (Chapter 4) and when the Malayan Union was constituted as the first attempt to re-cast the political structure of Malaya in 1946, Penang was included in the Malayan customs area. This drastic break with tradition roused considerable opposition, as did the whole concept of the Malayan Union itself of course, and free port status was restored, but to the island only. The situation was reviewed in 1956 by a Working Party[15] whose recommendation was that the island should remain duty-free, a conclusion strongly influenced by the views of the representatives of the three Chambers of Commerce (European, Chinese and Indian). This conclusion ignored the effects on the island's industries of cheap duty-free imports from overseas which already were restricting Georgetown's range of possible manufacturing,* the uneconomic nature of raw material imports from mainland Malaya owing to the export duties on commodities such as rubber and copra†, and the customs barrier that surrounded the obvious mainland market‡. By the late 1960s as the entrepot trade, the traditional *raison d'être* of free port status, continued to decline as a proportion of total trade, the anachronism of the position of Penang island outside the customs area became even more apparent and it came to be assumed, at least in trading circles, that free port status would in due course be withdrawn, and the withdrawal accompanied by the provision of extensive duty-free zones and warehousing facilities and provision for the prompt draw-back of duty already paid on goods subsequently re-exported.[17] The abolition of the free port status of Penang island is not likely to affect the shift of economic emphasis already noted from island to mainland but it could well assist industrial growth in Georgetown which has been practically stagnant since 1953, despite the existence there of the largest single concentration of population in north Malaya.

II. SINGAPORE

Trade & Industry in the Colonial Period

The foundation in 1819 of the East India Company's

---

* Cases were reported in the late 1950s of Hong Kong and Japanese shoes costing half the Penang price, of Thai bee-hoon (a rice-flour vermicelli) of high quality and low price causing the closure of local factories, and of cheap canned food from Singapore creating stiff competition for local canneries.[16]

† Georgetown oil millers have always relied on imported copra, especially from Sumatra, and the export duty on the mainland Malayan copra reinforced this dependence which, in view of the decline in the entrepot trade, is undesirable.

‡ And which subjected even weekend shoppers from the mainland to the tedium and irritation of customs examination and the payment of duty on the most ordinary domestic purchases.

settlement on Singapore island was, as seen in Chapter 3, the outcome primarily of Stamford Raffles's realization of the limitations of the location of Penang for the purpose of forwarding Britain's commercial interests in the archipelago. The very great commercial progresss of the colony, which led it rapidly to outgrow Penang and in due course to become the major trading centre in South-east Asia, peopled by the largest single concentration of overseas Chinese, is the basic factor underlying both Singapore's political difficulties vis-à-vis peninsular Malaya and its emerging role as the principal industrial area in the region.

Singapore island, some 24 miles by 14 miles in size, is roughly lozenge-shaped with a coastline indented by broad estuaries that are tending to become mangrove swamps and is separated from mainland Malaya by the mile wide Johore Strait. Intrusive granite, principally in a squarish north-central mass, underlies more than half of the island, which structurally is a continuation of the folds that extend southwards from Gunong Tahan on the Pahang-Kelantan border, but outcrops rarely at the surface. On the main central mass of the island the relief is low, round and smooth, though the surface, with an average height of no more than 200 feet, is broken by a number of steep hills described by Dobby as monadnocks standing above the advanced peneplanation of the Sunda platform.[18] West of the central granite mass occurs a sequence of sandstones and shales which dip steeply away from the granite and on which has developed a typical scarp and vale landscape. To the extreme south-west of the granite, a valley along the contact zone is succeeded by the 250 feet high Mt. Faber Ridge, an erosional scarp, broken by transverse valley incisions, that can be recognized beyond Keppel Harbour in Blakang Mati island. East of the granite lies a hundred foot platform of alluvial debris that reaches the south-east coast as 80 feet high cliffs and that probably evolved from a mainland drainage system during a higher sea level phase.

The initial harbour of Raffles's settlement consisted of an extensive bay on the south coast that extended from Mt. Palmer (about one mile south-south-west of the mouth of the Singapore River) and reached across the river mouth to the Kallang Basin. The banks of the Singapore River developed as the principal focus of warehousing, especially the present-day Boat Quay area on the river's right bank, and commercial activity spread to neighbouring 'Commercial Square' (renamed Raffles Place in 1858). By 1830, the town and its harbour facilities had spread westwards along the coast, the latter to the sheltered channel between the coast and the islands of Pulau Brani and Blakang Mati. All shipping anchored in the Roads between the mouths of the Singapore and Rochore Rivers and goods were landed across the beaches or on the banks of the Singapore River near which the earliest Chinese settlement grew up.

Raffles's Singapore, as already described earlier in this book, attracted both commerce and settlers very rapidly. The majority of immigrants were Chinese of a variety of dialect groups from South China but with Hokkiens, Cantonese and Tiechius predominating. Raffles planned his city on an ethnic basis with particular districts for particular racial or cultural groups. The European town was placed on a fairly extensive and well-drained site adjacent to the government area, which was established on the north of the Singapore River. The Arab and Bugis zones were confined between the coast and the Rochore River, beyond which lay a swamp, where the sea-faring Bugis could take advantage of the river mouth and coastline. The Chinese, who, Raffles presumed, 'from the number . . . already settled, and the peculiar attractions of the place for that industrious race . . . will always form by far the largest portion of the community',[19] were located next to the mercantile establishments on the south bank of the Singapore River, whilst the Indians were given an area also fairly close to the commercial core with a river frontage of over a quarter of a mile.[20]

The attraction of Singapore for the Chinese was based to a considerable extent on the advantages to be gained under the government of the East India Company that they had come to grasp during the previous thirty-three years of Penang's existence. The readiness with which the British welcomed to the island all newcomers who were likely to contribute to the expansion of its commerce was reinforced by the ideal location of Singapore as a centre for the ring of

Chinese trading ports in the western Nanyang.* The proportion of the total population represented by the Chinese grew rapidly (Table 2). By 1840 they were half the population of the colony and outnumbered the Malays, the next most numerous group, by two to one.

Singapore's early function as an entrepot for the South-east Asian region, serving as a collecting centre for the produce of the archipelago and as a distributor of the manufactures of Europe and North America, was carried out with limited harbour facilities, despite the generally continuing growth in the volume of trade. Apart from the cargoes and passengers that were landed direct from the mail steamers at wharves in the so-called New Harbour, between the south shore of Singapore and the small islands off the coast, as late as 1864 most goods were still handled along the banks of the Singapore River, especially in the circular basin formed by the river between its mouth and Elgin Bridge a quarter of a mile upstream. The right bank of the basin, Boat Quay, was lined with a complete crescent of godowns and almost the entire river frontage alongside them was taken up with the loading and discharging of lighters or *tongkangs* which ferried cargoes between the godowns and the ships at anchor in the harbour. It was estimated that, in the mid-1860s, three quarters of the island's trade, valued in total at some £12 million sterling per annum (p. 76), was handled in the Singapore River.[22]

The trading boom of the 1870s that followed the opening of the Suez Canal and the linking of Singapore to London by telegraphic cable (p. 76) stimulated—as it had in a smaller way in Penang—a considerable improvement of Singapore's waterfront facilities. During the 1860s the increasing use of the sheltered channel of New Harbour by the steamship

* Wang Gungwu describes the Chinese division of the 'Southern Ocean' into the eastern and western Nanyang by an imaginery line north-south through the centre of Borneo. To the east of the line, trade was centred on Luzon. To the west, where existed commercially more developed territories, there never had been a centre satisfactory to the Chinese. Since the decline of Palembang before the fifteenth century and since the fall of Malacca to the Portuguese, the Chinese had moved uncertainly to and from Siam, Johore and Java. By the last years of the eighteenth and the first decades of the nineteenth century the Chinese had closed their ring of trading ports in the western Nanyang by establishing settlements in the Sambas in west Borneo, in Bangka-Billiton and in the Riau-Lingga archipelago and several more on both sides of the Straits of Malacca. For this chain of ports both Batavia and Penang were comparatively remote.[21]

companies had been accompanied by the banding together of
commercial interests to improve port facilities, and the Patent

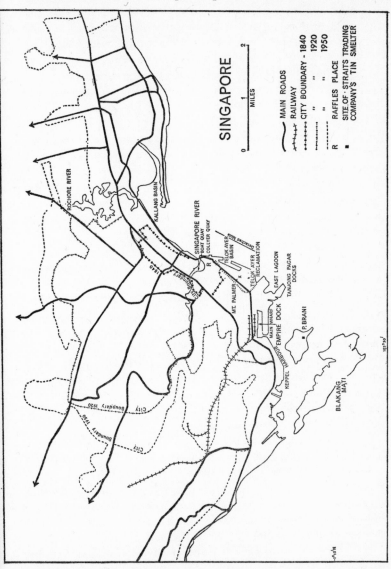

Figure 22. Singapore—City and Port

Slip and Dock Company was formed in 1861 and the Tanjong
Pagar Dock Company in 1863. As the volume of steamer

traffic increased after 1869, the Tanjong Pagar Dock Company expanded its facilities in the western anchorages—now known as Keppel Harbour—and subsequent amalgamations led to its achievement of a virtual monopoly of the port services except for those provided by the Peninsula and Orient Company. A clear division of the port subsequently emerged, with Keppel Harbour handling ocean borne commerce and the bigger vessels, and the Singapore River and Kallang Basin, at the mouth of the Rochore River, handling island trade carried by local craft. A direct road link between Keppel Harbour and the commercial centre of the port was not constructed until 1878, however, when the Settlements government began to reclaim Telok Ayer bay and to build the Anson-Robinson Road (Figure 22). Until this time, ninety per cent. of goods landed had finally to be transported by lighters.[23] Despite short-lived steam tramway services, an initially unsuccessful attempt to obtain an extension of the Singapore-Kranji railway through the town to the docks*, and even plans for a canal, bullock carts and handcarts constituted the principal means of conveyance of goods between the docks and the commercial centre of Singapore until superseded by motor transport in the 1920s. Slow and bulky, the bullock carts created great congestion as the volume of traffic grew, and were very subject to loss of goods by theft.[24] The extension of the Singapore-Kranji railway southwards from the Tank Road Station in 1906–07, was of no assistance in easing the traffic problem between the docks and the city centre, since it entered the docks from the west and merely served to link the wharves with Tank Road.

The most significant aspects of Singapore's trade between the opening of the Suez Canal and the First World War were, as they have already been seen to be for Penang, a very considerable increase in volume and value and a gradual re-orientation, with the Malayan peninsula emerging as the major single trading partner. As was noted earlier (p. 202), changes in the exchange value of the dollar make comparisons of the value of trade over a number of years misleading, but the nearly sevenfold increase in the tonnage of shipping

---

* Singapore was linked by railway to Kranji, on the Johore Strait, in 1902, with the city terminus in Tank Road (now part of Clemenceau Avenue).

cleared with cargo between 1878 and 1911 (Table 38) is a fair indication of the expansion of Singapore's commerce over the period. The growing importance of the Malayan

TABLE 38

SINGAPORE—SHIPPING & TRADE, 1878–1911

	Vessels cleared with cargo[a]		Value of Trade		
	Number	Tonnage	Imports ($'000)	Exports ($'000)	Total ($'000)
1878	1,923	1,048,236	47,259·3	40,021·9	87,281·3
1881	2,230	1,621,652	70,699·7[b]	58,001·2	128,700·9
1886	2,866	2,290,280	77,277·5	60,578·6	137,856·2
1891	3,453	2,609,906	103,012·2	91,725·5	194,737·7
1895	4,126	3,227,286	157,968·8	135,126·3	293,095·2
1901	4,715	5,135,912	254,128·3	213,108·8	467,237·1
1906	4,993	6,139,336	252,834·5[c]	228,872·7	481,707·2
1911	5,424	7,129,028	285,192·4	240,280·9	525,473·4

(a) excluding native craft.
(b) dollar valued at 3s. 9d. sterling.
(c) dollar valued at 2s. 4d. sterling.
Source: Straits Settlements Blue Books.

TABLE 39

SINGAPORE—PERCENTAGE OF TRADE WITH VARIOUS REGIONS, 1878–1911

	1878	1881	1886	1891	1895	1901	1906	1911
Malay Peninsula	7	5	10	9	14	16	18	16
Other Straits S.	8	7	5	4	4	3	3	5
Siam	6	8	6	6	7	7	8	7
Netherlands Indies	20	21	18	20	18	18	17	17
China	2	2	3	3	2	2	2	2
Japan	1	1	2	1	7	2	1	2
U.S.A.	1	4	4	4	4	6	5	6
Other Foreign	14	11	14	17	14	12	10	12
Other Brit. Cols.	23	19	20	19	17	21	21	20
U.K.	21	23	18	17	13	14	16	13

Source: Straits Settlements Blue Books.

peninsula to the trading activity of Singapore is very apparent from Table 39. By 1895 a larger proportion of the port's trade was carried on with the Malay states than with the United Kingdom itself, and a more detailed analysis (Table

TABLE 40

TRADE OF SINGAPORE WITH THE MALAY STATES, 1886–1911

($ thousands)

	1886		1891		1895		1901		1906		1911	
	Imports	Exports	Imports	Exports	Imports	Exports	Imports	Exports	Imports	Exports	Imports	Exports
Johore	4,397.6	3,036.5	4,691.4	2,930.7	8,199.0	4,591.5	11,072.4	5,530.1	8,833.9	3,820.3	8,787.0	5,268.8
Perak	59.1	63.9	1,324.8	80.5	4,468.2	844.6	13,337.6	2,861.2	11,237.5	6,298.6	10,907.8	7,582.0
Selangor	2,234.2	1,116.1	4,291.2	1,350.0	10,322.7	5,889.3	1,739.0	11,046.2	26,762.2	14,796.6	17,216.3	16,487.1
Sungei Ujong	278.7	191.8	971.9	561.6	1,480.9	964.6	5,435.8	2,236.3	8,494.3[a]	2,742.8[a]	5,567.5[a]	3,395.7[a]
Kedah	—	—	6.7	5.2	—	—	—	1.5	—	—	2.9	9.7
East Coast States	819.1	1,268.0										
Kelantan			191.6	318.5	300.6	322.3	969.8	703.3	1,232.3	844.0	1,724.1	1,779.6
Pahang			150.1	310.8	687.5	605.5	1,737.4	820.0	1,916.8	1,034.7	3,095.1	2,037.4
Patani			59.4	82.3	144.2	244.9	481.0	363.4	556.0	246.3	—	—
Singora			253.3	135.0	260.9	244.5	601.1	384.1	641.9	510.7	—	—
Trengganu			410.1	343.3	381.3	270.3	1,117.9	906.1	1,525.1	7,94.3	1,846.0	846.8

(a) Negri Sembilan

Source: Straits Settlements Blue Books.

40) of this trade shows that it was predominantly carried on with those states whose primary exports of tin and plantation products were rapidly growing. Trade with the Netherlands Indies was becoming proportionately less significant, but only to a minor degree, and its actual value continued to rise. A significant fall in trade with the other Straits Settlements reflected the increasingly independent links being developed by Penang, and the decline of Malacca as an entrepot for central Malaya as the centre of economic gravity moved north to Selangor. Trade with China, an important element in the commerce of early Singapore, had become much less significant, and Japanese trade, though erratic in the proportion it contributed to total Singapore trade during the period under discussion, was growing considerably in total value. It was particularly large in the 1890s when coal shipments from Japan to Singapore increased phenomenally, owing both to the relative cheapness of Japanese coal compared with Welsh and especially to the lifting in 1885 of a ban previously placed on its storage at Tanjong Pagar.[25]

As was true of Penang, the censuses of the Straits Settlements in the late nineteenth and early twentieth centuries give tantalizing statistical glimpses of the industrial activities of Singapore without providing material adequate for the construction of an accurate picture of the port's manufacturing status. The censuses of 1871 and 1881, which give a breakdown of occupations, show an increase of 45 per cent. in commercial employment in Singapore, a percentage increase proportional to total population growth over the decade, whilst industrial employment grew by only 13 per cent., but, as commented earlier (p. 204), 'industrial' as a description of the occupations so classified is rather misleading, since a large proportion of this category, in both years, was made up of boatmen, fishermen and labourers. In 1891, 1901 and 1911, the return of occupations was replaced by a return of manufactures, which had the advantage of providing a clearer picture of the types of manufacturing carried on in Singapore but failed to provide a measure of their relative contributions to the city's economy. The picture that emerges, however, as described in Chapter 3, is of a city whose manufacturing was limited to a narrow range of food and drink processing,

Q

the provision of building materials and of a few basic commodities such as soap and pottery. The major changes apparent in the breakdowns of manufacturing premises between 1891 and 1911 are a decline in the number of pineapple canning and packing premises, of sago manufactories and of rice mills (the result, presumably, of the concentration of these activities into larger, more highly mechanized, factories) and an increase in the number of sawmills. In 1887, however, was established the Straits Trading Co's tin smelting works on Palau Brani, (p. 91), which became the principal industrial undertaking in Singapore.

The export of agricultural produce from the mainland, especially from Johore, whose Chinese gambier and tapioca planters were pioneering the southern river valleys and both coasts in the second half of the nineteenth century (pp. 95–96), was an important element in Singapore's export trade (Table 40), and the rise of the rubber planting industry at the turn of the century added to the port's commerce. Particularly important during the boom period of the rubber industry between 1900 and 1910, however, was the growing influence of Singapore as a rubber market. Initially, the growth of the Singapore rubber trade was slow because estates sold their rubber in London, but in 1908 several European firms began selling small quantities in Singapore, where Chinese planters were also selling some of their lower grades through shops in the town. In 1911, the first local rubber auction was held by the Singapore Rubber Association, and during the First World War, when London auctions were temporarily suspended, Singapore became well established as a rubber market.[26]

By the end of the First World War, the pattern of Singapore's trade had clearly taken a new shape. The trend towards emphasis on mainland Malaya as its primary hinterland was strengthened by the increasing volume of rubber emanating from the peninsula and, with Singapore now established as a rubber selling centre, the port began to provide concomitant grading, packing and processing functions. The service and maintenance needs of the port, building and construction activity and consumer demand began to stimulate other manufacturing activities, but trade continued to dominate the economy. Commercial and financial services for the expanding trade were provided by predominantly British-owned commercial houses and banks, which mostly grew out of small nineteenth-century merchanting partnerships. The

TABLE 41

SINGAPORE—VALUE OF TRADE, 1915–1939
(in $ millions)

	Imports	Exports	Total
1915	338·2	303·9	642·0
1916	430·8	377·9	808·7
1917	528·0	491·8	1,019·8
1918	576·2	496·6	1,072·8
1919	727·0	720·3	1,447·4
1920	890·1	724·3	1,614·4
1921	484·8	415·8	900·6
1922	456·5	415·0	871·5
1923	580·3	512·8	1,093·1
1924	636·9	551·0	1,188·0
1925	1,001·5	899·9	1,901·4
1926	997·1	874·8	1,871·8
1927	930·6	791·6	1,722·2
1928	647·8	517·5	1,165·3
1929	640·2	511·0	1,151·2
1930	519·6	392·6	912·2
1931	330·6	273·8	604·4
1932	284·1	210·5	494·6
1933	254·0	230·6	484·7
1934	335·6	305·3	640·8
1935	335·6	319·0	654·6
1936	355·5	335·9	691·4
1937	469·2	456·1	925·2
1938	361·3	310·5	671·8
1939	414·9	405·8	820·6

Sources: Straits Settlements Returns of Imports and Exports. Malaya, Returns of Foreign Imports and Exports.

interests of these agency houses had expanded from the handling of the export trade in raw materials and import trade in manufactured goods, to direct and indirect control of plantations and tin mines and the wholesale and retail distribution of manufactures. Table 41 illustrates the value of Singapore's trade during the inter-war years and, as was true of Penang on the smaller scale, its annual fluctuations faithfully reflected the vicissitudes of the tin and rubber prices. Low trading values in 1921 and 1922 were followed by the temporary recovery associated with the Stevenson scheme and the aftermath of the Bandoeng Pool and a record trade turn-over was achieved in 1925. Thereafter values declined, to reach a trough in 1933, when the total value of Singapore's trade was the lowest since 1910. The agency houses were affected by the low prices through their tin and plantation interests as well as through the falling commercial turn-over which was exacerbated by the ability of the port's Chinese merchants to exploit the shift in demand towards cheap manufactured products from Japan and China. Most of the

TABLE 42

SINGAPORE—STRUCTURE OF TRADE, 1936
(in $ thousands)

Commodity Groups		Imports	Exports
0, 1	Foods, Beverages, Tobacco	67,309	33,947
2, 3, 4	Crude materials, Fuels, Oils	162,999	260,647
5, 6, 7, 8	Manufactures	43,632	3,768

N.B. Only commodities with a value exceeding $1 million have been included.
Source: Hughes and You, pp. 10–11.

agency houses were able to carry on through the depression years, however, thanks to resources built up over many years, and it was the small Chinese and Indian traders and the unemployed who bore the brunt and bitterness of the depression.[27]

An analysis of the structure of Singapore's trade in 1936 (Table 42) reveals its continuing emphasis on the import and export of raw materials and fuels. The import and export of rubber, and the import of tin ore and concentrate and the export of tin metal in blocks, ingots, bars or slabs represented the major proportion of trade in this category, but there was also a substantial volume of petroleum products handled. As a consequence of its location and its proximity to the oilfields of Sarawak, Sumatra and Netherlands Borneo, Singapore had become a major storage and distributing centre for mineral oils for the Far East, Africa and Australia, with installations on the islands of Pulau Sambu, Pulau Bukum and Pulau

Sebarok near the western entrance to the harbour.[28] Particularly noticeable is the very small value of manufactures exported, a fact which reflects not only the entire absence of any export-oriented manufacturing but also the very limited re-export of manufactured goods. Most imported manufactures (the largest single item being cotton piece goods) were presumably absorbed by Singapore itself—goods destined for Singapore's former entrepot partners in the South-east Asian region now were imported direct through ports such as Saigon, Batavia, Belawan and Surabaya.

During the interwar years, the population of Singapore grew consistently faster than did that of Malaya as a whole. Between the censuses of 1911 and 1921, the population of the island grew at an average rate of 3·2 per cent. per annum whilst the growth rate of Malaya was only 2·3 per cent. per annum; in the 1920s the difference was relatively less great, Singapore's average annual rate being 2·9 per cent. compared with Malaya's 2·7 per cent, a fact probably related to the influx of population to the west coast states during the prosperous years of the rubber industry in the middle 1920s. Between 1931 and 1938, Singapore's population grew at the high average rate of 3·5 per cent per annum, despite the depression and the quota on the immigration of foreign born male Chinese. The increase during the 1930s was particularly marked amongst the Chinese and Indian communities and was very probably due to an influx of unemployed labour from the mainland states, where the effects of the international tin and rubber control schemes were increasingly felt.[29]

By the 1931 census, the Chinese community made up three quarters of the Singapore population, compared with 72 per cent. in 1911. Especially noticeable during the period was the gradual increase in the percentage of Chinese females, who had made up only 26 per cent. of the total Chinese community in 1911, but accounted for 38 per cent. by 1931. The lack of quotas on alien Chinese female immigrants until 1938, as seen in Chapter 4, contributed to a further evening out of the sex ratio during the mid-1930s.

There were various improvements to transport and dockyard facilities in Singapore between the wars. The railway, which had reached Johore Bahru by 1909, was extended across the Johore Strait to the Kranji terminus of the Singapore line on a causeway in 1923 and, although this now gave the port direct rail communication with its principal hinterland, the traffic carried by the railway to the harbour represented only a very small proportion of inward or outward clearance.

Under the Straits Settlements Ports Ordinance of 1913, the Singapore Dock Board, which had been formed to take over the Tanjong Pagar Dock Co. Ltd. and the New Harbour Dock Co. Ltd., when these undertakings had been expropriated by the Settlements government in 1905*, was superseded by the government-owned, self-financing Singapore Harbour Board. The newly created Board proceeded with the construction of the present Main Wharves and the creation of the Empire Dock together with two berths to the west of it. This work, which removed most of the pre-existing wharves, was completed by 1918. Subsequently, other private wharves were acquired and extensions carried out in the early 1930s. In 1932 the Telok Ayer reclamation, commencement of which had begun following a consultant's report in 1901 and which had encountered heavy technical difficulties, was completed. The reclaimed area consisted of a long frontage divided by a tidal basin for lighters with depths alongside varying from six to twelve feet. One main intention of the construction of the quays and basin was to draw business from the ever-congested Singapore River—an objective not achieved, due primarily to conservatism on the part of the Chinese and Indian interests owning godowns and businesses on the Singapore River.[30] In 1934, Singapore's first civil airport was constructed, on land reclaimed from mangrove swamps at the mouth of the Kallang River.

During the later 1920s and early 1930s, efforts were begun to improve the residential areas of the city, especially following the Singapore Improvement Ordinance of 1927 which vested planning and slum clearance powers in the Singapore Improvement Trust. From 1927 to 1932 the Trust concentrated chiefly on the laying out and widening of roads and on the

* The two private undertakings, amalgamated in 1899, were unable to finance development on the scale demanded by Malaya at the time when it was on the threshold of great economic expansion. The government therefore took them over, on the payment of £3.5 million compensation.

opening up of back lanes through blocks of back to back buildings. Some swamp land that had been acquired for improvement was filled. Housing for the general public, other than under improvement schemes, was not started until 1936, after the government was convinced that private enterprise could not tackle the job.[31]

Although Singapore had more than doubled its population between the outbreaks of the First and the Second World Wars, the value of its trade in 1939, as a result of the depression, was less than a third greater than it had been in 1915 (Table 41) and the structure of that trade, as demonstrated by Table 42, was still dominated by the import and export of raw materials, the latter after some processing. Just before the outbreak of the Second World War E. H. G. Dobby summed up the economic role of Singapore by declaring:

> in no case does it add anything to value by manufacture; its function is purely that of handling, forwarding, shipping, reshipping, breaking bulk, distributing, collecting—in other words, acting as major carrier of the East. For this reason its population is one of go-betweens and middlemen, whose profit is more of a commission than value added by work.[32]

The only sign of manufacturing was the recent appearance of Bata Shoe manufactories to make use of local rubber, an idea which had 'been tried before and failed—so many of the natives prefer to go barefoot, and freight costs on piece goods defeat any advantage of cheap local manufacture'.[33]

Singapore since the Second World War

The major economic changes that have been brought about in Singapore since 1950 have been discussed in Chapter 5, and it remains necessary here primarily to consider some of the specific developments that have taken place in the port's trading activities and in its urban landscape, especially in relation to harbour and industrial growth. Singapore's trade since 1950, when in general it had recovered to its pre-war position, necessarily reflects the structural changes that have been taking place in the island's economy since that date and also certain, probably mainly temporary, interruptions to trading patterns caused by political events, especially by the 'confrontation' with Indonesia. Specifically, changes in the pattern of trade reflect differences between the character of the traditional entrepot trade and of the currently develop-

TABLE 43

SINGAPORE—PERCENTAGE OF TRADE BY VALUE WITH VARIOUS REGIONS, 1961–1969

A. IMPORTS

	1961	1963	1965	1966	1967	1968	1969
Peninsular Malaya	23·1	20·7	23·2	23·2	19·1	15·9	17·5
Sabah and Sarawak	5·7	3·5	5·9	5·5	5·2	4·7	4·9
China	4·1	5·8	5·9	6·7	8·8	9·1	6·7
Thailand	3·8	3·3	3·9	4·0	3·3	3·3	2·7
India	2·1	3·1	1·5	1·4	1·2	1·1	0·9
U.K.	13·0	11·7	10·9	10·0	8·0	7·8	6·7
U.S.A.	6·0	6·2	5·1	5·2	5·6	6·8	7·8
West Europe[a]	5·1	5·0	4·7	4·4	4·8	4·5	5·7
Japan	10·8	11·1	11·1	11·4	12·4	13·6	16·3
Australia	4·0	4·2	4·4	4·7	4·5	4·3	3·9
Hong Kong	3·5	3·3	2·9	2·8	2·9	2·8	2·7
Others	18·9	22·2	20·7	20·8	24·2	26·1	24·1

B. EXPORTS

	1961	1963	1965	1966	1967	1968	1969
Peninsular Malaya	28·4	31·5	31·2	26·9	23·6	19·4	16·4
Sabah and Sarawak	5·3	6·7	9·4	8·5	7·8	6·9	6·5
China	0·4	0·5	0·7	4·1	2·7	2·1	3·7
Thailand	2·7	3·0	2·3	3·5	3·7	4·4	3·8
India	1·5	1·1	0·8	0·8	0·6	0·5	0·8
U.K.	7·9	6·3	6·4	5·5	6·1	6·3	5·8
U.S.A.	7·2	7·2	4·2	4·8	7·0	8·5	10·7
West Europe[a]	7·4	6·3	4·9	4·6	4·7	4·8	5·6
Japan	5·6	4·3	3·7	3·7	4·5	7·1	7·1
Australia	2·5	2·7	3·1	2·1	2·1	2·3	2·6
Hong Kong	2·1	2·8	4·4	3·6	3·3	3·6	3·0
Others	29·0	27·6	28·8	32·1	33·9	34·1	34·0

(a) France, Italy, West Germany, Belgium and Netherlands.
Source: Singapore International Chamber of Commerce.

ing trade with its higher proportion of retained imports and domestic exports.

The general structural pattern of the trade of Singapore is largely determined by the structure of what traditionally has been called the entrepot trade since, of the two components of total trade, entrepot and home, the entrepot is the larger.[34] The definition of entrepot trade in the Singapore context, however, is extremely difficult since the term is used rather loosely to describe a trade in which much more than a largely merchandizing function is performed. A substantial element

TABLE 44

SINGAPORE—VALUE OF TRADE, 1949–1969
($ millions)

	Imports	Exports	Total
1949	1,304·7	1,053·4	2,358·1
1950	2,124·5	2,480·2	4,604·1
1951	3,593·7	4,016·0	7,609·7
1952	2,849·2	2,543·4	5,392·6
1953	2,324·6	1,980·5	4,305·1
1954	2,299·9	2,044·9	4,344·8
1955	2,865·4	2,781·8	5,647·2
1956	3,929·3	3,429·0	7,358·3
1957	4,062·1	3,478·1	7,540·3
1958	4,730·1	3,140·3	6,880·4
1959	3,908·3	3,440·3	7,348·6
1960	4,532·4	4,708·3	9,240·7
1961	3,963·3	3,308·5	7,271·8
1962	4,035·8	3,416·8	7,452·6
1963	4,279·1	3,474·5	7,753·6
1964	3,478·7	2,771·9	6,811·3
1965	3,807·2	3,004·1	6,250·6
1966	4,065·7	3,373·8	7,439·5
1967	4,406·5	3,490·6	7,897·1
1968	5,083·8	3,890·6	8,974·4
1969	6,243·6	4,740·7	10,984·3

Source: Singapore International Chamber of Commerce and Department of Statistics.

of manufacturing is also undertaken, it having been estimated that about half of all added value is derived from the processing of imported products.[35] Since 1965, the complete political separation of Singapore from peninsular Malaya, has made the latter Singapore's principal entrepot partner (accounting for an average of about 25 per cent. of Singapore's total trade over the period 1966–1969—Table 43), a change that is not entirely the result of definition alone, however, in view of the great decline in trade with Indonesia during the mid-1960s.* In general, it may be argued that the very considerable changes, both political and economic, that have affected Singapore since 1960 make any effort to distinguish entrepot from home trade of very limited value, the more so since it is almost impossible to do so statistically anyway. It is probably much to be preferred that Singapore's activities be referred to as entrepot-manufacturing which, following Blake's use of the term,[36] differs from entrepot-trading in that the production process *per se* shifts from the hinterland to the entrepot and involves the entrepot in a greater commitment of resources. In the rest of this chapter, therefore, no attempt will be made to distinguish a specific entrepot trade for Singapore.

During the period 1961–69, the value of Singapore's trade, excluding that with Indonesia, increased by 80 per cent., its general growth being only temporarily halted in the mid-decade by low world rubber prices (Table 44). At the beginning of the decade annual trade with Indonesia was worth about $1000 million, by far the most important element of which was the import of rubber, mainly from the small-holding sector, requiring cleaning, processing and grading.† After 1963 some profitable trade with Indonesia undoubtedly continued, by means of smuggling and barter deals, as well as by the consignment of Indonesian products, particularly rubber, to third countries such as Thailand or Japan for transhipment to Singapore. It has been suggested, nevertheless, that at least 70 per cent. of the pre-embargo trade between Indonesia and Singapore had been cut off by 1964.[37] There is no official indication of the extent of the recovery of the trade

---

* It is difficult to gauge the extent to which trade between Singapore and Indonesia has recovered since the end of confrontation because no statistics of trade between the two countries have been published since 1963.

† The precise measurement of trade between Indonesia and Singapore is difficult mainly because of substantial discrepancies between the trade returns of the two partners. Differences in statistical methods are a major cause of these discrepancies since Indonesian statistics present exports according to known destination and imports according to place of origin whereas Singapore records exports by country of first consignment and imports by country of last consignment. There was also an unknown volume of smuggling into and out of Indonesia, recorded as normal trade by Singapore, and some trade values not covered by Singapore returns because of barter deals and incorrectly recorded transactions. On the matter of different methods of recording trade statistics in general, see Grotewald, A., 'What Geographers Require of International Trade Statistics', *Annals of Association of American Geographers*, Vol. 53, No. 2, 1963.

since the end of confrontation as no figures are published, but it was believed, unofficially, that Singapore-Indonesia trade had recovered to its pre-confrontation level by the end of 1968.

A detailed analysis of the structure of Singapore's trade in the mid-1960s has been made by D. J. Blake.[38] By 1965, recovery from confrontation was well under way, and even without the Indonesian contribution, import values had returned to or exceeded those of 1961 for most commodity sections of the standard international trade classification (S.I.T.C.) except for section 2, inedible crude materials. This section, dominated by rubber, suffered from the 15 per cent. decline in rubber prices during the period 1961–65 as well as from the loss of the Indonesian rubber exports. In the mid 1960s Singapore appeared to occupy an intermediate position between that of colonial entrepot, which had characterized the port before the Second World War, and that of manufacturing entrepot, to which status the island state aspired, and this position is well illustrated by Blake's analysis of the pattern of Singapore's trade by country of origin or destination and types of commodity by commodity section*. In relation to the economically developed world, specifically Japan, the United Kingdom, the U.S.A., Australia and Hong Kong, Singapore's trade possessed a clear colonial character, with a predominance of imports of manufactures and exports of raw materials and foodstuffs. Trade with less-developed countries on the other hand, especially with peninsular Malaya, Sabah and Sarawak, Thailand and India, was dominated by imports of raw materials and exports of manufactures. This contrast reflected more than a traditional entrepot trade, which superficially would have produced a similar dichotomy, since Singapore's own industries were the source of many of the manufactures exported to its less-developed trading partners—this was particularly true of processed foods, petroleum refinery products, construction steel, garments, furniture and transport equipment.

The transition from an entrepot to a manufacturing economy is necessarily reflected in changes in the structure of overseas trade but certainly not by any decline in its importance

* As defined by the S.I.T.C.

TABLE 45

SINGAPORE—STRUCTURE OF TRADE, 1961–1969

A. IMPORTS—*Percentage of Trade in Each Commodity Group (by value)*

Commodity Groups		1961	1963	1964	1965	1966	1967	1968	1969
0, 1	Foods etc.	20·3	21·7	22·1	21·4	20·5	20·1	19·4	16·6
2, 3, 4	Crude Materials, Fuels, Oils	44·2	37·2	32·7	33·3	35·3	32·7	29·8	31·2
5, 6, 7, 8,	Manufactures	33·5	39·0	43·0	43·2	42·1	45·3	48·5	50·2
9	Others	2·0	2·1	2·2	2·1	2·2	1·9	2·3	2·0

B. EXPORTS—*Percentage of Trade in Each Commodity Group (by value)*

Commodity Groups		1961	1963	1964	1965	1966	1967	1968	1969
0, 1	Foods etc.	16·1	18·2	16·7	16·1	15·0	16·0	14·1	12·6
2, 3, 4	Crude Materials, Fuels, Oils	50·8	45·7	42·9	43·6	47·5	48·3	51·9	56·3
5, 6, 7, 8,	Manufactures	25·7	28·6	31·8	31·1	28·8	26·0	24·1	23·6
	Others	7·4	7·5	8·6	9·2	8·7	9·7	9·9	7·5

N.B. Figures for 1963–1969 exclude trade with Indonesia.
Source: Singapore International Chamber of Commerce.

(Chapter 1, p. 33), and this is well borne out by Singapore's experience (Table 45). Retained imports expanded sharply in the period 1961–65, from 35·8 per cent. of total imports to 49·1 per cent., the major part of this expansion being in response to the growth of manufacturing and construction activities. The most significant change in the pattern of Singapore's retained imports was the increase from 12·6 per cent. to 18·6 per cent. of the total represented by the machinery and transport equipment section, a section consisting predominantly of producers' goods. In respect of several other imports, the development of new manufacturing capacity in Singapore has encouraged a shift from the import of final products to that of inputs, sometimes with an associated change in source of supply. This shift is particularly apparent in the increased import of crude oil for refining in Singapore's refineries* and the decline of refined products imports.

The share of domestic products exports in total exports doubled between 1961 and 1965, export sales of manufactures growing at about 15 per cent. per annum with high rates of growth occurring in petroleum products, textiles, miscellaneous manufactures, metal products, furniture and transport equipment. In some cases, according to Blake, the growth of export markets was a permissive factor in the expansion of manufacturing industries, though most industrial growth— at least until 1965—depended upon the expansion of the domestic market i.e. was concerned with import substitution.

The considerable increase in the volume of Singapore's trade that took place during the 1960s, as well as technological advances in the shipping industry such as the development of containerization, made necessary various improvements in the port's cargo handling facilities. The mechanized handling of cargo was formally introduced by the Harbour Board in 1949, both as a long-term solution to the post-war problem of high labour costs and also with a view to speeding up turn-round and reducing damage to cargo.[39] Greater efficiency in cargo handling was alone inadequate to cope

* Located at Pulau Bukum (Shell), Jurong (Mobil), Pasir Panjang (British Petroleum), Pulau Ayer Chawan (Esso) with a fifth planned (1970) for Pulau Merlimau (Singapore Petroleum—a joint venture between Amoco International Oil, Oceanic Petroleum and the Development Bank of Singapore) (Figure 16).

with the increasing volume of cargo, however, and the recognition of the vital role of the port in maintaining and expanding the island's economy made developments essential. Between 1961 and 1963 over $11 million was spent on effecting further improvements at the eastern end of Keppel Harbour[40], where the new East Wharf project added four large berths with a total length of 2,500 feet.

Further developments in the East Lagoon were begun in the later 1960s in the anticipation of the operation of container ships in the Pacific and South-east Asia by the early 1970s. A project for the construction of container berths and handling facilities is being implemented in stages, with the reclamation of nearly 100 acres of land having been completed by mid-1968. The complex,[41] expected to be completed by the end of 1972, will provide a stretch of 2,250 feet of marginal wharves dredged to 41 feet LWOST for container vessels, and a cross berth of 700 feet for the feeder services that will inevitably grow as Singapore increases the transhipment responsibilities that will accompany its role as a container port. Developments elsewhere in the port provided increased godown accommodation at Telok Ayer Basin and Empire Dock as well as the 8,000 feet of wharves and various facilities for handling bulk cargo previously mentioned (p. 191) at Jurong.

With the exception of the tin smelting works on Pulau Brani, the traditional industries of Singapore had grown up in various districts of the urban complex in proximity to their local labour force and markets, to lines of communication or to harbour facilities. Development was on an individual basis, often by small family businesses, and whilst certain districts, (e.g. the lower Kallang basin) acquired a more distinctive industrial flavour than others, there were no clearly apparent manufacturing zones.* A move towards the establishment of larger, private industrial ventures in less congested parts of the island first became apparent just before the outbreak of the war with Japan and developed some momentum in the 1950s. At Bukit Timah, on the direct road and rail link between Singapore and mainland Malaya,

---

* In 1960 there were over 2,000 industrial concerns in Singapore, mostly small or very small. The most numerous were in the manufacturing and processing of fabrics (407), printing and publishing (176) and engineering works (172).[43]

Hume Industries—making pipes, conduits and asbestos sheeting—first occupied land in 1938, and the Ford assembly plant acquired a neighbouring site in 1941.[42] Both presumably were established with the intention of serving the entire Malayan market.

The post-war period saw further extensions of various private industrial units and also of these sponsored by the Commonwealth Development Corporation in what is now known as the Bukit Timah Industrial Estate. This project undertaken in 1951, had the object of stimulating the growth of small-scale and medium-scale industries by providing prepared sites with common services and facilities such as roads, electricity, water, sewerage and banking. The estate was located eight miles from the core of the city and outside the city limits. It had the advantages of lower property tax rates, cheaper cost of land and excellent transport linkages. A second industrial estate, aimed at encouraging the establishment of industries smaller than those at Bukit Timah, and within easy reach of the city labour supply and market, was established in the suburb of Alexandra by the Singapore Improvement Trust, and its successor the Housing and Development Board, acting as agents for the State Government.[44]

The activities of the Economic Development Board (p. 185) have, however, been primarily responsible for the development of industrial areas on the island since 1960. The redevelopment of certain city localities (e.g. Redhill, Tanglin Halt) as small industrial estates has already been described (p. 185) and it remains to examine further the major complex at Jurong.

Before development began at Jurong the area consisted of lines of hills rising to 250 feet with cultivated valleys and flats between. The valleys opened out into a flat swampy coastal plain covered with mangroves, with tidal flats in use as prawn ponds. Of some 16,000 acres, about 9,600 acres were occupied in one way or another by about 2,900 families, the remainder of the area being hill country or swamp. There were a few very small or old and abandoned rubber plantations, and sporadic formless hamlets whose inhabitants were engaged in fruit and vegetable farming and the rearing of pigs and poultry.

Both planning and construction began in earnest in 1961

and by the end of the year a new access road across the Jurong estuary was under construction, the road from Jurong village

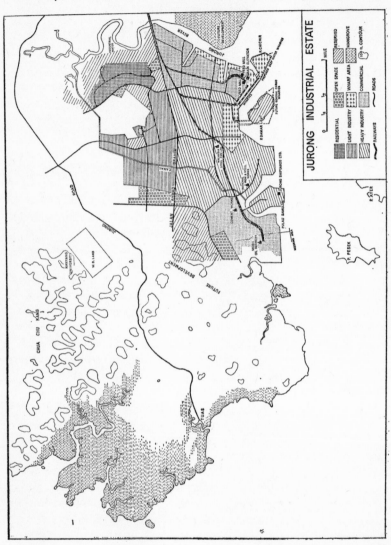

Figure 23. Jurong

southwards re-located, a railway link brought in from Bukit Timah and the first light industrial area set out. The Jurong estuary was closed by a bund and the impounded fresh water reserved for industrial use. By 1962 all areas for use up to 1967 had been acquired. The land surface was sculptured to provide sites for development—hills were cut to pre-determined levels, swamps, ponds, valleys and foreshores filled, channels dredged for navigation and drains and canals cut. Major hills were earmarked for retention as buffers, for reservoirs and for open space and others for the future mining of clays where suitable for industrial use. The costs of land acquisition were not high and much of the land was already state land.

The Japanese plan of 1960, which formed the basis of the original Jurong master plan, provided for water-front heavy industry and for light industry inland. Areas were also allocated for residential use, for the town centre, for basic services and utilities, including water reservoirs, roads, railways and wharves, for telecommunications purposes and as nature reserves. At the end of 1962, 55 applications for industrial sites at Jurong had been received and Singapore's first steel mill, National Iron and Steel Mills Ltd., located on a 20 acre coastal site opposite Pulau Samulun, was under construction. The steel mill was planned as the core of the water-front heavy industrial zone (Figure 23) and came to be associated with a shipbreaker's on an adjacent site and with the Jurong shipyard on Pulau Samulun, which was connected by bridge to the mainland. An oil refinery, cement works, power station, sugar refinery, grain elevator and feed mills were also located in this waterfront zone, which was planned with roads, railway, bulk and general cargo and coastal and lighter wharves to give ready access by land and sea.

Jurong is already Singapore's major industrial region and is destined to play the main role in the island republic's vigorous attempt to survive and grow as a viable economic unit. Industry at Jurong, whilst it will provide much needed employment for Singaporeans and is being planned as an element in a new town complex, is mostly capital intensive and, in many cases, highly automated. Essentially, it is expected to compete in overseas markets and to provide a sound export manufacturing base to the national economy.

The bulk of the industrial area will be located between the Jurong estuary and the Tuas area, with additions on the

R

east side of the Jurong River at Chua Chu Kang and on the adjacent islands. Residential areas are planned to enfold the co-ordinated industrial zones, protected and beautified by open spaces on hills and foreshores. The contrast between the functions and layout of Jurong and those of the commercial core of Singapore near and along Boat Quay illustrates more strikingly than any statistics the new post-colonial economy of the city-state.

III. KUALA LUMPUR–PORT SWETTENHAM

The Colonial Period

The central Malayan population concentration, focused on the Malaysian federal capital, Kuala Lumpur, is distinct from the two urban complexes already examined in that it has not evolved from an entrepot port but from the exploitation of local natural resources. By 1824, the small-scale and spasmodic tin-mining that had characterized the upper Klang Valley until the nineteenth century had developed to a stage where it was possible to list known mining centres and eight were named by Anderson[45] in that year, including Petaling and an intriguing 'Sungei Lumpur'*.

The Klang River rises in the vicinity of Gunong Sempah, a 3,951 foot peak in the Main Range on the Selangor-Pahang border and, in conjunction with its major tributaries, the Batu, Gombak and Ampang, occupies a well-defined basin between the Main Range and a western spur of sedimentary rocks that extends southwards as the Petaling Hills. The upper Klang basin is a highly mineralized area (Chapter 2, p. 53) and rich deposits of alluvial tin were laid down by the streams of the Klang system.

* The origin of the name 'Kuala Lumpur' has not been satisfactorily explained. The literal translation 'muddy estuary' is inadequate since, in Malay, it is far from common—if indeed any examples can be found—for 'Kuala' in a place name to be qualified by a descriptive adjective rather than by the name of the river or tributary that debouches at that point into the sea or a main river. Unfortunately Anderson's 'Sungei Lumpur', of which no trace remains, was probably north of the Batu caves in the Sungei Tua area[46]. The suggestion has been offered[47] that Kuala Lumpur is a corruption of Pengkalen Lumpur, mud jetty, first abbreviated by Chinese and then modified by false analogy. The fact that Klang was also known as Pengkalen Batu, stone jetty, lends credence to this idea. Gullick, however, doubts the explanation in default of any evidence of such corruption.[48]

Chinese mining in inland Selangor had begun at Kanching, in the upper Selangor river basin, in the 1840s and the moderate success of the area had demonstrated the possibility of tin deposits along the upper reaches of the nearby Klang. As described in Chapter 3 (p. 81), prospecting in the area occurred in the late 1850s and mining began in the Ampang district. The success of the Ampang mines was responsible for the establishment of a trading settlement at the site of Kuala Lumpur, at the junction of the Klang and Gombak rivers. Until 1880, when Kuala Lumpur was brought under British administration, the settlement and the mines around it were under Chinese control. For much of this period (1868–1885) the Capitan China,* Yap Ah Loy, who had connections with the Chinese capitalists of Malacca and Singapore, administered the settlement, which was involved in a series of bitter feuds with the miners of Kanching and then in a Malay civil war that seriously reduced tin output in the later 1870s. Selangor had come under British protection in 1874 but active control was first restricted to the coast, based on Klang, with Yap left almost supreme in the interior. Only when rapid developments took place in Kuala Lumpur in 1879, as the result of a sharp rise in the tin price, and a 30 per cent. population increase in one year revealed the inadequacy of the elementary municipal administration, did the British authorities move to Kuala Lumpur to assume direct control.

At the time of the appointment of the first British administrator in Kuala Lumpur in 1880, the town was restricted to a stretch of the east bank of the Klang river, between the present Market Street and Mountbatten Road (formerly Java Street) and bounded on the north-east and south by swampy ground in the vicinity of the streams. The town centred on Yap Ah Loy's large market (the present Old Market Square). North of Java Street, a Malay† quarter was located in Kampong Rawa, whilst the west bank of the

---

* The title 'Capitan China', which has a long history stretching back to the Portuguese period in Malacca, was the usual nineteenth century designation of the headman of a large Chinese village in the Malay states.

†Many of the local 'Malays' were actually of Sumatran origin who had been washing tin at Ulu Klang, probably before 1860. In Kuala Lumpur they were traders.

Klang was occupied by vegetable gardens bounded north and south by swamp and to the west by the higher ground of the Bluff (Figure 24). The early British administration located itself on the west bank of the Klang River in order to have a river barrier between itself and the Chinese town, and the Residency (moved in pieces from Klang), the houses of other British officials and the police barracks were built on the Bluff. The vegetable gardens were converted into a parade ground—ultimately to become the lawns of the Selangor Club.

In the 1870s Kuala Lumpur was essentially a trade centre and a link between the mines and the port of Klang, and as it developed it attracted traders from the port to settle upstream. Within a few years of the establishment of British administration much of the town was rebuilt—a necessity incurred by the considerable fire danger resulting from the narrow streets of palm-thatched houses—and an entire brick and tile industry had to be created in order to make possible the changes introduced by new building regulations. By 1886 there were 15 brick kilns and 6 lime kilns around Kuala Lumpur, though a number were forced to close when the building boom expired. A rough census in 1884 estimated the population of Kuala Lumpur at 4,054.[49]

The economic development of Kuala Lumpur was closely related to the tin mining industry, the industrial requirements of the mines and the varied needs of the miners creating trade and industry in the town. The British administration (especially in the person of Swettenham, who was Resident of Selangor from 1882 to 1889) realized the extent to which the economic progress of the Selangor tinfield was held back by the inadequacy of its communications. Yap Ah Loy had linked various of the mining areas to Kuala Lumpur by road, but transport from the town to Klang was by river and the upstream journey of forty miles along the meandering Klang River took three days. A road constructed in the 1870s between Damansara and Kuala Lumpur via Batu Tiga, to by-pass the great southward loop of the river, was badly made, and preliminary surveys were therefore undertaken in 1883 for a railway as an alternative. By 1886 the line was ready for use, and in 1889 yielded an annual profit of 28 per cent. on the capital invested in it. This profitability made extensions and improvements possible, including the bridging of the Klang River by the Connaught Bridge to take the line across from its initial terminus at Bukit Kudah into Klang. In the later 1880s and early 1890s, as mining developed at greater distances from Kuala Lumpur e.g. at Kepong, Rawang, Serendah and Kuala Kubu, radial lines were constructed out from Kuala Lumpur so that by 1895 Selangor had 70 miles of track, which in that year earned 11 per cent. on capital invested.

With efficient rail connections, both with tidewater and with the extensive surrounding mining area, the significance of Kuala Lumpur as the economic focus of Selangor necessarily grew. Improvements in mining techniques, especially the introduction of the steam engine which permitted the draining of mines to greater depths, accompanied the steady expansion of mining areas in inland Selangor which, by 1887, had spread as far as Ulu Selangor and Ulu Langat. Agricultural expansion, of padi, market garden produce and increasingly of export crops, took advantage of the local market and also of the transport network that made commercial planting an economic proposition (Chapter 3, pp. 98–101). By 1895 the population of Kuala Lumpur was estimated at 25,000, approximately half the total population of Selangor.

Commercial and industrial activity was, however, very closely dependent on the activity of the primary production of the surrounding area and fluctuations in the tin price were faithfully reflected by prosperity or recession in Kuala Lumpur. Industries, of a type already familiar in the Straits ports, were gradually established in the town—sawmills were set up in the 1880s (for building construction and railway sleepers especially), and the first ice and aerated water factory in 1888. Insurance companies and banks developed in the 1890s. General improvements to Kuala Lumpur as it grew included drainage and reclamation work to cope with flooding problems and to remove the swamp areas to the north, east and south of the town. The Klang River was first bridged by a permanent structure in 1883. A telegraph line linked Kuala Lumpur with Malacca (and thence with Singapore and Europe) by 1886, and schools (reflecting the increasing normalization of population structure) were built in the 1880s.

In 1895, Kuala Lumpur was selected as the capital of the newly founded Federated Malay States, a choice that increased its status, gave it a much more elaborate apparatus of government and set it apart from other growing mining centres elsewhere in Malaya, such as Ipoh, Taiping or Seremban.

The expansion of the export trade of the upper Klang Valley, both in tin and in plantation products, and the increasing need to import rice for the growing population as well as other commodities for mines, estates and the consumer, emphasized the need for improved port facilities at the mouth of the Klang. For many years before 1895, coastal steamers trading between the Straits ports and Selangor called at the port of Klang, twelve miles up the winding and muddy Klang River. Only small ships, drawing less than thirteen feet of water, could reach the jetties, however, and accommodation for increasing traffic was limited. The construction of the railway to the coast in 1886 had implied the necessity of providing wharves at the terminus, and alternative routes to two possible sites for a new harbour were examined.

Of the two sites, Kuala Sungei Dua (Deepwater Point) on the north Klang Strait offered considerable advantages as a port for ocean steamers but the railway extension from Bukit Kudah would have been forced to cross nine miles of mainly swampy country. The second site, Kuala Klang, although land locked and shallower, was more accessible from the landward side, and, largely on grounds of cost, this alternative was preferred.[50] All necessary work, which involved unexpectedly heavy expenditure, was completed by 1901 and administration of the new port facilities, named Port Swettenham in honour of the then High Commissioner for the Malay States, was handed to the Railway.

Port Swettenham was originally conceived as a port for coasting vessels but it was visited during its first few years by a growing number of ocean steamers and by 1908 had become a thriving, though congested ocean port. Facilities had to be improved, and the creation of a true ocean port at Port Swettenham was favoured by the economic expansion of the Federated Malay States, especially the rapid spread of rubber planting, as well as by political feelings concerning the desirability of economic 'freedom' from Penang and

Singapore*. Construction of ocean wharves began in 1912, and in 1914 Port Swettenham became a true ocean port.

Although built essentially to serve the expanding export economy of central Malaya, Port Swettenham from the first played a different role from that of the Straits entrepot ports of Penang and Singapore. To some extent this was due to the attitude of the major shipping companies who argued that an ocean port midway between Penang and Singapore was unnecessary, reduced speed in passage time and added to shipping costs. The Eastern Shipping Conference imposed a surcharge on goods other than rubber on the grounds that Port Swettenham had inadequate facilities for cargo handling and offered navigational difficulties to large ocean ships. The location of Malaya's tin smelting works in Penang and Singapore, and the connection by rail of the central Malayan mining centres direct to each in 1903 and 1923 respectively, effectively deprived Port Swettenham of the handling of one of its hinterland's major export commodities, and, in marked contrast with that of its rivals, Port Swettenham's trade showed a very great predominance of imports over exports from the first (Table 46). Port Swettenham, of course, also had no entrepot trade which, despite their growing dependence on their Malayan hinterland, remained an important element in the trade and commerce of Penang and Singapore. Port Swettenham's function from the start was clearly that of port to Kuala Lumpur and to a relatively small central hinterland. The nature of its trade and its degree of prosperity were closely tied to the economic role of Kuala Lumpur, and while this prosperity was obviously linked to the fluctuations in the world market for tin and rubber (as evidenced by the rises and falls in the volume of the port's trade especially in the 1920s and 1930s) it was the demand engendered by the overall urban growth of Kuala Lumpur that most clearly

* Despite their obvious economic interrelationships, the Straits Settlements and the Federated Malay States appeared to be jealous of their political separateness. Swettenham revealed this sense of separateness when he wrote, "The Malay States made, and paid for, the Province Wellesley Railway, and no benefit so great has ever been conferred on Penang in the history of that settlement".[51] Tregonning[52] comments on the 'antagonism and rivalry' and considers it an exemplification of the phenomenon observable elsewhere in South-east Asia of 'two opposing points of view typified by a dynamic ocean port and a traditional inland royal capital' but it is difficult to recognize Kuala Lumpur in the latter role especially in the late nineteenth century.

characterized Port Swettenham's role. In the period preceding the Second World War, imports passing through Port Swettenham consisted mainly of foodstuffs (especially rice), machinery, constructional material, coal (for the railway

TABLE 46

PORT SWETTENHAM—TONNAGES HANDLED, 1911–1938
(in long tons)

Year	Imports	Exports	Total
1911	207,894	37,570	245,464
1912	219,037	44,569	263,606
1913	250,852	53,795	304,647
1914	233,046	53,414	286,460
1915	171,345	53,542	224,887
1916	159,521	58,670	218,191
1917	144,267	64,228	208,495
1918	135,422	60,157	195,579
1919	141,875	68,505	210,380
1920	184,211	68,317	252,528
1921	140,934	63,415	204,349
1922	134,764	69,271	204,035
1923	184,660	71,716	256,376
1924	229,436	74,537	303,973
1925	272,889	87,129	360,018
1926	347,456	107,401	454,857
1927	418,945	93,360	512,305
1928	469,700	126,833	596,533
1929	440,779	161,059	601,838
1930	372,413	139,091	511,504
1931	254,725	120,496	375,221
1932	192,540	115,673	308,213
1933	204,052	148,678	352,730
1934	249,513	149,398	398,911
1935	262,751	133,912	396,663
1936	309,243	141,945	451,188
1937	400,749	169,806	570,555
1938	384,590	152,568	537,158

Source: Mon bin Jamaluddin (1963).

and power station especially) and manufactured products. Exports were dominated by rubber.

The functional role of Kuala Lumpur between the First and Second World Wars remained essentially what it had been before 1914. By 1911, its population had reached nearly 47,000 (Table 28) and commercial premises, residential, shop and terraced houses were built on an increasing scale in the years 1905 to 1915. The distinctively styled railway station and government offices had also been constructed. By 1921 the population had increased to over 80,000 and had reached more than 110,000 by 1931. Urban development, with associated road improvements, took place especially in the later 1920s, particularly in the business and commercial central area and in residential areas. The temporary improvement in economic conditions, associated with the implementation of the Stevenson scheme and the rise in tin production as increasing numbers of dredges came into operation, which culminated in the minor trade boom of 1929, was clearly the underlying cause of this expansion. The city, despite the degree of stability no doubt contributed by its administrative function, was still economically at the mercy of its export economy whose fluctuating fortunes determined the inflow and outflow of alien immigrants[53] as well as the income of many of its commercial undertakings. The lack of an alternative economic function that could partially cushion the effects of the unstable income earned from the production and export of primary products was as apparent in Kuala Lumpur as it was in Penang and Singapore.

Port Swettenham's fortunes reflected those of Kuala Lumpur its highest tonnage being recorded in 1929, and the pressure on its facilities in this short boom period highlighted their deficiences. A scheme was envisaged for the construction of additional wharves on the existing site, but the Imperial Shipping Committee, which reported on Port Swettenham in 1931, recommended the construction of all new wharves at Deepwater Point. The rapid worsening of the economic situation, however, effectively prevented any immediate expansion, and the Second World War was quickly to put out of court any developments that might have flowed from the improvements in trade that were becoming apparent in the late 1930s.

Kuala Lumpur–Port Swettenham since the Second World War

The emergence of the Kuala Lumpur–Port Swettenham axis as the major zone of population concentration in peninsular

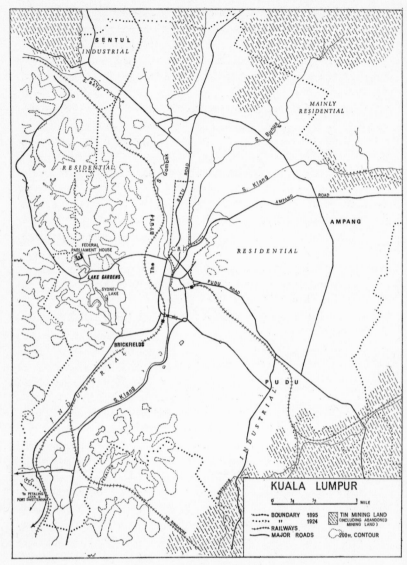

Figure 24. Kuala Lumpur

Malaya, and as the second largest in Malaya, is related
essentially to its position central to the tin and rubber belt
of the west coast states, a position reinforced by the pattern of

road and rail construction that links it with that belt, and with the Straits ports at each end of it. The selection of Kuala Lumpur as the capital of the Federated Malay States, certainly strongly influenced by this nodality, gave the town a 'national' political and administrative function, that accelerated its growth and that became of very considerable additional significance upon the creation of the Federation of Malaya in 1948 and its subsequent independence in 1957.

During its period as capital of the Federated Malay States, Kuala Lumpur had acquired a role as distribution and financial centre for much of Malaya's trade, though always subject to the commercial dominance of Singapore, and as the seat of a legislative council and centralized colonial administration. These roles were strongly reinforced after 1957, when financial and commercial independence from Singapore was sought, and when the new national capital was required to serve as the physical symbol of nationhood, as well as the seat of government. The economic policies of independence, however, especially those relating to industrialization, gave central Malaya, and particularly Kuala Lumpur, an additional new role.

The stimulus given to industrialization by the national development plans and supporting legislation led, as has been seen in Chapter 5, to the establishment and growth of a range of import-substitution industries, for the location of which the population cluster of Kuala Lumpur, with its good distributive network and its function as centre of the bureaucracy, was a major attraction. The existing industrial functions of Kuala Lumpur were located in suburban centres just beyond the city's commercial core, especially at Pudu, Brickfields and Sentul (Figure 24) and mainly consisted of railway workshops, engineering, sawmilling and the familiar range of 'naturally' protected metropolitan consumer industries. Elsewhere, small industries and repair shops were located amongst common retail and service facilities.

Although land was available for industrial purposes in Kuala Lumpur and new manufacturing concerns were established in various parts of the city, many of them unauthorized and occurring in residential and commercial quarters,[54] the principal expansion of industrial activity took place in the Klang Valley, some five miles from the city centre, in Petaling Jaya. Petaling Jaya was first conceived

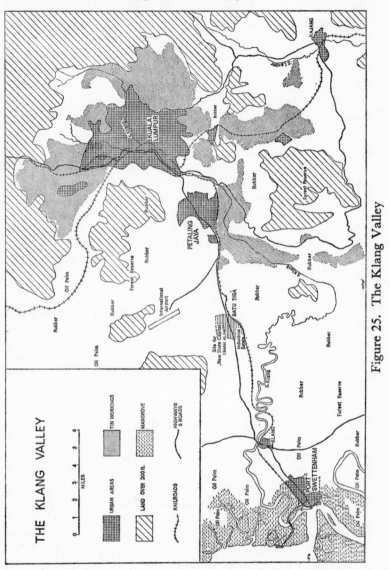

Figure 25. The Klang Valley

as a new town, and approximately 1,200 acres of land were acquired in 1952 by the Selangor State Government with the intention of developing a more modern and more agreeable mode of urban living, for at least some of the state's population, by combining the locations of work, residence and recreation.[55] Development, in fact, began in the form of a squatter re-settlement scheme in an attempt to solve the problem of re-housing the large number of migrants from the countryside who had established themselves illegally on vacant land in and around Kuala Lumpur especially as a result of the Emergency. The availability of loan finance for private home construction soon led, however, to the construction of extensive areas of high quality housing that contrasted most markedly with the mediocre, low cost timber dwellings of the resettled squatters. 300 acres in the west of the town were set aside for industrial use, but response from industries in the early years of Petaling Jaya was poor—by the end of 1955 hardly 6 acres of this land had been taken up.[56] This may have been due to the availability of industrial land in Kuala Lumpur itself, but probably mainly reflected the limited progress in industrialization in Malaya in general at that time.

At the beginning of 1955, the functions of administering and developing Petaling Jaya were handed over to a statutory body, the Petaling Jaya Authority. Empowered to raise loans for developmental purposes, the Authority proceeded to acquire land for an ambitious development programme until it either owned, or managed on behalf of the state govern-ment, about 4,000 acres. Rubber was cleared from the estate and small-holding land that had been acquired, roads and drainage were put in, lots demarcated, and some factory buildings constructed for renting on the 300 acres of industrial reserve. Land for building factories was made available at an economic price. From 1958, the combined effect of the Authority's activities and the Federal Government's industrial policies created an upsurge in investment in manu-facturing industry at Petaling Jaya and the rapid taking up of factory sites.

By the end of the First Plan period in 1960, more than 150 factory lots had been sold to enterprises producing processed foods, beverages, tobacco, pharmaceuticals, paints and chemi-cals, printed materials, tin containers, plastics, electrical

appliances and construction materials. About 80 factories
had actually started production. The initial 300 acres set

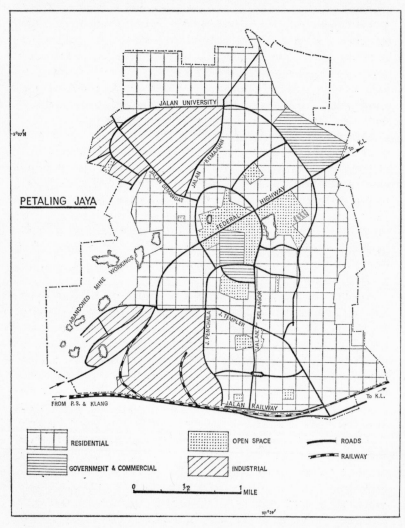

Figure 26. Petaling Jaya—Residential building continues to
spread, especially on the western side of Petaling Jaya.

aside for industry at Petaling Jaya proved inadequate to meet
the growing demand for factory sites and a further 300 acres

was allocated for industrial use north of the town in an area originally proposed for housing (Figure 26). This extension was less ideally located than the first area since it was not served by rail but it had good road connections with the new federal highway that linked Kuala Lumpur with Klang and Port Swettenham and sites were quickly taken up. A second smaller extension, of about 100 acres, was reclaimed from old mining land and opened up for industrial use west of the initial industrial reserve, but separated from it by the Federal Highway.

At the end of 1966, all 700 acres of industrial reserve had been allocated, and apart from a few acres of worked-out mining land that was being reclaimed for industrial use as well as for low-cost housing, there was no more factory land in Petaling Jaya. 210 lots had been allocated for the establishment of 207 factories, of which 42 had been granted pioneer certificates, which were employing an estimated 10,000 workers.

As early as 1961 it had become apparent that more industrial land than could be provided at Petaling Jaya was going to be needed in the Kuala Lumpur region, and the Selangor State Government sought additional land for the establishment of a second industrial estate*. The consideration of areas outside the Klang Valley ran into difficulties, amongst others of transport and water supply facilities, and the area finally selected lay at Batu Tiga†, between Petaling Jaya and Klang (Figure 25). By mid-1968, 33 lots had been allocated and 10 factories were already in operation employing nearly 1,500 people. The Batu Tiga estate is flanked on the north by the dual carriageway Federal Highway and on the south by the railway line, and is well served with electricity and water. The estate when completed will be larger than Petaling Jaya and will form part of a new town ('Shah Alam') eventually to become the seat of administration of the state of Selangor.

The growth both of population and of industry in the

* The planned expansion of industrial development beyond Petaling Jaya was accompanied in 1964, by the conversion of the Petaling Jaya Development Corporation (which the Petaling Jaya Authority had become in 1958) into the Selangor State Development Corporation. The municipal functions of the former corporation devolved onto a Town Board.

† The 'third mile' on the Old Damansara Road (see p. 88).

Klang Valley increased the demands on the port facilities at Port Swettenham, the volume of cargo passing through the port having almost doubled between 1957 and 1965, whilst the political separateness of Singapore and peninsular Malaya since the Second World War* was a further stimulus to the Federation Government to develop its own national port.

TABLE 47

PORT SWETTENHAM—TONNAGES HANDLED, 1957–1969
(in thousands of long tons)

| | Over Port Wharves | | | Fore Shore | Private Wharves | Grand Total In Port | No. of Ships |
	Dry	Liquid	Total				
1957	900	310	1,210	12	112	1,334	1,509
1958	858	309	1,167	22	105	1,294	1,733
1959	888	319	1,207	19	105	1,331	1,798
1960	1,003	364	1,367	21	227	1,615	1,746
1961	998	392	1,389	23	277	1,689	1,539
1962	1,058	459	1,517	28	364	1,909	1,740
1963	1,155	473	1,628	28	373	2,029	1,727
1964	1,152	365	1,517	26	497	2,040	1,728
1965	1,229	386	1,616	27	630	2,273	2,017
1966	1,260	440	1,700	28	400	2,128	2,077
1967	1,390	421	1,811	44	624	2,479	2,413
1968	1,563	478	2,041	40	917	2,999	2,590
1969	1,822	477	2,299	34	1,041	3,373	2,644

Source: Port Swettenham Authority.

In 1950 some 41 per cent. of peninsular Malaya's imports and 43 per cent. of its exports passed through Singapore, but by 1960 the proportion had decreased to 39 per cent. and 29 per cent. respectively, and to 23 per cent. and 8 per cent. by 1969.†

In addition to the population and industrial growth of the Klang Valley and the increased productivity of its rubber and oil palm estates which generated most of the additional trade, improvements in communications—especially roads—since the Second World War have enlarged Port Swettenham's

* Except for the short period of 1963–65 when Singapore was part of the Malaysian Federation.
† Figures do not include imports originating in Singapore or exports destined for Singapore.

hinterland. The construction of the Maran-Temerloh road in 1958 and the improvement of existing roads permitted the extension of Port Swettenham's hinterland eastwards as far as Kuantan and Kemamon, so that a large proportion of commercial activity in the state of Pahang now has its external links through Port Swettenham. Port Swettenham has now effectively taken over the trade of Port Dickson for virtually all commodities except petroleum products— a fact probably related, at least in part, to the removal in 1936 of the surcharge formerly levied by the Far Eastern Shipping Conference (p. 251) which gave Port Swettenham a decided advantage over the smaller ports of central Malaya including Malacca* and Telok Anson.[57]

The very considerable increase in the volume of trade passing through Port Swettenham was already creating severe pressure on the port's capacity in its limited site in the 1950s and the expectation that this trend would continue as the Klang valley attracted more industry and population made additional facilities essential. The original (Kuala Klang) site of the port, now known as the Old Port, had just over 1,000 feet of deep draught wharf for ocean-going vessels in 1958, and although there were possibilities of increasing this wharfage, the limitations of the site were such that any major expansion had to be elsewhere. The immediate needs of the port were met by a 'crash programme' in the Old Port, consisting of the addition of a coastal berth, an ocean berth with transit shed, three lighterage jetties with transit sheds and additional open storage yards, to tide over an interim period until a new site had been developed.

In 1956 the Federal Legislative Council authorized the construction of additional facilities at Deepwater Point on the North Klang Straits as a long term development project. The site originally recommended in the 1880s, and again in 1931 by the Imperial Shipping Committee, therefore was finally to be developed†. The project, begun in 1957, was

---

* Bonded zones are to be established at Malacca and Port Dickson in an attempt to attract trade from West Sumatra and Riau.

† Though this decision was taken *against* the advice both of D. F. Allen who, in his 'Report on the Major Ports of Malaya' in 1951 (admittedly just before the Korean War boom) did not think that 'the case for constructing new wharves at North Klang Straits can be sustained', and of an International Bank Mission.

initially to provide three berths, each 580 feet long, to be constructed on piles along the 6-fathom line. Wharves, 200 feet wide, were to carry two rail tracks and transit sheds and to be connected to the Old Port by a combined road-rail approach and a bascule bridge over the Klang River. The New Port started functioning in 1964. The original plan was modified to provide four berths, and further developments, involving the reclamation of 40 acres of land, are scheduled. By the end of 1972 it is planned that the port will have been

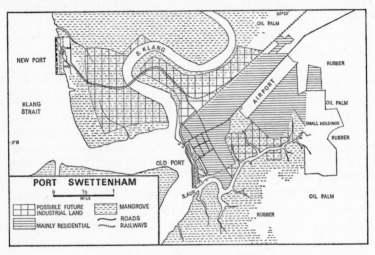

Figure 27. Port Swettenham

provided with further berthing facilities for both conventional and container ships. Goods handling is fully mechanized.

Although both the Old and the New Port are equally equipped to handle imports and exports, a division of functions currently operates with the Old Port handling exports and all liquid cargo (latex, palm oil, coconut oil, petroleum products, alkane, tallow and fuel oil) and the New Port handling mainly imports. The Old Port is also equipped to handle bulk wheat which is conveyed direct to the Federal Flour Mill.

A significant trend in the pattern of Port Swettenham's trade that has become apparent in the 1960s is the achievement of a more even balance, at least in terms of volume, between imports and exports. Whereas (p. 252) before the Second

World War import tonnages regularly represented between 65 per cent. and 75 per cent. of total trade, by 1967 their percentage had fallen to 55 per cent. Rubber, in sheet and latex form, was still the principal export in 1967 (just), but timber, iron ore and palm oil were exported in large quantities. Import trade was dominated by general cargo and petroleum, with chemical fertilizers, iron and steel and food imports also major components.

Port Swettenham's function is essentially that of handling the varied imports and exports of the Klang valley and its own industrial role is very limited. In addition to the flour mill in the Old Port, however, a wood chips factory has been established in the New Port and a tin smelter was opened at nearby Klang in 1964, a venture by joint Japanese-Malaysian capital, which suspended operations indefinitely at the end of 1969 owing to its doubtful ability to maintain sufficient production to operate economically. A provisional plan for the Klang valley region, though not yet finalized or officially adopted, suggests the designation of considerable areas between the Old and New Ports as industrial land, a location that would seem generally appropriate for processing of imports or any ultimate heavy industry.

The Klang valley, from Klang Gates to New Port, Port Swettenham, has already emerged as Malaysia's premier economic axis and the economic advantages to be derived from location in such a core area suggest that it is likely to continue to attract secondary industry more readily than any other part of peninsular Malaya. In view of the desirability of building as strong and economic a manufacturing sector as possible in the national economy there seem to be no grounds for other than assisting this development, though at the same time recognizing the need for careful and informed overall planning of the region to ensure the provision of essential services and amenities and the avoidance of the many familiar problems evident in older established urban-industrial regions elsewhere in the world.

REFERENCES

1 Cooper, E., 'Urbanization in Malaya', *Population Stud.*, 5, 1951
2 Macalister, N., *Historical Memoir relative to Prince of Wales Island in the Straits of Malacca*, London, J. H. Hart, 1893, p. 10

3   Scrivenor, J. B., *The Geology of Malaya*, London Macmillan, 1931, p. 6
4   Küchler, J., 'Penang. Kulturlandschaftswandel und ethnisch-soziale Struktur einer Insel Malaysians', Giessen, Giessener Geographische Schriften, Heft 13, 1968, pp. 9–10
5   Braddell, T., *Statistics of the British Settlements in the Straits of Malacca*, Penang, 1861
6   *The Right and Title of the Sea Frontage and Shore in Beach Street*, Penang Gazette Press, 1918
7   Allen, G. C. and Donnithorne, A. G., *Western Enterprise in Indonesia and Malaya*, London, Allen & Unwin Ltd., 1957, pp. 200–201
8   Straits Settlement Blue Book, 1911, p. W4
9   'Report of the Penang Chamber of Commerce for 1916', Penang, 1917
10 Courtenay, P. P., 'Changing Patterns in the Tin Mining and Smelting Industry of South-east Asia', *J. Trop. Geogr.*, 25, 1967
11 Ward, M. W., 'Major Port Hinterlands in Malaya', *Tijdschr. Econ. Soc. Geogr.*, 57, 1967
12 Allen, D. F., 'Report on the Major Ports of Malaya', Government Printer, Kuala Lumpur, 1951, p. 70
13 Penang Port Commission, 'Project for the Construction of Deep Water Wharves at Butterworth', Penang, 1967
14 United Nations, 'Industrial Estates in Asia and the Far East', New York, 1962, p. 246
15 Report of the Penang Customs Duties Working Party, Federation of Malaya Legislative Council Paper 51 of 1956, Kuala Lumpur, Government Printer, 1957
16 Reports of the Federation of Malaya Labour Department, Kuala Lumpur, October 1958, January 1959, February 1959
17 Unpublished 'Notes on the Economic Situation in the State of Penang, July 1968' prepared by the Chairman of the Penang Branch of the States of Malaya Chamber of Commerce
18 Dobby, E. H. G., 'Singapore: Town and Country', *Geogr. Rev.* 30, 1940
19 Logan, J. R., 'Notices of Singapore', *J. Indian Arch. E. Asia.* 8, 1854
20 Hodder, B. W., 'Racial Groupings in Singapore', *Mal. J. Trop. Geogr.*, 1, 1953
21 Wang Gungwu, *A Short History of the Nanyang Chinese*, Singapore, Eastern Universities Press Ltd., 1959, p. 19
22 Cameron, J., *Our Tropical Possessions in Malayan India*, London, Smith, Elder & Co., 1865, p. 57
23 Wikkramatileke, R, 'Focus on Singapore, 1964', *J. Trop. Geogr.*, 20, 1965
24 Bogaars, G., 'The Tanjong Pagar Dock Company, 1864–1905', Memoirs of the Raffles Museum, No. 3, 1956, p. 178
25 *Ibid.*, *op. cit.*, p. 135
26 Wilson, J., *The Singapore Rubber Market*, Singapore, Eastern Universities Press, 1958, pp. 26–30
27 Hughes, H. and You Poh Seng, *Foreign Investment and Industrialization in Singapore*, Canberra, Australian National University Press, 1969, p. 9–11
28 King, A. W., 'Plantation and Agriculture in Malaya with Notes on the Trade of Singapore', *Geogr. J.*, 93, 1939
29 Straits Settlements, Colonial Annual Report for 1938, p. 10
30 Allen, D. F., *op. cit.*, p. 15

31 Fraser, J. M., 'Town Planning and Housing in Singapore', *Tn. Plan. Rev.*, April 1952

32 Dobby, E. H. G., *op. cit.*

33 *Ibid.*, *loc. cit.*

34 Blake, D. J., 'Patterns of Singapore's Trade, 1961–1966', *Mal. Econ. Rev.*, XIII, 1, 1968

35 Richter, H. V., 'Indonesia's Share in the Entrepot Trade of the States of Malaya and Singapore prior to Confrontation', *Mal. Econ. Rev.*, XI, 2, 1966

36 Blake, D. J. *op. cit.*

37 Richter, H. V., *op. cit.*

38 Blake, D. J, *op. cit.*

39 Allen, D. F., *op. cit.*, p. 7

40 Wikkramatileke, R., *op. cit.*

41 Port of Singapore Authority, 'Report and Accounts for 1968', Singapore, 1969

42 Wikkramatileke, R., *op. cit.*

43 Economic Development Board, Singapore, Industrial Facilities Division, 'Development of Jurong New Town, 1960–1967', Singapore, 1967, pp. 8–9

44 United Nations, *op. cit.*, pp. 344–5

45 Anderson, J., 'Political and Commercial Considerations relative to the Malayan Peninsula etc.', Penang, 1824, p. 196

46 Gullick, J. M., 'Kuala Lumpur, 1880–1895', *J. Mal. Brch. R. Asiat. Soc.*, 28, 1955

47 MacFadyen, E., 'Note on the name Kuala Lumpur', *J. Straits Brch. R. Asiat. Socl*, 1916, reprinted in *Mal. in Hist.*, 5, 1959

48 Gullick, *op. cit.*

49 *Ibid.*, *op. cit.*

50 Mon bin Jamaluddin, *A History of Port Swettenham*, Singapore, Malaya Publishing House, 1963, p. 2

51 Swettenham, Sir F., *British Malaya*, London, Allen & Unwin, 1948, p. 279

52 Tregonning, K. G., 'Singapore and Kuala Lumpur: a Politico-Geographical Contrast' *Pacif. Viewpoint*, 7, 2, 1966

53 Hamzah Sendut, 'The Structure of Kuala Lumpur', *Tn. Plann. Rev.*, 1965

54 Concannon, T. A. L., 'A New Town in Malaya: Petaling Jaya, Kuala Lumpur', *Mal. J. Trop. Geogr.*, 5, 1955

55 McGee, T. G. and McTaggart, W. D., 'Petaling Jaya. A Socio-economic Survey of a New Town in Selangor, Malaysia', Victoria University of Wellington, Pacific Viewpint Monograph, No. 2, 1967, p. 3

56 Selangor State Development Corporation, 'Industries in Petaling Jaya', Petaling Jaya, no date, p. 5

57 Ward, M. W., 'Port Swettenham and its Hinterland', *J. Trop. Geogr.*, 19, 1964

Appendix 1

DEFINITIONS

1 *Geographical as used in this book*

MALAYA—Geographical term, covering the peninsula and its associated islands, including Penang and Singapore, from the Thai border as defined in 1909 (i.e. Malaya includes the states of Perlis, Kedah, Kelantan and Trengganu but not Ligor and Patani) to the Indonesian frontier north of the Riau archipelago.

SINGAPORE—The port and island of Singapore, included geographically in Malaya.

THE MALAYAN REGION—That part of South-east Asia centred on Malaya, understood to include southern Thailand, Sumatra, Java and Borneo; used in historical contexts before a satisfactory political nomenclature had crystallized.

PENINSULAR MALAYA—Malaya without Singapore but including Penang; the geographical area occupied by the Federation of Malaya (1947–63), and West Malaysia (1963–   ).

Neither of these latter terms can conveniently be used in certain contexts since each is tied to a particular political period.

MAINLAND MALAYA—Malaya excluding the islands, especially Penang and Singapore.

2 *Political*

THE STRAITS SETTLEMENTS (S.S.)—the colonies of Penang (with Province Wellesley), Malacca and Dindings, and Singapore, administered until 1942 as a Crown Colony.

THE FEDERATED MALAY STATES (F.M.S.)—colonial political entity created in 1895–6 and surviving until 1942, made up of the Malay states of Perak, Selangor, Negri Sembilan and Pahang.

THE UNFEDERATED MALAY STATES (U.M.S.)—the states of Perlis, Kedah, Johore, Trengganu and Kelantan which individually accepted British Advisers after 1895.

266

The S.S., F.M.S. and U.M.S. collectively can conveniently be termed BRITISH MALAYA.

MALAYAN UNION—A British political concept of a unitary state formed in 1946 of the three units of 'British Malaya' but without Singapore and abandoned in favour of the Federation of Malaya and Colony of Singapore in 1948

FEDERATION OF MALAYA—Political entity existing from 1948 to 1963, made up of the states of Perlis, Kedah, Penang, Perak, Selangor, Negri Sembilan, Malacca, Johore, Pahang, Trengganu and Kelantan.

FEDERATION OF MALAYSIA—Political entity made up of:
  (i) 1963–65, the Federation of Malaya (defined as above), Singapore, Sarawak and North Borneo (Sabah).
  (ii) Since 1965, the Federation of Malaya, Sarawak and North Borneo (Sabah).

WEST MALAYSIA—Political term used since 1963 to describe the area previously known as the Federation of Malaya.

EAST MALAYSIA—Political term used since 1963 to describe the territories of Sarawak and Sabah.

Appendix 2

AN ANALYSIS OF THE LOCATION OF CERTAIN MANUFACTURING INDUSTRIES IN PENINSULAR MALAYA

An analysis of the location of manufacturing industry in peninsular Malaya (West Malaysia) indicates that the degree of concentration varies amongst different types of industry. In an attempt to explain these variations, it might be hypothesized that industries that have a scale of operations such that a small number of establishments (one or two) can supply all or most of the market i.e. are indivisible, will show a high degree of concentration, whilst industries operating on a smaller scale will show lower degrees of concentration. It may also be hypothesized that, in a nation where most manufacturing industry at present is of the import-substitution type, the former group will show a marked preference for location at or near the major national market, whilst the latter group will show a tendency to be more regularly distributed amongst the country's urban areas. Data from the survey of manufacturing industry in West Malaysia collected in 1967* have been examined to test these assumptions. Unfortunately, much of the information in the survey is not entirely satisfactory for geographical analysis. A number of industries covered by the census are not tabulated on a state basis and there is no way of knowing what, if any, bias is introduced by these omissions. Further, the provisions of the Statistics Act, 1965, require, *inter alia*, that the identities of establishments must be safeguarded in the presentation of statistics.† In some instances this has led to the grouping of states in the tabulations, and in others to the omission of industries. Industries have been omitted when a grouping contains fewer than three firms, when one firm accounts for more than 75 per cent. of the total for any grouping and when two firms account for more than 90 per cent. of the total

---

* Department of Statistics, Malaysia, 'Survey of Manufacturing Industries in West Malaysia, 1967', Kuala Lumpur.

† The concepts and methodology used in the compilation of the survey are described in the introduction to the 'Census of Manufacturing Industries in the States of Malaya, 1963', Department of Statistics, Kuala Lumpur, 1965.

for any grouping. The major omission resulting from this policy is, of course, the tin smelting industry. For the purpose of this analysis, when states are grouped together in the tabulations, the figures given for the group as a whole are divided equally amongst the states included in the group. Where this results in fractions of a unit being assigned to a state the figure is rounded upwards. This equal division certainly has the effect of crediting a disproportionate share of the data to the less industrialized states with the effect of suggesting a lower degree of concentration than actually exists.

The data used in this analysis are the figures for *number of establishments* and *net value of output*. The industries have been grouped, according to the Malaysian Industrial Classification, into the following categories:

Category	Industries actually included in Analysis
1. Processing of Estate-type Agricultural Products in Factories off Estates	1121, 1123, 1331.
2. Manufacture of Foods, Beverages and Tobacco Products.	3021, 3054, 3055, 3061, 3097, 3098, 3140, 3200.
3. Manufacture of Textiles.	33.
4. Manufacture of Wood, Rattan, Mengkuang, Attap and Cork Products, Except Furniture and Footwear	3511, 3513, 3531.
5. Printing, Publishing and Allied Industries.	3810/3830, 3821/3822.
6. Manufacture of Chemicals and Chemical Products.	4191, 4192, 4199.
7. Manufacture of Non-Metallic Mineral Products, Except Petroleum and Coal Products.	4310, 4350.
8. Basic Metal Industries.	4421.
9. Manufacture of Metal Products, Except Machinery and Transport Equipment.	4520, 4530, 4563.
10. Manufacture of Machinery Except Electrical Machinery.	4623.
11. Manufacture of Transport Equipment.	4831.

Indices of concentration, using a Lorenz Curve technique similar to that used for the export specialization indices on p. 25 f, have been calculated from the available data with the following results:

TABLE (I)

PENINSULAR MALAYA—INDICES OF CONCENTRATION BY INDUSTRIAL
GROUPS

Industrial Group	Index in Terms of Number of Establishments	Index in Terms of Net Value of Output
1. Processing of Estate-type Agricultural Products	52·70	51·13
2. Food, Beverages and Tobacco	50·94	78·46
3. Textiles	80·01	90·85
4. Wood Products etc.	42·22	49·68
5. Printing etc.	66·51	90·28
6. Chemicals etc.	70·76	93·09
7. Non-Metallic Minerals	57·55	81·86
8. Basic Metals	67·20	79·71
9. Metal Products	70·65	83·54
10. Machinery	64·17	80·59
11. Transport Equipment	61·53	78·07

TABLE (II)

PENINSULAR MALAYA—INDICES OF CONCENTRATION FOR SPECIFIC
INDUSTRIES*

Industry	Index in Terms of Number of Establishments	Index in Terms of Net Value of Output
4191 Soap	63·03	99·05
4192 Pharmaceutical Goods	66·22	87·83
4350 Wire Products	66·82	92·23
4530 Concrete	74·71	92·33
4421 Iron Foundries	67·20	79·71
4623 Machinery and Parts	64·17	80·59
4831 Car Bodies	61·53	78·07

* 7 individual industries have been selected from the 28 industries covered by
the survey.

An examination of these tables reveals certain significant features,
namely:

1 There is a very high concentration of textile manufacturing,
both in number of establishments and in net value of output.
However, the high index of concentration in numbers of

establishments is the result of the location in Kelantan of 26
of the 48 textile manufacturing establishments recorded.
These are largely small, handicraft establishments, which
together are responsible for only 3·8 per cent. of the total net
value of output. The high index in net value of output results
from 74 per cent. of the total net value of output originating
from Johore, where 9 establishments are located. This is a
higher concentration than might traditionally be expected for a
textile industry.

2 There is a rather higher concentration of the food, beverage
   and tobacco industries than might be expected. This may be
   explained by the existence of large animal feed mills in Malacca
   and Selangor and of large tobacco products factories in Selangor.

3 There is a lower concentration of transport equipment industries
   than might be expected—in net value of output it ranks ninth
   of the eleven groups. It is believed that this ranking is un-
   realistic and is caused by the grouping of the data (for the
   reasons stated on p. 268) in such a way that a relatively high
   value of output has been apportioned equally between Penang
   and Pahang with the effect of suggesting a quite unlikely high
   net value of output for the latter state.

4 All groups and industries, except for the processing of agricultural
   products, are more highly concentrated in terms of net value
   of output, but it may be noted that the difference in degree of
   concentration measured by the two indices varies with different
   industries.

Industries Group/Industry	*Degree of Difference Between Indices*
Food etc.; Printing; Chemicals; non-metallic Minerals; Soap; Pharmaceuticals; Wire Products.	> 20
Textiles; Basic Metals; Other Metal Products; Machinery; Transport Equipment; Concrete.	10—20
Processing of Agricultural Products; Wood Products	< 10

The index for net value of output is considered the more significant
of the two indices since value of output is a more significant measure
of industrialization than number of establishments, which, as in
Kelantan, might be numerous but small. This index is, however,

undoubtedly an understatement of the true degree of concentration in a number of instances—such as transport equipment noted above—because, in cases where states are grouped together in the survey, values are evenly apportioned, thus 'spreading' the concentration unrealistically. A ranking of the industrial groups by the index of concentration in net value of output produces the following result:

TABLE (III)

PENINSULAR MALAYA—INDUSTRIAL GROUPS RANKED
BY INDEX OF CONCENTRATION

Rank	Industrial Group	Index of Concentration
1	Chemicals etc.	93·09
2	Textiles	90·85
3	Printing etc.	90·28
4	Metal Products	83·54
5	Non-Metallic Minerals	81·86
6	Machinery	80·59
7	Basic Metals	79·71
8	Food etc.	78·46
9	Transport Equipment	78·07
10	Processing of Agricultural Products	51·13
11	Wood Products etc.	49·68

It should be noted that all the indices of industrial concentration are significantly different from the concentration of population* (index = 36·22).

If states are ranked by net value of output for each industry group, Table (iv) is produced. The following matrix p. (274) is produced if industrial groups and states are ranked in accordance with the results of Tables (iii) and (iv) and the percentage of total net value of output of each industrial group is allocated to each state, Table (v).

This matrix reveals the predominance of Selangor as the preferred location for a very large proportion of the industrial activity covered by the survey and (with the exception of the textile industry) also the fact that the more highly concentrated an industrial grouping may be, the more likely is it to be concentrated

---

* Calculated from estimated state populations in 1967 extracted from Department of Statistics Research Paper No. 1, 'Estimates of Population for West Malaysia, 1967', Kuala Lumpur, 1969.

TABLE (IV)

PENINSULAR MALAYA—STATES RANKED IN TERMS OF NET VALUE OF OUTPUT

| Industrial Group | | | | | | | | | | | Total | State | Rank |
1	2	3	4	5	6	7	8	9	10	11			
1	2	3	1	1	1	1	1	1	2	1	15·0	Selangor	1
2	1	6	4	3	2	2	3	4	1	1	32·0	Perak	2
3	6	1	3	4	3	3	5	2	5	2	40·5	Johore	3
1	3	2	9	2	4	4	2	3	3	7·5	41·5	Penang	4
6	7	9·5	6	7	5	5	7·5	6	4	3·5	67·0	Negri Sembilan	5
4	4	6	5	8	7	9	4	7	7	6	69·5	Kedah	6
5	5	9·5	10	6	6	7	7·5	5	6	7·5	74·0	Malacca	7
7	10	6	2	9	9·5	6	10·5	8	8	5	80·5	Pahang	8
8	9	4	7	5	8	8	7·5	10	9	3·5	86·5	Kelantan	9
9	11	9·5	8	10	9·5	10	10·5	11	10	10	108·5	Trengganu	10
10	8	9·5	11	11	11	11	7·5	9	11	11	111·0	Perlis	11

TABLE (v)

PENINSULAR MALAYA—PERCENTAGE OF TOTAL NET VALUE OF OUTPUT OF INDUSTRIAL GROUPS BY STATE

Industrial Groups Ranked in Terms of Indices of Concentration	States Ranked in Terms of Net Value of Output										
	S	P	J	PN	NS	K	M	PA	KE	T	PE
Chemicals	83·5	6·8	4·4	3·6	1·0	0·2	0·3	0·05	0·1	0·05	0·0
Textiles	5·1	0·4	74·4	15·6	0·0	0·4	0·0	0·4	3·8	0·0	0·0
Printing	74·8	6·3	2·2	12·7	0·9	0·6	1·1	0·2	1·1	0·2	0·0
Other Metal Products	59·1	3·5	21·6	9·8	1·3	1·2	2·6	1·0	0·0	0·0	0·0
Non-Metallic Minerals	62·7	14·6	8·6	7·1	2·8	0·8	1·0	1·3	0·8	0·3	0·0
Machinery	34·8	48·0	1·8	8·3	2·1	1·6	0·6	0·8	0·8	0·1	0·1
Basic Metals	52·3	15·6	5·3	19·4	0·5	5·3	0·5	0·0	0·5	0·0	0·5
Food Drink & Tobacco	64·6	8·5	3·9	8·1	1·2	7·3	4·2	0·4	0·6	0·3	1·1
Transport Equipt.	51·1	16·9	0·1	12·8	2·3	0·1	4·0	12·8	0·0	0·0	0·0
Processing of Agric. Products	15·9	13·8	27·4	9·2	12·4	9·6	5·1	5·0	1·7	0·1	0·0
Wood Products	28·6	12·7	14·4	3·9	6·3	6·4	2·4	16·4	4·3	4·3	0·2

KEY:—S=Selangor. P=Perak. J=Johore. PN=Penang. NS=Negri Sembilan. K=Kedah. M=Malacca. PA=Pahang. KE=Kelantan. T=Trengganu. PE=Perlis.

in Selangor. In view of the inadequacy of the data available no more than such a generalized conclusion may safely be made.

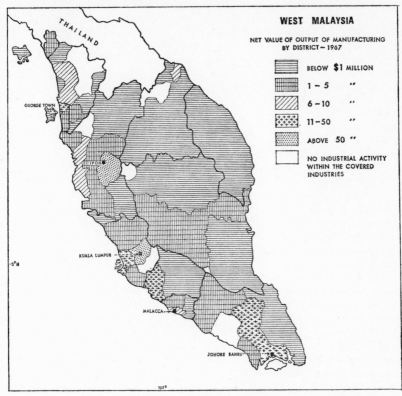

Figure (i). West Malaysia—Net Value of Output of Manufacturing by District, 1967

The accompanying map, Figure (i), based on the 1967 survey, illustrates the distributions in peninsular Malaya of industrial activity by net value of output.

Index

T*